Critical Essays on Indian English Poetry and Drama

Texts and Contexts

Critical Essays on Indian English Poetry and Drama
Texts and Contexts

Arvind M. Nawale

AUTHORSPRESS
Publishers of Scholarly Books

Worldwide Circulation through Authorspress Global Network

First Published 2010
by
Authorspress

Editorial
Q-2A Hauz Khas Enclave,
New Delhi-110 016
e-mail: authorspress@yahoo.com

Marketing
E-35/103, Jawahar Park
Laxmi Nagar, Delhi-110 092
e-mail: authorspress@yahoo.com

Critical Essays on Indian English Poetry and Drama: Texts and Contexts

ISBN 978-81-7273-562-3

Printed in India at Tarun Offset, Delhi.

Dedicated to my elder brother, Mr. Sunil M. Nawale,
Head, Project Operations, Large Projects,
Honeywell Automations India Ltd, Pune
For
His love and constant support and everything he had done for me.
It is he who saved my life from a severe cardiac arrest, providing
all care and expenses within an hour to get my coronary angioplasty
done and made me able to see the world again...

Dr. Arvind M. Nawale

Preface

Though foreign in its origin, English has been adopted in India as a language of education and literary expression besides being an important medium of communication among people of various regions. The beginning of Indian English literature is traced to the end of the eighteenth century and the beginning of the nineteenth, by the time when English had begun to be firmly established in the three major centres of British power in India: Calcutta, Madras, and Bombay. The place and status of Indian English poetry and drama before and after Independence are open to deliberation as critics contemplate diametrically opposite views on the achievement of poetry and prose in general. However, the recognition achieved by Indian English poetry and drama cannot be overruled.

Post-Independence Indian English poetry is both a disruption with the past and a continuation with it too. Modernity in contemporary Indian English poetry, which fundamentally means a break with the past, has manifold identifiable manifestations. It comprises a past-oriented vision, which is linked to a sense of loss and despair, a future-oriented vision, associated with a desire to re-establish the world and a present-oriented outlook, which is a historical and ambivalent. Similarly, the Indian English drama was promoted by the increasing interest of the foreign countries in Indian English literature in general and Indian English drama in particular. The journey of the Indian English drama has been on a swan song since then. Deviating from classical and European models, the contemporary Indian drama has been experimental and groundbreaking in terms of the thematic and technical qualities incorporated in it. It is not an outcome of any definite convention and it has established the groundwork of a unique tradition in the history of drama by scrutinizing socio-political and cultural issues.

My paper 'Arun Kolatkar's *Jejuri*: A Poignant Ode on Religious Bigotism' depicts Kolatkar's rebellion against institutionalized religion. It is an analytical study of Arun Kolatkar's *Jejuri* and the narrow outlook towards religion it projects. Prof. R.K. Bhushan Sabharwal's paper examines how Gopi Kotoor's poetry is the poetry of life and captures the ever-going panorama of life. Dr. Dinesh Kanwar Singh, in his paper, 'Quest for Empowerment: Revulsion and Reverse Sexism in Kamala Das's depicts reverse sexism in Kamala Das's poetry. In his paper, 'Ecowisdom in Keki N. Daruwalla's Poems "Wolf" and "The Last Howl"', Dr. Suresh Frederick attempts an in-depth analysis of the metrical patterns and free verse, and reflects on Keki N. Daruwalla's capacity to combine thematic concerns. P C K Prem focuses on the exhaustive approach in Indian English poetry. His paper 'Contemporary Ethics, Value-system, and Concept of Life in English Poetry in India' brings to light the contemporary issues associated with the growth and development of English poetry in India.

Ankita Khanna's paper 'Revelation of Borderline Traits in the Poetry of Kamala Das' examines the fierce originality, bold images, exploration of female sexuality, and intensely personal voice in Kamala Das's poetry. In 'The Magic World of Poetry and Poetic Art of Kulbhushan Kushal', Dr. N. K. Neb appraises the powerful and appealing imagery in Kulbhushan Kushal's poems which captivate the eye and the ear. Dr. Anindita Chatterjee's paper, 'An Analysis of the Poetry of Toru Dutt With Special Reference to Her "Sita"' addresses the thematic context of 'Sita'. Her paper also projects the writings of women in English in pre-independence India. Dr. Amit Bhattacharya depicts displaced generation in Kamala Das's *Treatment of Old Age* in his paper. Chavan Sandip, in his paper 'A General Review of Prevalent Themes of Kamala Das's Poetry & Her Poetic Stance' attempts to investigate the powerful feminist imagery and the emergent voice in the poems of Kamala Das.

Deepali Patil in her paper 'Sexuality as an Expression of Emancipation in Selected Women Protagonists of Vijay Tendulkar' gives an account of the resilience put forth by the women and accentuates the triumph proclaimed by women. Dr. A.J. Sebastian attempts a close reading of Ritwik Ghatak's "The Rack/The Torment. Dr. Anita Singh & Shyam Babu study caste, gender and sexuality reflected in Tendulkar's *Ghasiram Kotwal.* Dr. Shailaja Wadikar explores the conflict of body and soul in Tendulkar's *The Vultures* in her paper while Dr. Vishwanath Bite studies gender problem in Vijay Tendulkar's *Silence! The Court is in Session* in his paper.

'Representation of Women Characters in Post Independence Indian English Drama' by Dr. Vikas Raval primarily concentrates on the description of women and the stance manifested by them in the wake of patriarchal subjugation and cultural norms. Dr. Ibrahim Khalilulla's paper 'Interrogating The Savage and Bitter Indictment in Manjula Padmanabhan's *Harvest',* is an endeavour to comprehend the alienation and marginalization faced by the characters. Dr. Prafull Kulkarni studies social retribution depicted in Girish Karnad's *Tale-Danda.* Sophia Jaychandran in her paper 'Girish Karnad's *Tughlaq:* "Absolute Power Corrputs Absolutely"', brings to light the contradictions in Tughlag's ideals as he is not able to strike a chord between idealism and realism and has miserably failed in using his authority in a positive manner. Depicting the 'Social Transformation and Hidden Contemporary Realities in the works of Mahashweta Devi' is a major concern of SriLatha Golakoti. Her paper delves deep into the societal codes so rampant in the community. T.K. Kanthale's research paper 'Women in Vijay Tendulkar's Plays: A Socialistic Study' presents an all-inclusive portrayal of women in Vijay Tendulkar's plays. His paper looks into the causes as to why womenfolk form a major component in Tendulkar's plays, and the last paper 'Do Until You Die: Usha Ganguli's *Rudali',* by Durgesh Ravande draws our attention to the theatrical dimensions of the text.

The deep insights of the above scholarly contributors into the Indo-English writing would surely benefit the students, teachers, and researchers of Indian English poetry and drama. I am honoured and privileged in editing the papers of such scholarly contributors and present this book to the vast readership.

The present anthology has strictly followed blind peer review procedure while selecting the papers. I am thankful to Prof. P. G. Pandiya, former Head of my Department and former Chairman, BoS in English, S.R.T.M. University, Nanded (M.S.), Dr. R. M. Sangewar, former Head, Dept. of English, M.U. College Udgir (M.S.) and Dr. Ketaki Datta, a novelist, critic, translator and an Associate Professor, Department of English in Acharya Brojendra Nath Seal Govt College, Coochbehar, (W.B.) for reviewing, selecting papers, making suggestions and sharing with me in critical arguments.

I must record my deep sense of indebtedness to Sudarshan Kcherry, Managing Director, and the whole team of Authorspress, New Delhi for pursuing me to edit present volume. I must not forget to express my gratitude to my respected father Shri Manikrao Nawale and mother Sow. Mandakini Nawale, my brothers, Dr. Sanjay Nawale and Mr. Sunil Nawale, my sister Jyoti Khurpe, brother-in-law Prof. Manohar Khurpe, my father-in-law Mr. K. G. Tudame, my wife Manisha, daughter Apurva and son Amit for their inspiration and constant support.

Capt. Dr. Arvind M. Nawale

About Contributors

Dr. Arvind Nawale, Head, Dept. of English, Shivaji Mahavidyalaya, Udgir, Dist: Latur (M.S.). He has edited more than half a dozen books and is also on the editorial board of three international journals.

Prof. R. K. Bhushan Sabharwal, a veteran educationalist, creative writer, poet, motivator with international standing is at present working as a Professor and Head, Dept. of English, Lovely Professional University. He has published a number of papers and more than a half dozen books on English literature.

Dr. Kanwar Dinesh Singh, a Sahitya Akademi Award (HP)-winning English poet of India, is an internationally published writer, poet, critic, translator, editor and reviewer. He has authored and edited a number of books and is also Editor-in-Chief of *Hyphen*, An international journal of interdisciplinary studies in literature, art and culture. He is also Assistant Professor, Department of English, in Government Postgraduate College, Solan (H.P.)

Dr. Suresh Frederick, is Associate Professor & Head, Department of English, Bishop Heber College, Tiruchirappalli (Tamil Nadu).

P.C.K. Prem is a retired IAS officer from Palampur, Kangra (Himachal Pradesh). He is a renowned critic, poet, novelist and essayist and has written wrote many books of poetry and fiction.

Ankita Khanna currently works as lecturer in Sardar Vallabhbhai National Institute of Technology, Surat (Gujarat).

Dr. N. K. Neb is Associate Professor, Department of English in D.A.V. College, Jalandhar (Punjab). He is Editor-In-Chief of a national journal. He has authored three books: one each on contemporary literary criticism, fiction and poetry, and has co-edited five books on fiction.

Dr. Anindita Chatterjee is presently working as Head, Department of English at Taki Government College, (West Bengal). Some of her poems have also been published. She has been the co-editor of the *Newsletter of the Centre of Studies in Romantic Literature in 2006-07*, and regularly publishes in the leading English dailies of Kolkata.

Dr. Amit Bhattacharya is Associate Professor in English at the University of Gour Banga (W.B.). He has presented research papers on various topics and chaired sessions in a number of national and international seminars. He has also contributed articles to journals like *Pratyay: The Journal of the SCERT*, *Symposium: A Forum for Literary Dialogue*, *The Critical Practice*, *North Bengal Critical Review*, *Pallet*, *The Wesleyan Journal of Research, Appropriations, Atlantic Critical Review, Atlantic Literary Review, Salesian Journal of Humanities and Social Sciences,* etc. His many papers appeared in critical anthologies on Indo-Anglian Literature and New Literatures in English.

Chavan Sandip Pandurangrao, Asst. Professor, Department of English, Dayanand College of Arts, Latur (M.S)

Dr. Deepali Patil, Associate Professor, Department of English, S.B.B. alias Appasaheb Jedhe College of Arts, Commerce and Science, Shukrawar Peth, Pune (M.S.)

Dr. A.J. Sebastian, Associate Professor, Dept. of English, Nagaland University, Kohima (Nagaland).

Dr. Anita Singh, Professor, Department of English, Faculty of Arts, Banaras Hindu University, Varanasi. She is also

Co-Coordinator, Centre for Women's Studies and Development, BHU, and Editor of a national journal. & **Shyam Babu**, Assistant Professor, Dept. of Literary Theory & Criticism, School of English Studies, The English and Foreign Languages University, Hyderabad (AP)

Dr. Shailaja Wadikar is Asst. Professor, Department of English, School of Languages and Literature in S.R.T.M.University, Nanded (M.S.). She has authored a few books in Indian Writing in English.

Dr. Vishwanath Bite is Asst. Professor, Department of English in MBSK Kanya Mahavidyalaya, Kadegaon (M.S.). He has edited a few books and is also Editor-In-Chief of *The Criterion*, an international journal in English.

Dr. Vikas Raval is Assistant Professor of English at Institute of Technology, Nirma University, Ahmedabad (Gujarat). He has published several research papers at the national and international level.

Dr. M. Ibrahim Khalilulla, is Assistant Professor, Department of P.G. Studies and Research in English, Kuvempu University, Jnana Sahyadri, Shankaraghatta, Shivamogga District, (Karnataka).

Dr. Prafull Kulkarni, is Assistant Professor, Sharadchandra College, Naigaon, Dist. Nanded (M.S.). He authoured four books on drama.

Sophia Jaychandran, is Assistant Professor in English, Vanita Vishram Women's College of Commerce, Surat. (Gujarat).

Sri Latha Golakoti, is Assistant Professor in Dept. of English at GITAM University, Hyderabad. (A.P).

Tarachand Kanthale, is Assistant Professor of English, Babaji Datey Kala Ani Vanijya Mahavidyalaya, Yavatmal, (Maharashtra).

Durgesh Ravande is Assistant Professor in the Department of English of KKM College, Manwath, Dist.Parbhani. (Maharashtra).

Contents

1

Arun Kolatkar's *Jejuri*: A Poignant Ode on Religious Bigotism

—Arvind M. Nawale

> ...Our accounts of God are likely stories;
> But all the same legendary.
> Not one of them is full and final.
>
> (*Radhakrishnan*. 1963:27)

Satire on religious hypocrisy is not a new topic for literature. We can see its representation in British as well as Indian English literature right from Lagland to Modern Age. Right from William Lagland, who in his *Piers the Plowman* flings a ruthless satire on pomposity of religious fundamentalism of his age to Taslima Nasrin, who in her *Lajja* exposes bigotism of religious beliefs, many writers of literature wrote on hypocrisy and superstitions of religion. Chaucer in his *The Prologue to the Canterbury Tales*, Milton in his *Lycidas*, Dryden in his *The Hind and the Panther*, Jonathan Swift in his *A Tale of Tub*, T.S.Eliot in his *Gerontion* and many other poets wrote on pretence of religious beliefs and empty rituals availing nothing.

Arun Kolatkar, a Maharashtrian English poet, can be grouped among the above-mentioned poets who have satirized superstitions and empty rituals of religion in their poetry. In this connection his *Jejuri* (1968), a collection of poems, may be called as a poignant ode on religious bigotism.

Actually, Jejuri is a small town in western Maharashtra, located at a distance of about thirty miles away from Pune. This town is a place of pilgrimage because it has a temple devoted to a god by the name of Khandoba with statues of that god, some carved out of stone, and others cast in bronze and gold also. Maharashtrains have great faith in god Khandoba who is believed to be an incarnation of Shiva. Outside the temples, there are five sets of rocks into which the demons killed by Khandoba were believed to have been distorted. People from different parts of Maharashtra, and some even from other parts of India, go there to worship Khandoba and pray for his favor.

Kolatkar has not written the poem *Jejuri* to pay his individual tribute and homage to god Khandoba. In fact, he does not even fully or wholeheartedly believe in idol worship or the worship of gods. He believes this worship to be a kind of false notion, though he does not openly say so anywhere in the poem. The main target of the poet seems to expose hypocrisy of religious viewpoint and empty rituals, and this scepticism of his predominates in the poem.

In the poem, entitled "The Priest" the priest is a type of man who is more engrossed in his income than any kind of social or religious service. This poem depicts mood his as he waiting for the arrival of the bus which brings a crowd of pilgrims and tourists. The priest is, of course, not concerned about the religious aspect of pilgrims. He is more anxious with the offering which the pilgrims always make when they bow respectfully before the god Khandoba. The poet clearly satirizes the priest's worldliness and greediness. The priest is not a genuine priest in any sense of the word. Not only does his livelihood depend on the donations made by the pilgrims but he likes to enjoy the luxuries of life too. Milton, in his *Lycidas,* also notices the same drawbacks of religious ceremonies performed in the churches of his time.

In "A Low Temple", we see that a pilgrim has to light a match in order to be able to see the images of god in its light. The protagonist (whose name is Manohar and is partial projection of the poet himself) offers a matchbox to the priest who lights a match so that the he is able to see all the images one by one. The bronze image of the deity has an amused look on its face. A stone image of another deity seems to be smiling. Yet another image seems unsurprised by the presence of devotees. This interpretation seems to be amusing to the poet. Kolatkar's disbelief in the divine attributes of the statues at Jejuri is evident in this poem. Among the statues the protagonist sees one of the goddeses, which has eighteen arms. He asks the priest who this goddess is. The priest replies that it is the statue of a goddess having eight arms. Actually, however, the idol has eighteen arms, and the protagonist has counted the number. He naturally draws the priest's attention to the fact that the idol of the goddess has eighteen arms. But the priest still says that she has eight arms. Here one finds the difference between fact the belief, and our blind faith that we have.

In Makarand, the protagonist refuses to enter the temple of one deity when he is asked to take off his shirt and enter in temple to do the pooja. He rather prefers to smoke outside than to go inside shirtless for the worship. In other words, he objects to the very act of the worship of a stone or bronze image supposed to represent a deity.

It is very difficult for the poet to decide at Jejuri what a god is and what a stone is because any stone which a pilgrim picks up is said to be a holy stone personifying some god:

> What is god
> and what is stone
> the dividing line
> if it exists
> is very thin
> at jejuri
> and every other stone
> is god or his cousin (28).

A god's cousin is as holy as the god himself; and therefore, every stone deserves worship. Here, Kolatkar has ridiculed the blind faith of the pilgrims by saying that almost every stone at Jejuri is sacred because it is an image of some god. In the poem entitled "Chaitanya", the poet tells us sarcastically that the stones of Jejuri are sweet like grapes, according to people, and they try to eat them.

In "Heart of Ruin", the poet depicts in Jejuri a temple which is in ruins. The roof of this ancient temple is distorted exactly over the head of the stone statue of god Maruti. But nobody seemes to mind the mishap. Pilgrims no longer visit the temple because it is in ruins:

> The roof comes down on Maruti's head.
> Nobody seems to mind.
> Least of all Maruti himself.
> May be he likes a temple better this way.
> A mongrel bitch has found a place
> for herself and her puppies
> In the heart of the ruin.
> May be she likes a temple better this way (12).

A mongrel bitch has found the premises to be very suitable for giving birth to her puppies. The temple is no more a place of worship but it is still nothing less than the house of god. T.S. Eliot has also shown the same loss of faith and sterility of religion in his poem *Gerontion*:

> In depraved May, dogwood and chestnut, flowering judas:
> To be eaten, to be divided, to be drunk-
> Among whispers.
>
> *(Eliot 1988:474)*

In poem entitled "Yeshwant Rao", Yeshwant Rao is the name of one of the many gods. This god is believed to have no head, no hands, no arms, and no feet, in fact, none of the limbs, which every other god possesses. He is regarded as the patron of the headless, armless, and feetless people. He is only a second-class god whose statue has been installed outside the main temple and even of the outer wall, as if he deserved only a place among the tradesmen and the lepers:

> Yeshwant Rao
> mass of basalt,
> bright as any post box,
> the shape of protoplasm
> or a king size lava pie
> thrown against the wall,
> without an arm, a leg
> or even a single head.
> Yeshwant Rao.

> He's a god you've got to meet.
> If you're short of a limb,
> Yeshwant Rao will lend you a hand
> and get you back on your feet (46).

People who have lost a leg or an arm or a hand, go to worship this god in the belief that he would restore to them their lost limbs—when a god, who is himself maimed, is supposed to have the power to make the bodies of maimed human beings whole!

The catalogue of gods contains references to gods who are better looking; gods who seek worshippers because of the gold offerings which they are likely to make; gods who want to take possession of the souls of their worshippers; gods who claim to endow their worshippers with the power to walk on a bed of burning coals; gods who claim to have the power to bless the barren wives of their worshippers; and so on, as the poet satirizes the hollowness of religion.

"The Railway Station" is the concluding poem of the whole sequence. After visiting the temples the poet decides to go back home by a train instead of a bus. But, on arriving at the railway station, he finds himself in a very scratchy situation. The railway station, according to the poet, is another meaningless temple, and the station master is like a two-headed god who inhabits the place. There is a dog as also a bitch in the Maruti temple. The poet's impressions of the temple are juxtaposed with those of the incompetent and hollow railway station at the end.

In this way, *Jejuri* is a poignant ode on religious bigotism as Kolatkar's satirical lash exposes and whips the blind beliefs, pretentions and duplicity of religion, religious places and its rituals. But here the satire is not harsh like that of Alexander Pope who used decisive language to expose the hollowness of Dr. Arbuthnot. The satire in *Jejuri* is rather milder and indirect like that of Mackflecknoe in which Dryden changed the vulgar to the aesthetic and the low to the sublime. Kolatkar might have knowledge that religion is the most sensitive part of human life, so it should be handled carefully.

Works Cited

Eliot, T. S. 1988. *The Golden Treasury*. Edited by F.T.Palgrave. Delhi: Oxford University Press.

Kolatkar, Arun. 1976. *Jejuri*. Bombay: Clearing House. (All the page references in parentheses are to this edition only).

Radhakrishnan, Dr. S. 1963. *The Hindu Views of Life*. London: Unwin Books.

2

Defining Poetry to Define Infinity in Finite: A Study of Gopikrishnan Kottoor's Poetry

—R. K. Bhushan Sabharwal

After reading Gopikrishnan Kottoor, I felt that he is not only one of the most scholarly and learned poets but also innovative in British, American, Commonwealth and Indian Poetry in English. His versatility in creative writing puts him, without a speck of doubt, at the forefront among the generation of New Literature in English. He is not only a profound poet but also a novelist, a playwright, a writer of children's literature, a translator and a transcreator, besides being the editor and the founder editor of *Poetry Chain*. He has retained writing as his first love, though going scrupulously with his professional compulsions also enhance his competence. However, it is not fair on the part of the literary fraternity that he is still deprived of his due in India.

Gopi, I love him to address him as such and hope that he also loves in the same spirit, is not a casual poet but seriously rooted in the art and tradition of poetry. So reading him definitely acquaints us with his broad concept and vision of poetry so deftly and delicately expressed in his poetic accomplishment. His poetic talent is richly gifted and he makes full use of his grooming, practice and performance. I place him among the poets of high order and meaning in the golden treasury of world poetry. Himself being finite, as we all lesser and lower mortals are honoured to be, Gopi is deeper and defines poetry to define Infinity exploring the relativity felt genuinely and rarely. He makes a solemn declaration of his manifesto as a poet to introduce us to the meaning of poetry and its lasting beauties, in "The Man in the Mist", the first poem in *Victoria Terminus*. The reader will decide whether it is a declaration or a dedication to the splendid design of book. He says:

> . . . What began
> as a wild desire, a wetness under the forest leaves,
> turns cold, the sun takes on the words
> spoken by the lips of rain, the fragrance of white hidden flowers
> mating in the open air. Each whisper turns over to a shade
> love cannot hold beyond the secret words of the night,
> spoken lover to lover, laid upon the bed of desirous lips.
> Who cries after all this? And why?

In the Third Section, *Painted Wagons Rolling* of *VT,* he says in "A Good Poem"*:*

> Still earth,
> On the museum walls of night
> are masterpieces of sleep,
> and the wind painting lifeless trees,
> The grasshoppers here are eminent authors.

This is true poetry—passionate, sensuous, mystical, philosophical, metaphysical, meditative and nothing short of divine. Gopi stands respectfully among Spenser, Milton, Shelley, Keats, Tennyson, Browning, Yeats, Houseman, Spender, C. Day Lewis, Whitman, J.P. Fernando, Tagore, Sarojini Naidu, Nissim Ezekiel, Keki N. Daruwala Shiv K. Kumar, Kamala Das...... sorry for the list of the adored and decorated continues beyond the limitations of space.

Defining poetry in this way to define the infinity, the finite Gopi weaves bewitching poetic patterns. This becomes the poetry of "criticism of life" with milkmaids of *poetic truth* and the lingering fragrances of *poetic beauty* with escape and expression of personality playing hide-and-seek with the reader. Gopi alone could do so. Others cast their own spell of music and magic. Gopi stands away and apart to treat the reader with the delight of his own fare. It is not a poetry of illusion or elusion. It is a poetry of musings loaded with moods and memories of the happenings that go on happening in the open theatre and stadium of life marking it with subtlety and simplicity. He captures this panoramic movement with the rare honesty and straightforwardness of the artist who sees the truth, views it to tell, without hurting the viewer or the viewed, with a telling effect.

Stark realism in its complete sensuality drained into poetry, *moving* poetry, the poetry of life in its natural and live moods and modes and the moments that capture the ever-going panorama of life, not confined to some specific places or spaces in a metropolitan city but in all big or open places—Gopi makes it all a happening poetry. Each poem, a concise or concrete statement, becomes an epigrammatic poetry. Here both the realism and naturalism create a representational beauty felt and seen in Chaucer's *Prologue to the Canterbury Tales,* Ted Hughes's animal poems and Imtiaz Dharker's metro poems. The tones and tunes may vary but the themes sparkle in surprise and delight. The flow in Gopi's poems invites no irritations of expression and imagery but endears us to life to hug it and love it to adore and live it with a sense of purely personal understanding that strengthens our belongingness in these callous and cursed times.

Vers libre is the *joie de vivre* of Gopi's poetry, and we feel the freshness of his poetic technique. At places, it has the touch of poetic frenzy, the silence of the seas scaring us with their depths. Rich poetic phrases coined and used by him resound with music meaning and even magic and they leave the reader in grief and pain of the situation. The psyche of the poet works at different levels—personal, psychological, religious, familial and inter-relational. He has built up an inimitable phenomena of relativity raising the ordinary to the lofty as all these are eternal indispensable components of human life. Maybe here the situation warrants involvement of the reader in an equally eloquent manner. The simple lyrical expression of emotion, thought and sentiment is a melody of "unified sensibility". I don't know whether Gopi realized it, even remotely.

The purpose of the present study is to analyse poetically Gopi Kottoor's *Victoria Terminus* which appears to me to be his poetic journey of life from his childhood to the present level of his professional accomplishment via adolescence and youth. It makes undoubtedly a fascinating graphic poetry in this regard, its own kind in poetry anywhere, especially Indian poetry in English. However, the present requirement of this specific paper is far from sufficient and cannot fulfil its aim. However, I shall set out in the direction and pause after walking a little distance from where I shall only point to the rest. *Victoria Terminus* is an achievement of rare poetic excellence in Indian poetry in English. Its four sections:

1. Father, Wake us, In Passing;
2. Mother Sonata;
3. Painted Wagons Rolling; and
4. Victoria Terminus.

are so arranged that they create a unique design of the movement of life—slow, brisk, leisurely, lonely, lively in its grim, gloomy, grieving, gay and vibrant gait. These are the poems of powerful dramatic tensions. It is a drama of his emotions, a play of his endurance with overwhelming calm, control and poise. The sea under tremendous pressure making a frantic controlled bid to surge and seethe, merges into the ocean to experience harmonious relief. The "impassioned speech," "lofty tone," "mighty voice," announcing to the world dying father's grief and the son's illimitable pain make a living portrait of both the father and the son in the First Section with the continuity of love for the loving light of the mother in the Second Section. Then there is a shift of mood in which the painted wagons roll into the Victoria Terminus halting the poetic journey of the bard, perhaps to refresh himself, to rejuvenate himself for the challenges of the next start. Gopi Kottoor is a widely mobile poet with a wider scholarship of classical and modern Oriental and Occidental literatures.

I shall take up only the First section of the book—*Father, Wake Us, In Passing*—for the present purpose and also focus—on the portrait of his father and father-son relations depicted so truthfully and faithfully. This is the prime aspiration of true poetry and the great poet fulfils it. Gopi has done it well in all the 42 numbers of this section. He tells us that it is a *poem-cycle on the death-bed of father in coma, following a brain-haemorrhage.* I shall deliberately overlook the live details of the ICU, the latest medical technology and the process of treatment and the reports, responses and reactions there. Although the poet says that it is neither *In Memoriam* (Tennyson) nor *an elegy* (Thomas Gray), yet it is the latest interpretation of those two masterpieces of British English Poetry. It is a superb blend of trembling and weeping with invisible tears, sensitivity and tenderness, agony and anguish, light and flame, with the consistently running undercurrent of pain and passion that merge into the metaphysics of the psychology and philosophy of the son. It is not a pretension, not an exhibition, not even the necessity of expression but the unchecked smooth spontaneous flow of pure love across the occasional rough tall grasses, bushes, overhanging boughs, stones and rocks. It is a complete poem of intensely lacerated father and loving son, and intensely lacerated son and loving father. I don't think any other poet has written anywhere with such an intensity for a father. I also wrote about my father ("My Memories of My Father in my *Sentinels of the Soul)* and the pain is still excruciating but I salute finite Gopi for this ennobling and elevating attempt in his infinite abundance here!

Gopi adores and idolizes his father, though:

> I know you'll want me to come
> because we have hurt each other the most
> ....
> ....
> I've been your vagabond
> you have been my wound
> and I,
> the notebook of poems,
> your pet,
> you would carry with you
> across the river of life.
>
> —Number 4

This number is a beautiful summing up this relationship underlining the poet's accomplishment and, perhaps, his wish fulfilled. The poet wanted to be like his father:

> Tall handsome lover,
> the secret dream of all that I wished to be,
> who could hold the beautiful women of the world
> in your smoking hand.
>
> —Number 5

> My once, awesome six feet one,
> You towered above us as we listened to you.
>
> —Number 35

His dear dad was a lover of foliage, white roses, hill stations, a keen watcher and observer of the colours of birds, who turned many hands of high ranking state officials and remained "good natured sir."

In fact, sufferings harden the sensitive and when such sufferings are dead, poetry wakes up in them:

> I have now set out to do the things
> you loved most about me.
> About a gift of poetry.
> Never wrote like this before,
> perhaps, never again, must,
> ....
> for you hold my hand
> and I write on.
>
> —Number 14

Gopi realizes how he gave jingling tears to his dad who was always seriously concerned for the well-being and progress of his son. His father had a commanding personality, a perfectionist with aristocratic habits, a respected and feared and magnanimous bureaucrat, a lover of nature and aesthetics, a force and an authority with a roaring voice; his stern exterior concealed the tenderness and silken love of the rose.

> father, my once handsome young man.
>
> —Number 18

You were a good man.
....
....
Through the pastures of your years
as we grew,
your light flickered for us all....
—Number 19

The poet has a very subtle and clear imagination and he sees and feels from his fathomless sea each and every moment of father failing, lingering and falling and shares the same with us with his profound poetic potentiality. He proudly remembers the fair charms of his so gifted dad:

You were so fair.
Your colour attracted you to the birds.
Now, all the birds have flown.
—Number 20

The sight of the father in deep pain and agony transports Gopi into the labyrinths of religion and spirituality. He has regrets, stubborn concealments of true emotion which he is consciously trying to wrap in his blushing boldness. He says:

Did I ever love you?
I do not think I ever cared
if I ever loved you at all.
—Number 24

What a confession! He has traveled across the oceans to touch him, to wake him up from his recently learnt art of sleeping peacefully. There is not a moment of ease for him now; his mounting pain becomes a mounting tension and Gopi has shown a rare control, calm and poise. He can't hide the fact:

You are shepherd,
It is a pipe you are blowing,
You are blowing it downhill
Where pain grows its bursting buds......
—Number 25

The poet's fierce pain to see the father in this condition is felt in these lines:

Why were you chosen
to play the cripple,
to play, turning slowly to bone,
to be a memory of flesh
hanging shred
upon cold blood trees?
—Number 5

The father endured infinite pain in silence which ennobled his appearance and the Master showed Himself:

In pain He carved mountains of silence,
stuffed bright yellow butterfly wings
into the mouths of fiery red ants.
So, the story goes and goes.
—Number 32

God is the Creator of man and beauty, and He is a great artist to camouflage it with pain, the song of which humanity listens, sings and hums in tunes infinite. Here the poet expresses most poignantly the pain and agony which very few artists have the beauty to reveal:

It is the God of death dancing.
Amma, pray that father must die.
You are the one who's holding him back now.
If you let him go, he'll be happy.
We'll all be happy. Let god take him.
—Number 31

Gopi Kottoor tells us that his father lived in two eras: black and white. We can understand that his complete personality had been cast in these two widely variant cultures and social systems and he managed his whole life at home, at work and in social relations in that design. We do see and relish the writ and print of that design on what the poet is. He says:

Father, you belonged to the black and the white era.
You roared with a drone of a world war 2 plane

over our childhood sky,
and shone like our brightly laced Murphy radio.

—Number 26

This great dad smoked his Players sending up the curls of smoke. Each and every action of his dad brought back the reminiscences of the poet's earlier years under the terrible affections of this great soul. When we go down Gopi's memory lane with him, we too experience a live revival.

So many things refuse to die,
without you.

—Number 28

Fathers are needed all the time. Their presence makes us carefree and solemnly guides the course of our daily life. Otherwise life goes amiss at many places a number of times and we yearn for the advice of "the roaring drone" of our life. It is too late, Gopi! I too am rolling in pain with you.

His dad was a living inspiration to him in his poetic occupation and he would ever motivate him against his will. The poet's will will not work before dad's persistent motivation. The poet says:

I do not want to write these poems,
But you don't seem to want to make me stop.

—Number 30

Such a flow of thought and emotion interplay with each other in unusual images and words compounding into new expressions and technique of construction. That is what lends freshness of fragrance to his poems and we inhale its whiffs that intoxicate us and we wake up in pastoral regions populated with metro-culture. Gopi acknowledges his debt to his dear dad for prodding him on to write poetry and for making the final finest sacrifice for him by saving his poems on the shelf like pigeons and he carried them on him like coloured feathers (Number 37). His subtle immortal ambition to rise like phoenix from his ashes is the finest stroke of poetic sensibility:

and let me rise,
flaming
in your ashes.
—Number 37

Gopi must relax and comfort and give eternal relief to his Bhishma Pitamah lying on the tip of arrows waiting for the heavenly relief. He says:

after all these years
the time has now come
for me to obey you, father.
....
....
Must you die, father.
Decide your time,
I have the bow, and the arrows by my side.
—Number 40.

The last of the father, when he was brought out on a bed of wheels, was unexpected in the expected and the inevitable happened. Now distant like the Mars, the father left the legacy of his redness in the colour of the blood of his children, and they want to retain and preserve the dust-storm of his precious dust. So, dear idol, we look to you to:

Be our magic mountain, magic sleeper,
we'll keep your lesson,
that pain is all the treasure we have here on this earth.
Go back in now.
....
Come back,
And, wake us, in passing, in paradise.
—Number 41

There is a visible touch of the metaphysical beyond in these lines marked by hope and faith in the reunion. The last Number 42 closes this First Section on a completely different note merging the festivity into the freedom of the soul.

The entire construction of artistry the wounded and the bleeding poet is a lavishly rich compensation to both the wounded. Gopi's wounds—old, open, unhealed and gone dry—are more aching. And no amount of compensations, in whatever spirit offered and bequeathed, has ever made up for the losses. However, in the present cursed times of deliberate dereliction or compensation for a consideration, we shall speak goldenly of your service and it will shine in the pearls from our eyes. This is a pointer to what it is to have a father above and how it is to be without him above!

This specimen of Gopi's poetic accomplishment has raised and multiplied our genuine hopes that his tallness will overshadow many in the noble tradition of great poetry anywhere!

Works Cited

Kottoor, Gopikrishnan: *Victoria Terminus, Poems: Selected and New;* Authorspress, New Delhi, Edition 2010.

3

Quest for Empowerment: Revulsion and Reverse Sexism in Kamala Das

—Kanwar Dinesh Singh

Gender equality refers to providing equal opportunities to men and women, and in order to achieve that equality the need for empowering women was felt and, therefore, as of today, efforts have been made to make women self-confident through education and economic independence by providing them with a number of opportunities. Empowerment here refers to enable women to take control over their lives, pursue their own goals, live according to their wishes, desires and preferences, develop self-reliance and be able to make their own choices, and priorities and speak their minds. The term 'empowerment' has a variety of connotations and suggestions, but in literary gender-based discourses, it addresses women as victims of social discrimination and exclusion from decision making, and participating in matters of household as well as social and political positions on an equal footing with men, as discussed in the movement called feminism. After India got independence, quite a few of the women writers of India, especially those writing in English, began voicing their feminist proclivities as manifest in the works of women poets like Kamala Das, et al.

Kamala Das is regarded as the pioneer of modernism and feminism in Indian women's poetry in English. She is said to have brought about a revolution in the literary arena, especially in the field of women's writing, with her candid articulation. Most of her poems voice her quest for women's empowerment and gender equality, but in doing so, she seems to be countering the sexist bias of men, by subverting the whole traditional family structure in Indian society. She writes with a sense of antipathy and *reverse* sexism, as evident in her autobiography, *My Story* (1976), novel, poetry and short fiction published between 1965 and 1996. The present paper focuses on antipathy, revulsion and counter-sexism used as tools for securing women's emancipation and empowerment in the family as well as society as voiced in most of her poems. The discussion is based on an analysis of select poems from Das's poetic corpus, which include five volumes of poetry, *Summer in Calcutta* (1965), *The Descendants* (1967), *The Old Playhouse and Other Poems* (1973), *The Anamalai Poems* (1985) and *Only the Soul Knows How to Sing* (1996), besides a brief overview of her autobiography, *My Story* (1976).

Das's acrimony and revulsion against the system seems to have originated from her sense of frustration in her marriage. Her frustration is so highly pronounced that she seems to have no restraint on her verbal effusions, which range from emotive to vituperative modes of articulation. Her discomfiture in the given circumstances is articulated in her parlance, as through bestial imagery in the poem "Composition": "Now here is a girl with vast / Sexual hunger, / A bitch after my own throat." (Das: 1967: 31).

Where sexism refers to sexual oppression of women, which can be seen across almost all the cultures across the world, the term 'reverse sexism' has been used to describe the antipathy and prejudice expressed by women against men, as the radical feminists have come out with precisely the same type of prejudice which they so ardently oppose. In her essay, "The Myth of the Myth of the Vaginal Orgasm," Jill Johnston (1982), expresses reverse discrimination in a quite belligerent and sophistic manner:

> The man retains the prime organ of invasion. Sexual congress between man and woman is an invasion of the woman, the woman doesn't get anything up to participate in this congress, and although a woman may be conditioned to believe that she enjoys this invasion and may in fact grow to like it if her male partner makes rare

> sacrifices of consideration in technical know-how, she remains the passive receptive hopeful half of a situation that was unequal from the start. The fate that woman has to resign herself to is the knowledge of this biological inequity.
>
> (Johnston: 1982)

In a similar tone, Kamala Das articulates her revulsion and antipathy against the sexual congress, in her very first sexual encounter, which she describes no less than an "unsuccessful rape":

> I asked for love, not knowing what else to ask
> For, he drew a youth of sixteen into the
> Bedroom and closed the door. He did not beat me
> But my sad woman-body felt so beaten.
> The weight of my breasts and womb crushed me...
>
> (Das: 1973: 26)

Das was not happy with her marriage, as it was not fixed with her consent. As she reveals in her autobiography, *My Story* (1976): "there was nothing remotely Gandhian about my wedding" (p. 87). She describes her husband as an oversexed, lecherous person, having least or no emotional warmth at all. Gradually, she developed distaste for him: "I wanted conversation, companionship and warmth. Sex was far from my thoughts... I had hoped for a more tranquil relationship . . . I had no need at all for rough hands riding up my skirts or tearing up my brassiere" (p. 84). She found herself to be a "victim of a young man's carnal hunger" (p. 85). She describes marriage as a painful and humiliating experience. Her descriptions of love and lovemaking are mostly anti-erotic. In a poem "In Love", Das's corporal/anatomical imagery presented with a sense of revulsion clearly manifest her sense of antipathy against her man making love to her:

> He talks, turning a sun-stained
> Cheeks to me, his mouth, a dark
> Cavern, where stalactites of
> Uneven teeth gleam, his right
> Hand on my knee, while our minds

Willed to race towards love;
But, they only wander, tripping
Idly over the puddles of
Desire . . .

(Das: 1965: 14)

To Das, sexual love is a rape when it is not combined with emotion. Here, she sounds to be echoing the credo of the feminists, as put forth by radical feminists and lesbianists, the Leeds Revolutionary Feminists: "A rose is a rose and so is 'penetration', any act of penetration being tantamount to 'rape'" (Evans: 1982). An extreme case of reverse sexism can be found in the *SCUM Manifesto* written by Valerie Solanas (1983) and released in 1983 by the Matriarchy Study Group in London, SCUM being the acronym for Society to Cut Up Men, where blatant statements such as the following are made: "To be male is to be deficient, emotionally limited; maleness is a deficiency disease and males are emotional cripples . . ." (Solanas: 1983). Even Kamala Das says there is "boredom and the ennui of meaningless sexual encounters" (Rahman: 1981: 49) in lovemaking. She describes her disconcerting experience in "Convicts":

That was the only kind of love
This hacking at each other's parts
Like convicts hacking, breaking clods
At noon. We were earth under hot
Sun. there was a burning in our
Veins the cool mountain nights did
Nothing to lessen heat.

(Das: 1967: 26).

She abhors the marital love turning into lust and woman only gratifying the ego of her man, as depicted in the poem "The Looking Glass": "Stand nude before the glass with him / So that he sees himself the stronger one / And believes it so, and you much more / Softer, younger, lovelier." (Das: 1967: 25). Here, she seems to be endorsing the viewpoint of the radical feminists who consider penetration as a symbolic act of oppression because it is the oppressor (man) who enters the body of the oppressed and the penis is the tool of oppression. Thus, Das's metaphors, imagery and idiolect insinuate a kind of *reverse* sexism, reacting against the oppressive-compulsive strains she experiences in marital relationship. She tries even extramarital love, several times, but does not find her soulmate. Every lover she encounters proves only a substitute, as she laments in her poem "Substitute": "After that love became a swivel-door / When one went out, another came in,/Then I lost count, for always in my arms/Was a substitute for a substitute." (Das: 1967: 7). Such a confession, however, speaks of her own psychosexual anesthesia and emotional instability as she censures all men coming into her life.

Das's poem, "An Introduction" from her maiden number of poems entitled *Summer in Calcutta*, in an autobiographical-confessional-assertive mode, voices her strong revulsion and rebellion against the tradition-ridden male-dominated Indian society that imposes undue restraints on women. This poem is the voicing of her feminist credo in a quite self-assured and aggressive manner. The poem presents her self-portrait from childhood to adulthood, which is fraught with several bitter-sweet experiences of physical/sexual development, self-discovery, socialization, and identification and comparison of self with others. She feels that she constantly swings between sin and piety, between love and perfidy, and between elation and desolation. She empathizes with others, finding similitude in tribulations experienced by her as well as by others. She finds herself repressed at times, but, in any case, she has the grit of asserting herself: "I too call myself I". Poems like "Summer in Calcutta", "The Dance of the Eunuchs", "The Freaks", and "My Grandmother's House" from her first collection also deal ironically with her yearning for love and emotional fulfilment. In "My Grandmother's House", she expresses her disappointment at not receiving the love and affection that she used to receive from her grandmother in her house at Malabar. The death of her grandmother comes to her as a big jolt that shatters her completely because now she finds no one capable of providing her with the desired succour in her moments of dejection. Her husband and even other men from whom she seeks love prove only a mirage, as none of them can rise beyond their selfish interests. The poems such as "The

Descendants", "The Invitation", "Convicts", "Substitute" and "The Looking Glass" from her collection *The Descendants* too have the recurrent theme of the pursuit of love and sexual fulfilment. The title poem of her later volume *The Old Playhouse and Other Poems* raises the question of self-respect, identity and free will of a wife. She depicts how a wife is humiliated and reduced to a servile and subservient woman bogged down by dull and dreary domestic chores and complying silently with the commands of her husband. Besides, it expresses a woman's reaction against sexual slavery she undergoes with her male partner. She describes how she has lost her "will and reason" and "Beneath his monstrous ego", becomes "a dwarf." The poems such as "The Prisoner", "The Stone Age", "Glass" also voice her protest against patriarchy and sexual monopoly of men.

Kamala Das is regarded as a confessional poet for most of her poetry is fraught with autobiographical content in a reminiscent mode, and especially revealing those private experiences of her life which an average Indian woman would not prefer to divulge. She has very candidly expressed her feeling of dissatisfaction with her marriage, and her state of emotional vacuity, her sexual cravings and her urges for clandestine extra-marital relationships which are not approved by the traditional Indian society. Speaking freely and publicly of her private and personal experiences and feelings includes her in the category of confessional writers. The man-woman relationship with diverse aspects of love, marriage and sexuality forms the major strain in her poetry. In most of her poems, she emphasizes on the various shades of love; often the failure or lack of love in her subjective context. But as she talks about discontent in love / lovemaking and marriage, it has a strong undercurrent of her longing for emancipation from a bond that has been imposed on her, without caring for her wishes and desires.

In many a poem, Das raises her voice against the convention of arranged marriage that never cares for a woman's inherent wish, and does not allow a woman to take part in decision-making even when it concerns her own life. Her poem "My Grandmother's House" deals with a woman's quest for love and tenderness, besides voicing anguish of being married to a stranger who was never her choice and with whom she has altogether lost her ego, self-respect and dignity. She expresses her deep anxiety for not receiving the warmth of love in her present relationship with a man, as she had received from her grandmother in her early childhood. She wistfully recalls her childhood days spent in the house of her grandmother where she had received selfless and unconditional love: ". . . I lived in such a house and/Was proud, and loved . . ." (Das: 1990: 45-46). She compares and contrasts the ambiance she has found in her childhood with the atmosphere now she finds with the man she is putting up with or is just pulling on life with. However, she does not mention whether the man whom she addresses to be her "darling" is husband or a lover. Besides, she mentions strangers she comes in contact with from whom she seeks reciprocation of love:

> . . . I who have lost
> My way and beg now at strangers' doors to
> Receive love, at least in small change?
> (Das: 1990)

In the new environment, she has a feeling of strangeness without any promise of emotional fulfilment. A sense of alienation disconcerts her and creates in her an aversion to the present milieu. Struck with the memory of her grandmother's house, she nostalgically pines for reliving the past: "How often I think of going / There . . . ." (Das: 1990). Although the poem is in a subjective tone, yet it concerns the predicament and destiny of a traditional Indian woman, which is ordained or planned for her by the others, rarely in keeping with her wish or will. After marriage, in keeping with tradition, an Indian woman is compelled to leave her parents and all blood relations behind for a stranger's house. With the change of place, a woman has to face the difficult duality of shifting love and loyalties, and accepting and adapting to the new atmosphere and in doing so most of the time she has to compromise against her will with the given circumstances and conditions. Kamala Das's viewpoint in this poem is both feminine and feminist. She is feminine in her urging for the motherly love and showing concern for her grandmother and having emotional attachment with the reminiscences of the past. But, she sounds to be a feminist in voicing her predicament in her relationship with the male partner. She censures him harshly for not providing her with the same warmth of love as she has received in her childhood from her grandmother. Her yearning to "pick an armful of / Darkness to bring it here to lie / Behind my bedroom door like a brooding / Dog . . ." (Das: 1990) bespeaks of her lonesomeness and need for a loyal companionship and describes her state of being as inferior in the male-ruled world like that a dog tethered to its master's stake. Her simile and metaphor, as also her tone, are full of antipathy and rebellion against the male-governed system and articulates her inherent wish to subvert it for enabling women to live on her own terms and go by her choices and yearnings.

However, the poet's view is too pessimistic. She sounds to be overcritical of the connubial bond and too skeptical and disrespectful of the traditional Indian family system and values. There is a big paradox in the poem, which is felt towards the end of the poem when the poet expresses her powerful urge to be loved and to "beg now at strangers' doors to / Receive love, at least in small change?" (Das: 1990). Here the poet seems to be seeking love in reciprocation from those whom she loves, and in doing so her own loving is not selfless or unconditional. It is love of a very ordinary and lower level when one talks of reciprocity in love. True love is never give and take. In being confined to self and anticipating selfless loving or reciprocity of love ("at least in small change") from others ("strangers") makes the poet sound too self-centred and pessimistic about others. One needs intensive self-exploration to enable oneself to deserve love and respect from others. Besides, Das talks about begging for love at the doors of the "strangers", which is again self-contradictory as she is seeking love from people who are strangers and for whom she scarcely has any feeling of belongingness or closeness. The poet's diction is both inapt and inept in articulating the actual feeling.

Das's another poem "The Old Playhouse" voices in an even stronger rebellious tone and with greater antipathy, her reaction to the conventional patriarchal organization of the

Indian society that oppresses and suppresses women. The poet questions the specific customary and stereotyped gender roles prescribed to men and women by the male-governed society. The norms in the society are mainly manoeuvred by the males, and the females are the silent conformists to those norms under oppressive-compulsive circumstances. The patriarchal society deems man to be dominating, aggressive, assertive and superior, and woman to be secondary, subordinate, servile, subservient, submissive and yielding. Das depicts how a woman as wife is, under the "monstrous ego" of her husband, reduced to a "dwarf", that is, a person living in servility and submission; a person shorn of identity and individuality:

> . . . Cowering
> Beneath your monstrous ego I ate the magic loaf and
> Became a dwarf . . .
>
> (Das: 1973: 1)

The husband has been depicted not just suppressing the wife physically and sexually, but also repressing her emotionally and psychologically: "I lost my will and reason, to all your / Questions I mumbled incoherent replies" (Das: 1973: 1). The female persona of the poem, which is most probably the poet herself, expresses her disappointment and dissatisfaction over her botched connubial ties. She likens herself to a swallow and her husband to a captor who has tamed her completely. He has subjugated her with his physical power, restrained her freedom and has even deprived her of the comforts that she has enjoyed in her pre-marital life:

> You planned to tame a swallow, to hold her
> In the long summer of your love so that she would forget
> Not the raw seasons alone, and the homes left behind, but
> Also her nature, the urge to fly, and the endless
> Pathways of the sky.
>
> (Das: 1973: 1)

After marriage, she has realized that her husband is a self-seeking and highly egotistical man, having no concern for her inner cravings. He has been taking pleasure in her body and in making love with her, but has been totally indifferent to her emotional needs. In his pursuit of physical gratification, he remains ignorant of the fact that he has been finally failing in providing the requisite emotional warmth of love to his wife. To him, a wife is a mere housewife and sex-object, conforming to his corporeal desires. She presents a revolting description of her husband's bestiality in lovemaking:

> . . . You were pleased
> With my body's response, its weather, its usual shallow
> Convulsions. You dribbled spittle into my mouth, you poured
> Yourself into every nook and cranny, you embalmed
> My poor lust with your bitter-sweet juices.
>
> (Das: 1973: 1)

The experience of lovemaking has been depicted scruffily with a sense of revulsion. The husband remains concerned with gratification of his senses through the swerves and quivers of the wife's body. Here the husband maybe successful in pleasing his wife physically but he proves a total failure in providing her the craved affection and emotional satiety. The wife has found nothing except lessons on how to conform to the husband's will and ego: ". . . every / Lesson you gave was about yourself." (Das: 1973: 1). She laments the lowly, subordinate position she has been put to by her tyrannical husband:

> . . . You called me wife,
> I was taught to break saccharine into your tea and
> To offer at the right moment the vitamins.
>
> (Das: 1973: 1)

Kamala Das depicts how a woman is shorn of her dignity and self-respect as she is reduced to a mere housewife bogged down by the lacklustre quotidian routine, performing all domestic chores. The wife's self-identity is lost somewhere in her slavery to her conceited and egocentric husband. She feels smothered in her husband's house reeking of his masculine whiff. Even the "cut flowers / In the vases have begun to smell of human sweat": ". . . Your room is / Always lit by artificial lights, your windows always / Shut. Even the air-conditioner helps so little,

/ All pervasive is the male scent of your breath." (Das: 1973: 1). Devoid of singing, dancing and rejoicing, her mind is like an old murky and messed up 'Playhouse': ". . . There is / No more singing, no more a dance, my mind is an old / Playhouse with all its lights put out." (Das: 1973: 1). The poet-persona is fed up with the ambiance of the husband's house, and decides to free herself of it. She is determined to leave the house devoid of love and care. She finds that her husband has been a powerful man subjugating her physically and sexually and never providing her with the emotional care and concern which is certainly killing her bit by bit: " . . . The strong man's technique is / Always the same, he serves his love in lethal doses." (Das: 1973: 1). Like Narcissus, as it were "haunted / By its own lonely face", she feels beleaguered by the intensity of her craving for love, which can be realized solely by emancipating herself from that ravening environment, even through suicide, if she finds no other way out. She longs for a "pure, total freedom":

> For, love is Narcissus at the water's edge, haunted
> By its own lonely face, and yet it must seek at last
> An end, pure, total freedom, it must will the mirrors
> To shatter and the kind night to erase the water.
> (Das: 1973: 1)

The poem voices the angst and ire of the average Indian woman, especially belonging to the middle and lower classes, who as a housewife leads a life of bondage, conforming to her husband's absolutist yardsticks. She hardly finds any emotional fulfilment in her marriage. The conjugal relationship to her is no more than a bond of the master and the slave.

Evidently, Das's writings can be read at least as a critique of oppression and victimization of women in a patriarchal society, besides her longing for women's emancipation and empowerment. She has frequently employed the context of her own marriage and sexual encounters to depict the condition of women vis-à-vis sexual politics in the Indian society. But, Das's quest for women's emancipation and empowerment is fraught with gross revulsion and a kind of *reverse* sexism, thereby showing her aggression, anger and estrangement from any relationship of love with men. But, as she reveals in *My Story* (1976), she wrote her autobiography as a commercial publication, in the form of a series of articles for a popular magazine and, therefore, one cannot deny ambiguity, affectation and artifice in her writing, as Shirley Geok-lin Lim observes, "the spiritual impulse and the commercial intention are both evident in the dialogic, ambiguous, and contradictory features of the text" (Lim: 350). In one of her writeups, published in *Indian Express* ("Flair", *The Express Magazine*, 29 December 1996), Das made a mawkish statement that Indian men were losing their masculinity. In a quite cynical and sceptical way, she mentioned certain sexual aberrations and abnormalities distorting the masculine identity of men. It was again with a commercial point of view and with a little bit of notoriety and mischief to tantalize and provoke her readers she wrote all that. It was "not out of her sociological thinking but because of her own persecution complex" and "being broodingly resentful towards her personal experiences that she attempts at justifying herself by a flamboyant feminism" (Singh: 2004: 148).

Das's commercial viewpoint in her writing outright puts a question mark even on her integrity and authenticity as a writer. As, in *The Waffle of the Toffs*, M. Prabha observes, Kamala Das has offered "sex loaded poems" and such a stuff has been a "real change for the hungering Indian male" (Prabha: 224). Indeed, such writings may create a sensation and may have a certain nuisance value to provoke the readers, but cannot be said to provide a genuine picture of the society. Besides, as it pertains to a very delicate bond between the sexes, such opinionated writings may lead to reciprocal hatred and even worsen the problem rather than settling it. Such terms of emancipation and empowerment founded on an individual writer's whims and fancies and "sexual hunger" (Das: 1967: 31) may lead to a bitter kind of schism in the Indian society, which has a longstanding and accepted system of values for running family in a smooth manner with mutual understanding, respect and tolerance. The need is to work out solutions for problems in the system rather than devising counter-mechanisms to aggravate them.

Works Cited

Das, Kamala. *My Story*, New Delhi: Sterling Publishers, 1976.

____ . *Summer in Calcutta*. New Delhi: Everest Press, 1965.

____ . *The Descendants*. Calcutta: Writers Workshop, 1965.

____ . *The Old Playhouse and Other Poems*, Madras: Orient Longman, 1973.

____ . *Tonight, This Savage Rite. New Delhi: Arnold Heinemann, 1990.*

____ "My Grandmother's House", *An Anthology of Commonwealth Poetry*, ed. C. D. Narasimhaiah, Madras: Macmillan, 1990, pp. 45-6.

Evans, M. *The Woman Question*, London: Fontana Books, 1982.

Geok-lin, Lim Shirley. "Terms of Empowerment in Kamala Das's *My Story*", in *De/Colonizing the Subject: The Politics of Gender in Women's Autobiography*. Ed. Sidonie Smith & Julia Watson. Minneapolis: University of Minnesota Press, 1992.

Johnston, Jill. "The Myth of the Myth of the Vaginal Orgasm", in M. Evans, *The Woman Question*, London: Fontana Books, 1982.

Prabha, M. *The Waffle of the Toffs*, New Delhi: Oxford University Press & IBH, 2000.

Singh, Kanwar Dinesh. "Das's feminist camouflage", *Indian Express*, 13 January 1997.

___ . *Feminism and Postfeminism: The Context of Modern Indian Women Poets Writing in English*, New Delhi: Sarup & Sons, 2004.

Solanas, Valerie. *SCUM Manifesto*, The Matriarchy Study Group, London, 1983.

4

Ecowisdom in Keki N. Daruwalla's Poems "Wolf" and "The Last Howl"

—Suresh Frederick

Keki Nasserwanji Daruwalla (1937-) has established himself as a significant vocal voice in Indian English poetry. His poetry sprouts from the life around him. He is a poet with an impressively developed social conscience. F.A. Inamdar in *Critical Spectrum: the Poetry of Keki N. Daruwalla,* says that Keki's poetry is the "poetry of social comment" (http:// books.google.co.in). Daruwalla is a recipient of the Sahitya Akademi Award and the Commonwealth Poetry Award. He has published many books, consisting chiefly of poems and two fictional works. Some of his important works are *Under Orion, The Keeper of the Dead, Landscapes, A Summer of Tigers and The Minister for Permanent Unrest and Other Stories.* He has also edited a collection of poems entitled *Two Decades of Indian poetry*.

Keki N. Daruwalla speaks out in support of the subaltern. Gaurav Kanthwal in "Voice of a Subaltern Subject" says, "His is a voice of a subaltern subject (To Writers Abroad) continually bringing forth the pluralities of India, its contradictions, harmony and diversity of experiences, all attributing a distinct identity to the nation and itself" (www. tribuneindia.com). The poems of Keki N. Daruwalla are known for their richness. This richness is derived from the presentation of the suppressed. He acts as the voice of the voiceless.

Ecocriticism speaks for the voiceless earth. This approach is earth-centred and all the other approaches are eco-centred.

This way of looking at literature started with the publication of William Ruecker's *Literature and Ecology: An Experiment in Ecocriticism* in 1978. According to Michael P.Branch, William Rueckert was the first one to introduce the term "Ecocriticism" into the vocabulary of literary theory. This term is widely used in the United States of America and many other parts of the world, but in United Kingdom the term "Green Studies" is used. Some of the ecostudies focus on the anthropocentric vs the biocentric, culture vs nature, ecojustice, ecofeminism, pocoecocriticism etc. "Since these are in the formative years, it is very difficult to confine this in a bottle and say that it is ecocriticism" (Jha 127). Renowned ecocritics like Scott Slovic and others accept the "multitudes" present in Ecocriticism. "There is no single dominant world-view guiding ecocritical practice—no single strategy at work from example to example of ecocritical writing or teaching" (Coupe 160). One of the aims of ecocriticism is to "emphasise ecocentric values of meticulous observation, collective ethical responsibility and the claims of the world beyond ourselves" (Barry 264). The term 'ecological wisdom', or 'ecosophy', is a philosophy of ecological harmony or equilibrium. It was introduced by Norwegian philosopher Arne Naess in 1973. Even though, many feel that Arne Naess "does not go far enough" (Palmer 214), his term has done enough to go deep into literature.

Keki N. Daruwalla brings into focus the voiceless animals. Through two of his poems, "Wolf" and "The Last Howl", the poet brings into centrestage, the wolf, an animal which is despised by human beings. In the long list of wild animals hated by humans, the wolf appears prominently. The wolf is the largest member of the canine family. Gray wolves range in colour from grizzled gray or black to all-white. As the ancestor of the domestic dog, the gray wolf resembles German shepherds.

Wolves live, travel and hunt in packs of around six to ten animals. The packs include the mother and the father wolves, called the alphas, their pups and several other subordinate or young animals. The wolf packs are established according to a strict hierarchy, with a dominant male at the top and his mate not far behind. The alpha female and male are the pack leaders that track and hunt prey, choose den sites and establish the pack's territory. Wolves develop close relationships and strong social bonds. All of a pack's adults help to care for the young pups by bringing them food and watching over them while the others hunt. They often demonstrate deep affection for their family and may even sacrifice themselves to protect the family unit. These social animals cooperate on their preferred prey—large hoofed mammals such as deer, elk, and moose. Wolves are also known to eat beaver, rabbits and other small prey. They also eat smaller mammals, birds, fish, lizards, snakes, and fruit.

Through "Wolf", Keki N. Daruwalla brings a live image of the wolf before the eyes of the reader.

> Fire-lit
> half silhouette and half myth
> the wolf circles my past
> treading the leaves into a bed
> till he sleeps, black snout
> on extended paws.
>
> ("Wolf" 1-6)

In a fire-lit place, the outline of the wolf appears dark against a light background. For the poet, the wolf is half real and half myth. The wolf circles the past life of the poet as it walks on the leaves and makes them into a bed, with a black nose and big paws, till it sleeps. The wolf is a real animal, with flesh and blood. Humans have the tendency to make animals part of a myth and extirpate them. Wherever interactions between wolves and humans occur, the wolves frequently feature in the folklore and mythology of those cultures, both positively and negatively. The dark black nose and big huge paws made the humans fear this majestic animal. The gray wolf has longer legs and bigger paws, compared to coyotes and dogs. Their paws are also extra-large. Because of such paws, Gray wolves are easily able to walk on a variety of terrains.

The size and the colour of the animal has a different impact on the humans.

> Black snout on sulphur body
> he nudged his way into my consciousness.
> Prowler, wind-sniffer, throat-catcher
> his cries drew a ring
> around my night;
> a child's night is a village
> on the forest edge.
>
> ("Wolf" 7-14)

That black-coloured nose on the sulphur-coloured body has pushed his way into the consciousness of the poet. The wolf is branded as an intruder and it sniffs with the help of the wind to kill humans. In reality the truth is the other way round. Humans have intruded into the habitats of the wolf and indiscriminately killed them and other wild animals. Though once abundant over much of Eurasia and North America, the gray wolf inhabits a reduced portion of its former range due to the widespread destruction of its territory, human encroachment, and the resulting human-wolf encounters that sparked broad extirpation. Humans are afraid of the howling of wolves. Wolves are well-known for their terrifying howl, which they use to communicate. A lone wolf howls to attract the attention of his pack, while communal howls may send territorial messages from one pack to another. Some howls are confrontational. Much like barking domestic dogs, wolves may simply begin howling, because a nearby wolf has already begun. The total misunderstanding of the appearance and the howling of the wolves makes children fear the animal in the middle of the night.

The stories told by others, especially the mother to make the child to obey, become true to a child in the beginning and also when they are grown-up.

> My mother said
> his ears stand up
> at the fall of dew
> he can sense a shadow
> move across a hedge
> on a dark night;
> he can sniff out
> your approaching dreams;

there is nothing
that won't be lit up
by the dark torch of his eyes.
("Wolf" 15-25)

No doubt, the wolf is very sensitive to sound. With its large ears, it can listen even to a pin falling. Their auditory perception is very sharp, as they can hear up to a frequency of 26kH. But their sense of smell is relatively weakly developed, compared to that of some hunting dog breeds, as it is able to detect carrion upwind no farther than two–three kilometeres. Because of this, they rarely capture hidden hares or birds. So the child need not worry that its dreams will be sniffed out by the animal. The poet writes about the eyes of the wolf. Their eyesight is not as powerful as that of the dogs, though their night vision is the most advanced. Surely, the eyes of the wolf will lit up a dark night like a torch.

In the last stanza, Keki N. Daruwalla writes, "The wolves have been slaughtered now" ("Wolf" 26). The poet concludes, "A hedge of smoking gun-barrels / rings my daughter's dreams" ("Wolf" 27,28). Thus the child once afraid of the wolf cannot see or hear the wolf. He can only stare at the smoke from the barrel of the gun. In reality, the wolf, which survived the ice age, is considered a pest and a threat to the livestock and is hunted extensively by the humans. This poem unmistakably brings out the plight of the wolves, suffering in the hands of human beings.

The next poem, "The Last Howl" reinforces this suffering and the death of animals.

From steppe and tartary wolf stories came.
We heard them as children, thrilling with fear.
The cossack serf who hurled himself at them
was soon devoured, coat, cap and beard,
while master and children galloped to a safe haven.
("The Last Howl" 1-6)

The stories about the wolf come from steppes, the huge grasslands of Eurasia, chiefly in the Ukraine and Russia and Tartary, a vast region of eastern Europe and northern Asia was controlled by the Mongols in the thirteenth and fourteenth centuries. It extended as far east as the Pacific Ocean under the rule of Genghis Khan. Thus these stories are not from a nearby locality but from far-off places. As a child, the poet heard the story of a Cossack serf, a person in a condition of servitude, required to render service to a lord, commonly attached to the lord's land and transferred with it from one owner to another as well as a member of a people of southern European Russia and adjacent parts of Asia, noted as cavalrymen especially during czarist times, who was devoured fully (stress on coat, cap and beard) by a wolf while the master and his children dashed off to a safe shelter.

The poet moves from the far-off story to the reality.

> This was wolf country; whether the night was as black as
> a raven or moon-yellow as their pelts, the packs held sway.
> As they bayed a moment came when sorcerers threw salt
> in the fire and prayed for a spurt in the exorcizing flame.
> The wolves never left; their myths increased, glowing in
> the dark like fireflies. When people talked of salamander
> fires they had glimpsed a swarm of wolverine eyes.
>
> ("The Last Howl" 7-16)

The place where the poet lives was once a place full of wolves. There is no difference between a full moon night and a new moon night and wolves filled the place. Sorcerers tried their best to send away these animals in vain. People started telling stories about the wolves. When the people talked of the legendary salamander with fires, they had glimpsed a multitude of wolverine eyes. The name salamander is applied to both a mythical and a real creature, the one inspired by the other. The name comes from the Greek for "fire lizard". The real salamander is an amphibian, not a lizard. The salamander is a tailed amphibian. Salamanders are cold-blooded animals (their temperature changes with that of their surroundings). They have soft skin that is usually moist and must have a humid if not wet environment. Most species are found on land; a few are strictly aquatic. Land salamanders are often found under stones and logs. The legendry salamander was believed to be a creature of fire. The level of its elemental association varied. Sometimes it was simply fire resistant or would put out fire. At other times it was said to live in fire; sometimes it was even said to be born in fire. It has been said that salamanders were created when glass-blowers stoked their furnaces continually for seven days and nights. Already the salamander referred to in the poem is imaginary and the wolf is also elevated to that level.

The gardener also has a story to tell.

> My gardener said, however cold the first bleak light of day
> where once a wolf-flank had rested for the night
> the leaf-loam steamed as he slunk away.
>
> ("The Last Howl" 17-20)

The gardener said that on a cold day, he saw the flank of the wolf touch a leaf-loom and the loom boiled with smoke as the wolf walked away. So the wolf also has the power of the fire spitting salamander. Humans elevate animals to the level of a deity. Peter Barry in his important book on criticism, *Beginning Theory* writes, "Nature, then, isn't reducible to a concept which we conceive as part of cultural practice (as we might conceive a deity, for instance, and project it out onto the universe)" (252).

The poet does not want to reduce nature to a cultural practice and feels that the stories are hard to believe because the wolves of the locale are very small.

> Near home they were smaller, less than hip high and grey
> of flank, bellying forward at dusk to nibble at our villages
> as the wilderness shrank. They hunted in pairs, one
> caused a diversion, circled the village, bared his fangs,
> snarled. The other raced down the street and carried away
> a child.
>
> ("The Last Howl" 21-27)

These small grey wolves hunted in pairs and one day one of those wolves carried a child from the street.

A total change takes place in the behaviour of human beings after this act of the wolf.

> All the hungers of the world were caged in their bellies and hungers for the wild. After the last rabbit had bounced out of his hutch and the porcupine had shed his quills and the last swamp deer had slipped on bitumen and the barasingha had been felled by a telescope, they turned their snorkels to the moon and howled for the last time the howl of no hope. They sniffed the wind and moved into rnyth, into childhood dreams, allegory, fiction; and catching a scent of their own death they tracked it to extinction.
>
> ("The Last Howl" 28-38)

People indiscriminately killed all the animals in the vicinity. They have killed rabbits, porcupines, and different kinds of deer. The wolf left this biosphere with its last howl. Now the wild animals can be seen only in childhood dreams, allegory and fiction. This poem also tells how humans push the animals to extinction.

Glen A. Love in "Revaluing Nature" says, "The most important function of literature today is to redirect human consciousness to a full consideration of its place in a threatened natural world" (Glotfelty 237). This most important function of literature is vividly brought out by the poet. The poem "Wolf" is an embodiment of visual treat, where the figure of the wolf is brought before the readers' eyes. The poet warns of the total extinction of the wolf from the face of the earth. India has lost a vast majority of wolfs to human greed. Throughout all of North America, wolves were once common, but were killed in most areas of the United States by the mid-1930s. The same is their plight in many other countries. The second poem tries to give a reason for the killing of wild animals. Why did the dogs in the area not steal a child? This is purely because the dogs, which are another form of domesticated wolves, are well fed. The humans have taken over the habitat of the wolves and destroyed the food chain. J. Baird Callicott writes, "According to the ecological 'community concept', each species occupies a niche, role, or profession in the economy of nature. Just as in the human social microcosm there are farmers, truckers and doctors, each specializing in a particular task, so in the natural microcosm, there are producers (the green plants), consumers (animal of all sort), and decomposers (fungi, bacteria and the like)" (Palmer 152,153). The wolf is not allowed to have its niche. The humans want to take over all the territories available. Just like any other domesticated animal, the humans want the wolves to live on the leftovers. But the majestic and wild wolf does not budge and fall into the predetermined pattern designed by the humans for the wild animals.

In "The Social Construction of Nature", Terry Gifford asserts that 'Wild', as in wild ecosystem, is "richly interconnected, interdependent and incredibly complex" (Coupe 176). Surely left alone in the forest, the wild animal would have lived without disturbing any one. The humans look for ways of destroying the wild animals because they feel that the wild animals are useless to them. In "Oikopoetics", Nirmal Selvamony writes, "Even animals were ranged in a hierarchic order—the domestic and the wild" (4). In the human made hierarchy, domesticated animals are given importance and wild animals are rejected as useless. Here the dog which is a domesticated form of wolf, is given importance and called a friend of man whereas the wolf is rejected and butchered. Even the proverbs involving the wolf give a negative colour to the wolf. Gary Snyder says, "Wildness can said to be the essential nature of nature" (Coupe 127). Without wildness, nature cannot exist. "Black Elk's rhetoric routinely implies the egalitarianism among all the children of Father Sky and Mother Earth—human animal or non-human animal or plant" (Palmer 152). This kind of egalitarianism among the human animal, the non-human animal and the plant is the need of the hour. Instead of living in amity, the humans have become the predators who predate on wild animals. This will not last for ever. Cheryll Glotfelty in her introduction to *The Ecocriticism Reader: Landmarks in Literary Ecology,* wants the ecocritics to look for the "ecological wisdom" (xv) in a work of art. As a reader also, one has to understand the underlying meaning of a text and come to informed conclusions. The human animal, the non-human animal and the plant should become a biotic community to overcome further destruction.

Works Cited

Barry, Peter. *Beginning Theory : An Introduction to Literary and Cultural Theory*. Manchester : Machester UP, 2002.

Coupe, Laurence. ed. *The Green Studies Reader: From Romanticism to Ecocriticism*. London: Routledge, 2000.

Daruwalla, Keki N. *Landscapes*. New Delhi: OUP, 1987.

Glotfelty, Cheryll and Harold Fromm. (ed.) *The Ecocriticism Reader: Landmarks in Literary Ecology*. Georgia: The University of Georgia Press, 1996.

Inamdar F.A. *Critical Spectrum: the Poetry of Keki N. Daruwalla* (http://books.google.co.in)

Jha, Gauri Shankar. *Indian English Poetry: Recent Explanations*. Delhi: Authorspress, 2008.

Palmer, Joy A. ed. *Fifty Great Thinkers on the Environment*. London: Routledge, 2004.

Selvamony, Nirmal. *Tinai 1*. Chennai: Persons for Alternative Social Order, 2001.

http://www.tribuneindia.com/2006/20060709/spectrum/book5.htm

5

Contemporary Ethics, Value System and Concept of Life in English Poetry in India

—P.C.K. Prem

It is difficult to define "Value". It is indefinite and yet it exists in many concrete forms in a man. If a man holds firmly to certain religious teachings, principles or words which are desirable and positive and which transparently assist man and society to make lives better and harmonious then he can be called a man of value system. It is interesting to evaluate the measures that are taken to safeguard value system which is more or less highly sophisticated, stereophonic and chiselled to suit individual's demands, particularly at a time when inconsequential politicians, not statesmen (for statesmen is a rare phenomenon now) determine ethics, values and morality in august houses when chairs and sandals are thrown at one another to arrive at a decision. This is what a kid in a nursery or a student in a learning institution or a scholar in a university learns while so-called system-drivers whether-politicians or bureaucrats or—intellectuals whosoever they are—sit cozily on seats of power with valuable possessions of glib tongue, soft-anger, aggrandizement, aggression and amassing instinct.

Earlier a man not only worked and earned for individual happiness but for the society also but now it is the self. Earlier it was self-restraint that mattered; now it is restraining others and even those in pursuit of truth and service..

Values or ethics or morals can be defined, yet the dividing line is thin. As times change, values undergo relative transformation. Ethics also change and so also the morals affect life with the shifting textures of period. Questions of endurance and stamina do matter. If one goes back, it could be called tribal value system when wholesome survival or self-preservation was paramount.

Origin and Background of Poets' Ethical Perception

Values are closely linked to self-discipline and self-control. If one tries to interpret values philosophically, one encounters satisfying and dynamic revealing moments where life becomes serene and meaningful for, Hindu theology stretches the meaning of values to spiritual dimensions which determine man's existence not on earth only but it goes beyond to teach man the art of becoming immortal. It is possible to have men of value system, honesty and integrity if sincere efforts are made. Perhaps this sacred thought continues to throb in the hearts of all right thinking men, the poets appear to believe here. To have a healthy workable ethical structure, it is better to create an atmosphere of poise and harmony.

Here the words of Swami Chinmayananda are quite appropriate when he observes: "All the great thinkers, through their varied philosophical flights, have, in their final conclusions, realized the need for programs to evolve the individual. By disciplining and thereby improving the individual, every culture tries to raise the tempo, quality and beauty of the total national life. A world ordered for progress, through improved individuals constituting the community, is the direction which all philosophers and scriptural prophets preach and work...this will sound as a strange conclusion to all those who are educated in our modern concepts of the materialists." But if "Politicians strive to bring concord into social life and maintain law and order in the community. Economists conceive schemes and plans to increase the wealth in the nation and redistribute it with equity and justice" (*The Art of Man-Making* 1, 2). The world would become a better place to live. Here he reminds us of what kind of values Mahatma Gandhi wanted in social and political system.

It also enshrines the value based life of which John Ruskin speaks about and more recently to which Mahatma Gandhi often referred to. It is this virtuous and arduously inculcated value-system that works wonders in all spheres of life from individual to society and then it extends to the health of a nation. Much earlier Confucius usually thought as a great teacher of morals and ethics, always insisted that a man must imbibe qualities of virtues, ethics, loyalty and truthfulness. A relentless struggle to cultivate good qualities, to be explicit and simple here is an anxiety one detects and realizes when poetic minds are cautiously analysed.

Swami Krishnananda makes is quite transparent when he interprets values or ethics and observes: "As *ethics* philosophy engages itself in the ascertainment of the nature of right and wrong, good and bad. It deals with the nature of moral standards and moral judgments, the rights and the duties of the individual, the society and the state, the national and international good, the nature and function of the conscience, and the like." (*The Philosophy of Life* 18)

If analyzed without creating confusion it is quite clear that one must comprehend the implications of various meanings of 'good' and 'bad' and only then meaning of 'values' or 'ethics' will become evident. In the present context, before we come to examine the lyrics of Indian poets writing in English, a question arises as to the relevance of value system in the modern life-pattern. Are values relevant or already dead if not relevant? This thought will cudgel many intellects. A pessimist would bluntly tell that ethics or values or morals or...are already dead. If postmortem of the last half a century is undertaken, not a very magnificent picture will emerge. Though a splendid growth in all spheres of life stuns and bamboozles and a loud applause is reserved for many yet it is difficult to believe that ethics or values or morals or integrity or honesty have, in any case survived. Those responsible for materialistic growth also owe an answer to the history yet to be written, as to who killed ethics or morals. It is an institution of such unprincipled people who thrive under the shelter of favours, imprudence and nepotism that is responsible for the existing deterioration in the system. In this respect, it has to be examined if democracy as an institution or a system has survived or not?

To what extent has our education contributed to the unassailability of the virtues honesty and integrity? Where is the law really helpful? Is law honest? If such inconvenient questions are asked, the answer will be a pointblank no. To keep alive ethics is possible only if some really crazy and moral-obsessed men lit the flame of honesty and integrity not by the power of any institution or working system but by individual concerted efforts "to create and recreate" (to borrow Bernard Shaw's words) strong pillars of invisible forces of values in a resilient continuity. It is a great Vedic philosophy that enjoins a man to discharge his duty.

Swami Mahesanand Giri has appropriately defined values, when he observed: "Truth is one of the fundamentals of ethics. Actually all the virtues are considered by some as merely corollaries of this. Natural laws, ethical laws, religious laws, spiritual realizations are but the truths of those respective branches. All laws are thus expressed truths. To speak an untruth is only the grossest aspect. Even a truth spoken to hurt others or in a way that hurts others is considered an untruth. Shankara has emphasized this virtue beyond all others." (*Vedanta Philosophy for 21st Century* 11)

Truth is very important and if it is made a guiding principle of life, society will be a much better place to live. If one is worried about the happiness of others and works hard in that direction, it is a gratifying experience. It could be interpreted as a strong foundation of value-edifice.

Modern Life's Obsession with Physical and Material Considerations and the Poets' Sphere of Worries

Contemporary times are so complex and subtle that man's existence is exclusively dependent on the power of money. Materialistic considerations reign supreme in modern man's psyche. The malady is overwhelming and extensive, and culture is polluted, thoughts are spurious and feelings have gone astray where man measures everything with the strength of money. Many poets regret the fast growing strength and sphere of money which is crucial to the measuring of warmth in relations. A lack of moral qualities in life leads to a valueless system.

O. P. Bhatnagar speaks of values which affect life in a definite and positive way even if certain criteria to obey principles of life determine man's thoughts and actions. Man has still not learnt to live a harmonious life. Man was born free, Bhatnagar appears to suggest but exploitation continues and thus man lives with "tyranny, exploitation and rapes" while for a happy future, he prays and then turns to philosophy of values.

> So many years in sun and rain
> Has our freedom grown
> But far down in villages
> I' am the same –
> Oppressed, ill treated,
> Humiliated and strange.
> ... .
> I live in a languid sublimity of suffering
> With tyranny, exploitation and rapes
> Mixed with prayers, philosophy and fasts.
> ("The Still Questions," *The Audible Landscape* 13)

Man is very clever and selfish and in order to survive, he utilizes all available options from honesty to hypocrisy and untruth. Not for a moment, he diverts attention from the realities of life even while values are crushed and cultural heritage is wounded. Bhatnagar talks of pragmatic philosophy of ethics. Thoughts that make man's life better are essential in the modern context when instincts of survival rule the minds and hearts of people. Bhatnagar bemoans the terrible loss of values in life which is the essential cause of sufferings and miseries.

Here, one is also attracted towards a Christian thought which says that "...we must be self-restrained and live good and religious lives here in this present world, while we are waiting in hope for the blessing which will come with the appearing of the glory of our great God and savior....He sacrificed himself for us in order to set us free from all wickedness and to purify a people so that if could be his very own and would have not ambition except to do good." Bhatnagar sounds very relevant here. Man is hypocritical in words and behaviour and whatever he accomplishes in life; it is the consequence of false worship, fake obeisance and duplicity. Money and insincere conduct almost establish the depth of relations among men. Thus a silent deterioration takes place. Man knows and understands but still he shuts his eyes to the realities of life. Hypocrisy and love for money are other names for values now, when O. P. Arora says: "Why do you always paint nude?" He smiles: "Simple; there is more money in it." ("The Visitor," *The Creeping Shadows* 43). Elsewhere he says: "Deeds are nothing—/ seeds may be the best, / but you many not harvest. / Virtue is fleeting—/ by one turn, wrong or right / darkened may be what was white" ("Mirage," Ibid. 58). Even God is not spared. Manas Bakshi is somewhat vocal that man has even learnt to bribe God and everything on earth is available in his power.

> We have bribed that God
> With flowers, sweets and fruits
> When love for life
> Is lost to its roots,
> We have even changed
> The colour of God
> As we change religion into commodity
> For a vote-linked plot.
>
> ("God's Dilemma," *The Midnight Star* 14)

In the contemporary egalitarian set-up, it is a policy of votes which decides the fate of a region or a nation. The poet says that "Hypocrites turned public figures / Have yet to give Him more, / That cherished God is now, perhaps, / Seeking an escape door" (Ibid. 14). It is a general observation that the rich and the powerful often give more money to God to renovate its abode. This age survives on bribes and shares in unhealthy and valueless deeds, and here even God is not left untouched. Man makes Him a party to all scams and scandals as powerful people pay obeisance with bags full of money.

Here values are interlinked when questions of growth, progress and individual aspirations arise, and on the other hand, a region is defined as an offshoot of religion to hoodwink the gullible populace in a vote-catching apparatus where ethics get the lowest priority.

The modern man is exceedingly motivated and malicious. His insatiability and lust have left no scope for sublime human instincts to exist. The situation is beyond redemption when one finds that the invisible power-God wants to run away from the world. Material considerations govern the psyche of man and all the worldly affairs have an indelible stamp of mammon; and only wealth determines the morals and principles, values and ethics of man and now it is left to man to measure the depth of value system or maybe its disintegration. It is not money that builds up ethical foundation, it is man, but alas man in the contemporary world has lost his identity and distinctive presence. There exists nothing outside which adds sanctity to the life of a man. Right and wrong conduct of man is fast becoming irrelevant. Words and deeds grope in the dark for meaning.

On the other hand, D.C. Chambial is a poet of measured tone and words. Here, he speaks in a directness which is not his usual poetic quality. Corruption is a virtue of life in totality and it is like "flies" which is the cause of all the sickness in the society that is strongly inbuilt in the value-body a man follows:

> We are the denizens
> of such an age which breeds
> corruption like flies
> Those entrusted with
> the task to give a just
> and ethical rule, lead
> the vice and corruption
> to guillotine: feed
> them instead.
>
> ("The Tempest," *Gyrating Hawks & Sinking Roads* 15)

This symbolic use of 'flies' in fact stands for an absolute contaminated society. All evils and corrupt deeds are like flies which pollute the society. Chambial makes it apparent that people entrusted with the job to offer sleaze-free and transparent system are responsible for perpetuating such evils in the society. Perhaps rulers of the day have lost morals and values for which Indian Vedic culture and traditions are known.

Tragically enough, corrupt practices are considered an inseparable part of the value system of those now ruling the nation. As one will observe further, such strong indictments of people guiding the system are quite normal. This truth of unethical lifestyle is known to the people in power and interestingly these people also speak of ethics. Here, deeply repulsive and abhorrent feelings assault a man of integrity and logic for sheer double speak govern rulers' psyche, he understands. So nothing happens, and in silence they laugh and then mock at the pathetic words of moral teaching. Those who wish morality and values to prevail in life are ultimately despondent, crestfallen, beaten and finally face extinction. Bijoy Kant Dubey is sad and unhappy at the fall in quality of life around. With a heavy heart he remembers Gandhi, the great Mahatma of twentieth century who lived for peace and harmony. Bapu, as he was often called endearingly, fell to a bullet. He painfully recalls the tragic incident and regrets that people have forgotten the values he stood for. The poet with an aching heart says:

> Save, save us from bloodshed,
> From vengeance and carnage.
> We need you earnestly,
> The whole of India nay, the world...
> Your truth, non-violence, love and peace
> Humanity needs you
> O believer in universal brotherhood!
> Man riots for faiths but know not
> They in essence.----
>
> ("Bapu, Bapu-," *My Collected Poems* 35)

Erosion of ethical standards has led to irreparable loss in life as materialistic tendencies take roots. Distorted and disoriented values compel the poet in K. V. Dominic to say that the present disparities in the society exist because of the evil influence of wealth. He is appalled to observe a terrible gap between the rich and the poor. This hiatus has created yawning crevices even in human relations. A devouring gap between the exhibition of wealth and scarcity of even bare necessities of life causes nightmarish experiences. Life of slums forces even human beings to create fissures in warmth where earning livelihood brings forced separation.

> An old man and his wife resided there;
> sitting at the phone with sighs and moans,
> longed for the calls from their sons abroad.
> Not far away were the slums of the city;
> three generations lived in each hut;
> grandpa, grandma, their sons and their wives,
> and their little kids sleep in a room!
> ("A Nightmare," *Winged Reason* 23)

An ugly fall in the quality of life and values makes lives wretched and poor. To earn a livelihood is all right but then to forget old parents, speaks of an ailing social set-up. An advocate of socialistic pattern of society, Dominic in almost all the poems stands for the cause of the poor, and always speaks against the injustice and humiliation the poor people meet at the hands of the rich. An awful chasm between the rich and the poor appears to be perpetual. It is a predicament of the poet that despite sensitivity and a genuine desire to alleviate the sufferings of the poor and the neglected segment of the society, he is incapable of translating sublime thoughts to realities of life. It is difficult to disagree with the sensitive poets when they woefully lament over the loss of ethics and morality in private and public life. It is also observed that poets do not consider that the poor can be dishonest or corrupt. If the poor are corrupt, it is because the society compels them to become dishonest and immoral.

If quality of values is further examined, one finds that man is responsible for the grief-stricken declining qualities of life. In the modern set up, perhaps man does not want an ethical life to survive. R. A Janakiraman bemoans at the value-structure, that man rears up. Man is so much changed and degenerated that he believes in the power of money, and leaves nothing as a memorable heritage when he says, "Children measure all things by money; so they've sold all virtues for money! / After giving up all the good virtues / what use in crying about high ideals!" ("The Death of Virtues," *Arteries* 41). He regrets that at home children do not learn anything worthwhile, and parents only concentrate on materialistic achievements in life. Suresh C. Jaryal is quite unhappy when he observes an obvious fall in the quality of life. Ambitions in man play havoc and this attitude result in total discontentment and disillusionment. Material considerations are determining the level of relations in life and society. He is pained to observe:

> Everybody looks irrationally egocentric
> Everything is worked out in terms of money
> Truthfulness and purity of heart
> Propriety and honest are few and far between
> Life seem to be discernibly moved
> Towards the materialistic pole.
>
> ("Changing Faces," *Changing Faces* 37)

There are simple and pleasing images, and involved use of language is meticulously avoided. Jaryal's lyrics in plain words speak of a truth that cannot be contradicted. He speaks of life on earth and the falling standards of man along with principled value-system. Money-power is gradually eroding the spirit of real man, he says. But he still has hopes when he says that "for the revival of mankind on the Earth / for the sustainable happy bright future!" man must awake. Poets generally appear optimistic. Even while they see darkness around, rays of hope continue to cheer them up and this message they wish to convey. Man must strive and stay awake to catch right time and opportunity.

Deliberations on Corrective Measures and Imminent Premonition of Total Failure

In a way it always reveals the incapacity of an individual to fight against awe-filled magnitude of social ailment. Or is it that the poets hint at an easily foreseeable collective approach to correct the system? Poets are quite aware but know that in the absence of robust mental and moral health, nothing can be accomplished. Despite awe-inspiring media blitz, no ruler in the world has been able to infuse lofty and honest values around. Conceivably, it is the rulers and elites who vociferously profess that they are the benefactors of the people but cannot afford to live an ethical life; and so the polluted moral life continues.

Value system is not punctured as it appears on the surface. On the other side, Pashupati Jha paints a depressing picture of a mother who in a valueless social set-up, sells body to equip home with food. The words like "freshly squeezed", "night-out" and "orphaned" tell a harrowing tale of exploitation:

> But lo! What greets me
> first, the moment I step out—
> a mother of one freshly squeezed
> clutching two notes with beaming Mahatma
> stealthily rushing from a starred hotel
> to her home before the darkness
> is driven out by the peeping sun;
> her night-out is the only
> means to feed her family, untimely
> orphaned in the riot last year.
>
> ("Nature and Man," *Mother and Other Poems* 39)

This disastrous situation is also the handiwork of society in which her husband died. Nothing is left in life when fanaticism and religious frenzy rule the minds and hearts of people, the poet regrets. It is a heartrending commentary on the affairs of man where a woman has to auction her body so that she feeds her hungry children. What kind of value system we nurse is a tormenting and despairing question.

Here a mother stands for all the women who, in the existing sophisticatedly organized and primed social, economic and political structure, are often driven to a world of glamour and flesh trade irrespective of the status women enjoy. One has to go into the logic of old brothel houses, gambling-dens and liquor-venders, and consequent closure in a fractional manner. Many answers will stare blankly raising fresh questions about contemporary morality. This scenario also puts question marks on the so-called five-starred living and flesh trade coming to light in many regions without showing signs of disappearing. This is one of the most reprehensible blots on contemporary life. In an age, when feminism is strongly advocated and is also made a political weapon with those solemn pledges of elevated participation of women in the affairs of men, if flesh trade continues to thrive secretly, it is not an encouraging reflection on the behaviour and attitude of society. Motilal Jotwani in an entirely different but realistic manner makes values a personal matter. Each man perhaps harbours and lingers on with the thoughts and feelings of selfishness and greed without an inkling that he too is a contributor to the falling standards of moral principles in life. He narrates his reactions to different people he confronts every day, and how impishly and disingenuously or perhaps with a counterfeited and superficial display of good behaviour keeps a smiling face. But it is all charade and smugness. He knows that he does all this to extract more benefits so that life moves effortlessly without undue strain on values or money. He conveys succinctly what he feels:

> I smile at everybody.
> I smile especially
> at the grocer for
> the little tilt
> favouring me as he weighs
> my daily necessaries,
> so costly these days.
> … …
> By evening I have spent
> All my smiles for favours
> … …
> And I have no smile left
> To take home.
> ("Smiling," *Alien There is None* 36)

To derive undue benefits with obvious intention to harm none is hypocrisy and an indication of falling ethics. To keep one's integrity intact is not easy in the present corrupt system. What Jha tells can happen only when society harbours such fetid and putrefying value system tacitly about which P.K. Joy is also worried about though differently. Joy is pained at the working of mischievous and doubting minds.

Howsoever virtuous feelings a good man may nurture for women and morals, others will always view his relationship with the fair sex with suspecting eyes. It requires a very high degree of moral strength where a relation with a woman can be looked at from a different perspective. Man, and for that matter, even a religious priest, ought to understand this reality of life. For, scandals and acts of moral turpitude are born in such equations. At this stage, the poet is trying to reveal a truth which many hesitate to agree. It is this attitude of society towards ethical values of life which is the root cause of many contemporary ailments.

It has happened even with God but to talk of a mortal man, he observes contemptuously:

> Lately when I was a business man you saw unclean
> motives in employing good looking girls in my office.
> And when I was dutifully helping my wife in shopping
> You teased me for my dealings with the provision-vending
> girls Fed-up, when I withdrew into a world without women
> Now you are calling me 'an impotent coward!
> ("You Have Never Spared Me," *Forced Smiles* 44)

A malicious working of a man's intentions is given a beautiful description that gives glimpses of a society in which we live. Man is now low in quality of head, and heart and even pious intent is viewed and interpreted with spite and distrust. It also shows to what an abysmal depths men fall when eying a woman. There is something radically wrong somewhere. Man has yet to learn to live ethically, and if he goes back to find defence, it is a mere pretence.

Here it is worthwhile to recall the words of Confucius and Swami Krishnananda who emphasized the significance of 'good' and 'bad' and how they linked the meanings to values and ethics. On the other hand, if Gandhi and Ruskin spoke of moral attitude, they did not mean different. Man's life, in simple words, is a journey between 'the good' and 'the bad' and if 'the good' predominates, it is called a life of meaning and if 'the good' conquers, it is life of ethics, to be more explicit.

Dr S. Radhakrishnan observed "Ethical principles are but general rules for the guidance of human conduct and owe their significance to the developing society in which they arise....Morality is a working arrangement and its sanction is social necessity. As morality is a matter of convention, society has a right to alter or amend it, if it judges such modifications in the line of its interests. There is no God commanding us into a prescribed mode of behaviour. Ethical rules are objective only in the sense that they are independent of this or that individual and not in the sense that they are unconditional commands or that they assume that 'good' is an unanalysable and ultimate quality" *(An Idealist View of Life 19)* . He spoke of a lasting truth which, if man accepts, he could make life happy and better.

To this direction, English poets in India appear to be working. It is an incessant fight between good and bad with various shades and shadows. In the poetic endeavour, the poets continue to spread the message of good and virtuous life, and in the process touch on various areas where ethics assume different meanings but the fundamental objective to serve man remains intact. From this stage one begins to enquire into the role of religion.

To carry forward the argument, one conveniently finds out that the religious people of different hues are just perpetrators of immoral life. They seem eager to establish ashrams, meditation halls and cyclic method of organizing religious discourses whether near the seats of Gods or otherwise but it really does not happen. They, in the garb of such philanthropic and selfless activities, only amass wealth for personal use, and here a terrible nexus of politicians-bureaucrats-elites works wonders. Recent revelations about the functioning of such people and the orgies, scandals and scams surrounding them, are not in any case harbingers of a value-based future. Either man learns to live with this truth or is virtually condemned to live a life of the plagiarized, fictitious and sick value system with regrets without a happy life. To this hypocritical attitude and pretentiousness, Chanakya refers quite often when it is said that it is only the weak man who pretends to be a saint. Truly powerful men are rarely inclined towards a saintly life. One has to read in between the lines to know the correct meaning of the great man.

At times one is tempted to find reasons at places of ostensible goodness because poverty and hunger are afflicting many areas of the world. It is all the more glaring when it happens in a world full of intellectual and material richness. Increasing poverty and consequent misery agitate the mind of Aldous Mawlong, a sensitive poet. At a busy bus-stand where beggars crowd in with a begging bowl in hand, one notices people with healthy strong bodies eating rich food while ignoring the pleas of hungry child:

> Nowadays I frequent
> the busy bus terminal
> and I have seen
> the rich and the poor
> the cruel and the kind;
> Portly passengers
> would disembark each day
> And brush my pleas aside
> Then I would watch as they enter
> and devour
> paranthas fried in ghee.
> … …
> Once a man said, 'God bless you child.'
> I was too young, of course
> to understand what he meant.
> ("From the Eyes of a Beggar Child," *April Fairy* 31-32)

The protagonist self-effacingly gives expression to feelings of perennial inadequacies in the value-apparatus where the famished and the poor live without hope of a better future. Man is egocentric and self-absorbed, and does not have sentiments of compassion and sympathy for the less fortunate. Love, empathy and understanding constitute foundation of strong value-system. In the present scenario, the poet highlights total apathy of the affluent. This scene at the bus-stand is emblematic of heartless attitude to those requiring love and warmth. He raises moral issues like Joy, Dominic and Sharma. P.K. Majumdar is a different kind of poet. He is anxious about the man's future and attaches significance to values in life. He is worried about the deteriorating environmental health. He ascribes it to the values man cherishes. An extreme sense of aggrandizement and naked greed persuades man to wreak havoc on nature, the poet opines. If man does not protect the green land of the world, it'll prove dangerous to humanity, the poet observes.

> Water the trees save all the greens
> Better delay building more shrines
> Trees for ever are the best neighbour
> Who your living on earth earnestly favour
> ... ...
> Save all the greens water the trees
> Let the world rejoice in sapling planting sprees.
> ("Water the Trees," *Where Time is Dead* 14)

Closely connected to poverty and affluence, values get suitable meaning. It is the convenience of people of these two classes. There is no third category. The message may carry prejudiced or bitter connotations but the latent meanings are quite apparent. To the poor, rich appear as an embodiment of lust and greed and the rich also do not hold the poor in high esteem. It is lack of will power and hard work that perpetuates poverty. Man or for that reason society cannot tilt the balance to benefit a particular class despite what Marx, Ruskin or Gandhi say. Total equality is impossibility. This singular fact is often ignored by the poets but realities are painful.

If one wishes to come to a reasonable conclusion, one has to admit a hard fact that value system undergoes changes with the passage of time. A total reformation is not possible. To eradicate evil practices is difficult. To be pragmatic, one has to accept realities. To reach an ideal state is not possible; man must realize, and reconciling to these truths of life, can provide much needed relief to miserable hearts, for in the world it is difficult to find a man who is totally happy. Poverty, hunger, scarcity and exploitation rule the real world of man and there the tale reaches a conclusion. Bipin Patsani is again a poet who grumbles about shallow value system we nurture and hold fast. Now we have learnt, he desolately observes, to lead a "corrupt", "immoral" and "snobbish" life and our concept of life and values in life are totally distorted and decrepit. The areas of functions and qualities, to which a man imparts a dignified name of values or ethics or morality or honesty etc. are no longer valid and pertinent.

We have been so corrupt
And immoral in our attitude,
So snobbish in our perception
And blinded by opportunism
That drums, bombs and swamis
Of centuries and a cart-load of Gandhis
Won't be able to wake us Indians
To a single enlightened morn,
Unless we have the courage and will
To have visions of our own
Like those seers who chose an inward turn.
("Cultural Stasis" *Voice of the Valley* 63)

In fact, it is man who has eaten into the vital of a healthy value composition. Unfortunately, we want to resurrect a rotten life style with "cart-load" of ancient heritage, saintly wisdom and Gandhism. To one's utter horror, no religious or great man can redeem lives of total immorality, he appears to say. If man does not turn inwardly to see a true life, it will be waste of a precious birth. At another level, the poet is convinced that if a man begins search within, envisions future and chooses a life of pious people, enlightenment is certain.

In other words, many poets seem to say that

> ...right actions may often be called good as opposed to evil actions. But we shall avoid the phrase 'good actions' and consistently use the phrase 'right actions' (as opposed to 'wrong actions')—*a positive attitude to look at things*— ...Moral philosophers have conceived of the ethical ideal in various ways. Some have thought of it as pleasure and others as happiness. Yet others considered the notion of duty or obligation as central to ethics, while others again think of the goal as perfection.
>
> (*The Message of the Buddha* 230-231)

Principles and quality in life have eroded to such a grotesque extent that it is not only difficult to uphold sanctity in human relations where materialism of the present age is breeding violence and scorn but to survive in this whirlpool of terrifying realities of life is also atrocious. P. C. K. Prem appears to say:

It is admiring your girl friend
and straightway spreading into the bed

> when a waiting wife snores
> and you enjoy a cup of coffee
> with extra characters
> and that you condemn yourself
> in bitterness of accumulated wrath
> when a helpless father pleads
> and sons kill him
> to usurp and devour him.
> ("A Simple Equation," *The Bermuda Triangles* 35-36)

In the above few lines, the poet gives four different pictures where human relations suffer but still continue to live and it is also a deplorable portrayal of bonds where morals do not exist. It is unforgivable that man has brought human bonds to this precipice where the entire mankind is gradually crumbling. If life is perpetuated by killing a relation, it is a sad commentary on human life and relations. It is interesting how Gopichand and Nagasuseela view life's values when they observe: "Smoke, eat, drink and sex / Engulfing the bones of spring / Age no bar at all" (*Mushrooms* 26). However, at an entirely different level, K. V. Raghupathi raises questions about nature, environment and pollution. He is quite at ease while dealing with metaphysical questions of life. He feels profoundly hurt at the contemporary ideals a man upholds. At times, he does throw momentary glances at earthly joys wherein he tries to find answers to esoteric questions. Worldly and corporeal pleasures are apparently transitory he knows but still he is desirous cf finding answers so that he can explain the mystery to a man of ordinary rank.

> Once caught in rain
> shivering like a frightened squirrel
> he crept into a hovel
> to rest a while
> Warmth; you need
> fulfillment I need
> she said
> To conquer this world of misery
> and control the past and future
> come, come
> shed all your brooding

scoff all reflection and contemplation
quench all your passions
let me help you become Buddha
take my hand and sleep with me.
("A monk lost in a brothel," *Small Reflections* 67)

This short lyric makes crystal clear that a destitute in fears slips into the bed of his woman who assures him release from miseries and worries of past and future; and asks him to satisfy her for therein is hidden, a real Buddha. After the passions are quenched, a man is at peace and thinks deep of realities and philosophy of life, he seems to say. But it requires a man of deep understanding and rectitude to face consequences after a jaunt of carnal pleasures. A totally dispassionate attitude is required to understand a deeply embedded struggle between the flesh and the spirit. Man may try to find a rationale behind the sex urges and relates these to spiritual aspects of life but here man has to be psychologically strong to arrive at a philosophic solution. To rationalize experiences of earthly pleasures is not very easy. A. Raju, another poet, speaks in "A Millennium for the Undeserved" (*Sprouts of Indignation* 56) of the distorted value system where "superstitions" and "false practices" do not provide joy and happiness to man. In the name of religion people are killed while social plunder and violence extenuate sufferings of man:

All my wishes
Are crushed in the darkness
Of superstitions
And false practices
... ...
and with fear I visualize
the advent of an age
of holy massacres
and social arsoning
and natural calamities
as curses for those who're undeserved
of a third millennium!

Obviously the poet throws adequate hints at gruesome killings in the name of religion. When he talks of "social arsoning" it is in truth a totally butchered social constitution where nothing exists which could be called ethically sound. Poet's worry about the current socio-religious issues is natural. Even today, after many years of self-governance, one unmistakably observes and realizes that secular thought is still facing violence, and communal hatred guides men with negligible aberrations. A fanatic approach to religion without the thought of man and humanity, is contributing to the disturbing social imbroglios. An inveterate idealist in Mohammed Fakhruddin pertinently observes: "Respect Human Rights, / Egoism kills humanism; / World State stops all fights" ("Haiku 41" *Haiku Self-Exploration* 61). It is a painful dilemma of well-meaning people that they have failed to ensure a violence-free society. Hazara Singh always paints an optimistic picture even if there is darkness around. He says: "World has plenty for the basic needs of all / But not enough for a few avaricious cliques / All aspire to advance free of fear and want / Co-existence alone sustains such a yearning" ("Non-Violence," *Destination* 3). It is difficult but that the efforts continue is enough to strengthen belief in the optimistic outlook of life. Hopes still brighten areas of darkness in life though one may not be aware of. If natural disasters bring sufferings, these are because of man's callousness as he thinks little of maintaining balance in nature; and wantonly abuses natural resources.

Materialism and Consumer-Culture in Life and Devaluation of Moral Values

Possibly it will take time to formulate reasonably honourable edifice to which a man can adhere to. In almost analogous vein, all the poets are immensely worried about the dreadful devastation man spills on everything he catches hold of. Srinivasa Rangaswami also regrets the loss of values in the life of a contemporary man where absolute consumer-culture has taken roots resulting in wearing down of human relations and where a prurient psyche kills instinctive excellence of heart. To go ahead to transcendent pastures of life remains a delusion. Intelligence is nothing now but merely a mechanical implement to live and interpret life as is apparent in the lines below:

Man, a super-intelligent, has become
a robot, without a heart.
'Use and throw' consumerist culture
has overrun inter-personal relationships.
Media meant for education and entertainment
Is out to purvey
Prurient fare publicly.
Desolate is the scene...
("Would You the Promise Keep?" *Brave New Wave* 21
Indian English Poets 24)

A depressing scene awaits man where mechanical living will customarily determine future. A utilization theory will finally evaluate man and his benefits to the society after fully analyzing his definite contribution. Here is the crux of man's life. It is apparent to what extent media is influencing man and culture. One is already witnessing awful functional approach to relations. Abnormally sex-dominated and squalid nature in man about which Srinivasa Rangaswami speaks in "Would You the Promise Keep?" is a reality now. A similar sexual overture is much more treacherous and despicable among the sophisticated and urbane, T.V. Reddy suggests in the following lines:

Wearied of her thorny journey
her two minds merge into one
as she decides with a dry smile
to spread her youthful beauty
like a red carpet to the MD,
who draining a bottle of whisky
tempts her with a lure and a leer,
and ensures her rise in status
before the sun-rise.
("The Typist Girl," *The Broken Rhythm* 34)

It also tells garishly of the collapse of probity where even a woman is unhesitant to manoeuvre with bodily charms for a rise in status for these are characteristics of a consumerist culture. If one stretches the thought further one is aghast to witness a frequent display of such disgusting link-ups in relations simply to earn more and enjoy more without least worrying about ethical standards. Rajkamal Shiromani hints at the horrifying manifestation that materialistic obsession and insatiability will consequently descend on man when he observes so concisely:

> What we need is money
> In this twenty-first century
> to buy 'everything'.
> ... ...
> Which civilization
> We're heading to and for what
> Money, terror, lust?
> ("The 21st Century," *You & My Haiku* 62)

A frightening scenario is foreseen that shatters love for life if fascination for worldly luxuries continues to govern man's life.. When I.H. Rizvi talks about the human behaviour in the present context, he is quite forthright. The hardest wounds are inflicted by those who are intimate. It is a generally accepted psychological and philosophical meaning one infers about relations and earthly realities. This injury is not only physical, it hurts the soul too. He says: "She had been nursing it since long / And it was almost healed. But someone of the same tribe / Of wickedness flung hard a stone at her.../ And ran as fast as she could, / But could not save herself / From the curious eyes of the crowd." ("Honesty," *Unfading Blooms* 2)

Man often indulges in invisibly restrained aggression one observes, when he just mocks at the values man should stand for. Strangely enough, it is culture of physical violation building up deep and strong basis in the present social set up. I.K. Sharma, one of the major poetic voices, in beautiful poems regrets the modern attitude of teachers who have lost the confidence of pupils. At present intellects and hearts of this age do not permit students to believe even teachers, and perhaps the fault lies somewhere else. Honesty as a value of life now is empty and sans piety and dignity. A man living a life of honesty no more gets an expected respect. He can't afford decent education and comfortable life to his family in an age of materialism:

He cannot send children to convent schools
nor give them an ounce of milk impure,
nor wrap them in rags to face winter
nor get them a toy on their birthday
nor buy a gift for his sweetheart
in memory of their wedding day.
("Honesty," *The Native Embers* 15)

'Honesty is the best policy' is no longer a legitimate avowal; for, modern values rooted in acquisitiveness and material gains do not recognise old virtues. Poverty crushes an honest man so much that he cannot even dream of providing food, shelter and other comforts of life to family. Had he not been honest, he would have lived a life of luxuries. It is a reprehensible worsening of value system where a man of principles and integrity is bound to suffer and live under constant threats of poverty, scarcity and hunger. If one throws a glance at the events taking place outside, one finds that the corrupt are often set free. It is big fish that eats the small fish. That is the law of nature, and it is a jungle rule of barbarity and animalism. And this is man's location in life where the present socialistic pattern of society has pushed him to. Time is now, to think over. I.K. Sharma does not say bluntly but he means it. K.N. Sharma, in moderately terse words, talks about the commercialization of moral values. In other words, man has little use of fine values in life. Values have attained export quality. Maybe, the poet has the impression that Indians have a craze for everything Western and whatever smacks of Indian culture is an anathema to them. India used to be a rich country and here the poet hints at the high quality goods which were once exported to other countries, and this quality he links to cultural ethics, Indians nourished at that point of history. Now there is nothing left to export, so ultimately, if morals are exported, perhaps these can bring easy money since there is nothing left to be exported and India is now a backward country, he appears to say. He sadly observes:

Today the moral values
are canned, labeled
and are made ready for export.

They are not for domestic use.
The sale is one.
Honesty is mashed;
Integrity is pickled in lumps,
Goodness is sliced;
Truth, a dear merchandise,
is packed in capsules.
All are to be sold for foreign exchange—
the easy money.
("Today, the Moral Values," *The Whiff* 65)

Ethical values in medical profession have deteriorated during the recent years and it needs no revelation. When N. P. Singh talks of immorality in professional life, he underlines the mental state of a sick society. In fact, almost all the wings of the present governmental system are indefensibly worthless and immaterial. Doctors easily forget the professional principles and exploit the victims for money, and then they are not reluctant or averse to extract physical pleasure. It is loss of professional quality in doctors playing havoc with a highly respected profession. Now it is a school for scandals.

A young doctor
Offered to examine a young
Girl who had a backache.
He commanded her
To strip herself-partially
And Lie down on the patient's bed.
... ...
Was given a benefit of doubt.
The victim failed to identify
The accused in the court.
Why did her mother
A key witness
And the lady doctor
Also fail to identify
The accused
It is difficult to fathom.
("Miracles," *Millennium Blues* 83)

Where to go from this delicate and hazardous living style, is the disputable question that bewilders a sane man.

An absolute fall in professional ethics is an operative-fashion now, and everything that leads to money, pleasure and luxury is valued in medical profession. It remains unsaid whether the poet hints at other professions. But sufficient innuendoes make the meaning evident. The sickness is all—pervasive and other professions cannot claim ethical quality of life. The collapse is complete these days as even the mother or close relations of the victims fear to divulge the harsh truth for fear of public shame and ignominy. In the background, perhaps the poets are aware of the ignominious sale and purchase of human organs, and perfidious commercialization sans minimum quality expertise while treating patients with just a few exceptions. Not only at the personal level but at the official level there is frightening fall in quality conduct.

Corruption in professional ethics is not only restricted to medical areas; it is perfidiously discernible in all other professions, one can witness. Lalit M. Sharma, in a few words speaks about love, lust and woman while talking of value system that man adores. In a state of intensity of passions, a man only watches the bodily beauty of a woman, and sleekly and astutely forgets the relations, namely aunt, a cousin, or a pledge. Here civilization gets a huge beating. Morality is reduced to a string that looks like a snake and so must be killed or thrown away. Thus man's ethical values suffer as passions and lust thrill and excite:

> Loud the voice of lust
> Louder its echo in your mind, who
> Like a blind man is sure of the ways
> And yet slips into
> a ditch.
> Conscience finds a man
> Drunk, half sunk in the marshes,
> Craving to crawl to the land
> That can support him
> If he would stand.
>
> ("The Lure of Lust," *The Brown Tree* 28)

Lust and love drives man to a dark endless conduit like a blind man, and these thoughts prick conscience. Ravi Nandan Sinha, the poet, speaks of the official apathy and calculated moves to orchestrate sufferings of the people undergoing hardships during famine. At the bureaucratic level many lengthy plans on papers are made, words are spent, sympathy is recycled like polythene bags, and nothing perceptibly beneficial happens in the lives of the people. The poet says:

> Parched villages wait
> For their allocated share
> Of official sympathy.
> ... ...
> Famine is news.
> Seminars will be organized, speeches made,
> Old scores settled, political gains calculated
> Pain never sold so well.
> ("Famine," *Continuity: Five Indian English Poets* 228)

While alleviating miseries and agonies of the people, even if at the empty assurance level, the political gains are visualized and to that extent help is extended. One realizes an offensive feeling of selfishness among politicians while values are just crushed. This metaphor, if extended further, will reveal inadequacies in the system. Man is now absolutely self-seeking. There are virtually no efforts to strengthen character. Poets are anguished and much troubled. It is not poets for that matter, all men who think of future of mankind, nurture these thoughts.

Unfortunately, the poets with one voice are deeply troubled. Wide spread erosion of values in contemporary life is the cause of disillusionment and cynicism. But it is the basic reason that one often forgets. To sit back and regret may not be the solution. Man is realizing that it is difficult to stick to principles and morality in the present set-up. Hopes are still alive. At times the poets hint at solutions which do not appear pragmatic. However, it is often observed that poets wish definite action by those who decide for others. If the head of the family, in internal and external conduct conforms to certain minimum social norms and if a practical view is adopted with regard to ethics; and humanitarian attitude guides life's deeds, it will help immensely. If man's welfare is kept in mind while discipline is maintained, children will learn and adhere to quality in life, otherwise an anarchy will take birth and that is precisely happening now. It extends to society and then the nation and thus ethics undergo transformation with an ugly exterior. People know that it is a theoretical approach to life but then elders of the family, society and the country have a moral responsibility to provide a clean heritage to posterity. It is big question, the poets raise. Another harsh reality of life is also revealed here which is related to the truth of elder, aged and those who guide others. Are they sincere, honest and upright and ethically strong? Perhaps one day, this question will have to be attended to. The day is not far off when man understands man and the spirit of man's dignity. Possibly evils of animosity and revulsion will be relegated to the background and there will originate "the flame of love which *will burn* all impurities", the poets seem to reaffirm this unflinching faith in man. With an apology to Confucius one is constrained to say that to lead a 'good' and 'ethical' life "is the law of God" and to acquire these virtuous qualities "is the law of man".

Works Cited

Arora, Om Prakash. *The Creeping Shadows*. Delhi: Unique Publications, 1985.

Bhatnagar, O.P. *The Audible Landscape*. Aligarh, SL Publications, Raghubirpuri, Aligarh 202001, U.P. India, 1986

Chambial, D.C. *Gyrating Hawks and Sinking Roads*. Maranda: Poetcrit Publications, 2002. 1996

Dominic, K.V. *Winged Reason*. New Delhi: Authorspress, 2010. .

Dubey, B.K. *My Collected Poems*. Uday Publications, Medinipur, 2002.

Fakhruddin, Mohammed. *Haiku, Self-Exploration*. Bangalore: Poets International Society. 2007.

Gopichand P. & Nagasuseela P. *Mushrooms*. Allahabad: Cyberwit.net. 4/ 2 B, L.I.G, Govindpur Colony. 2009

Janakiraman, RA. *Arteries*. Bhubaneswar: The Home of Letters. 2001.

Jaryal, Suresh C. *Changing Faces*. Ranchi: Writers Forum. 1999.

Jha, Pashupati. *Mother and Other Poems*. New Delhi, Creative Books, Shanti CB 24, Naraina, New Delhi 110028, 2005.

Jotwani, Motilal. *Alien There is None*. A Writers Workshop Publication, Calcutta. 1989.

Joy, P.K. *Forced Smiles*. Madras, Indian Writers Press, C 23, Anna Nagar East, Madras 600102, 1988.

Majumdar, Pronab Kumar. *Where Time is Dead.* WW Publication, 2005

Manas, Bakshi. *The Midnight Star*. Kolkata: Cambridge India, F 46 Dakshinapan, 2 Gariahat Road (South), 2009.

Mawlong, Aldous. *April Fairy.* New Delhi: Sanchar Publication House, 1992.

Patsani, Bipin. *Voice of the Valley*. A Writers Workshop Publication 1993

Prem, P.C.K. *The Bermuda Triangles*. A Writers Workshop Publication, 1996.

Raghupathi, K.V. *Small Reflections.* A Writers Workshop. Publication, 2000.

Reddy, T.V. *The Broken Rhythms*. Madras 600042, Poets Press India, 1987

Rizvi, Iftikhar Husain. *Unfolding Blooms (Poems)*. PBD 1984.

Raju, Alexander. *Sprouts of Indignation*. Dragon Publications, Kottayam, Kerala, 2003.

Sharma, Kedar Nath. *The Whiff.* Dharamshala: Wisdom Books Publishers, Himachal Pradesh, 1991.

Sharma, I. K. *The Native Embers.* Jaipur Publishing House, 1976.

Sharma, Lalit M. *The Brown Tree.* A Writers Workshop Publications. 1984.

Shiromani, Rajkamal. *You and My Haiku*. Patna: ICLLC Publications, 2010.

Singh, Hazara. *Destination*. Ludhiana: Foil Printers, 2007.

Singh, N.P. Millennium Blues. A Writers Workshop Publication, 2004.

Jayatilleke, K.N. The Message of the Buddha. London: George Allen & Unwin Ltd. 1975.

Prem, P.C.K. *Contemporary Indian English Poetry from Himachal*. Delhi: Konark Publishers Pvt. Ltd., 1992.

Raghupathi, K. V.*Brave New Wave, 21 Indian English Poets*. Jaipur. Book Enclave, Shanti Nagar, Jaipur 2009.

Rizvi, I. H. and N. F. Rizvi. *Origin, Development and History of Indian English Poetry*. Bareilly: Prakash Book Depot, 2007.

Singh, R. A. *Continuity: Five Indian English Poets*. Jaipur: Book Enclave, 2003.

Swami Maheshanand Giri. *Vedanta Philosophy for 21st Century* Bharatiya Sanskrit Samaj, Delhi 110054, 1985.

6

Revelation of Borderline Traits in the Poetry of Kamala Das

—Ankita Khanna

Borderline Personality Trait (BPT) is characterized by consistently unusual ways of thinking feeling and interacting. It is associated with unstable self-image, feelings, behaving and relating to others. In order to be diagnosed with BPT, the sufferer must experience at least five of the following symptoms: unstable self-image, unstable relationships, severe impulsivity, repeated suicidal tendencies or threats, chronic feeling of emptiness, inappropriate anger, transient paranoia or dissociation.

Time and again many eminent personalities, around the globe, have been associated with Borderline Personality Trait. Biographer and journalist Sally Bedell-Smith says of Diana, Princess of Wales, "While one cannot say with certainty that Diana had a borderline personality disorder, the evidence is compelling." The author continues, "The most important factor setting the borderline personality apart from those with other disorders is early parental loss—in Diana's case the departure of her mother and the emotional withdrawal of her father for several years following the Spencer divorce."[1] During Diana's lifetime, someone close to Prince Charles consulted both a psychiatrist and a psychologist, who agreed that her behaviour "fit the description of the borderline personality in quite extraordinary detail." It has been speculated that Marilyn Monroe had Borderline Personality Trait due to the fact that people with the trait usually have turbulent relationships, rapid mood swings, great anxiety over real or imagined abandonment, and suicide attempts, and she fit this profile. Besides, names of Angelina Jolie (*Self-Injury, Volatile Relationships, Sexual Confusion, Eating Disorder*), Courtney Love (*Substance Abuse, Possible Eating Disorder, Inappropriate Anger, Shame, Self-Injury*), Lindsey Lohan (*Dangerous Driving, Substance Abuse, Eating Disorder, Unsafe sexual behavior, Possible Self-Injury*), Britney Spears (*Dangerous Driving, Substance Abuse, Bipolar, Eating Disorder, Inappropriate Anger*) and Amy Winehouse (*Self-injury, Substance Abuse, Volatile Relationships, Sexual Confusion, Impulsive Behavior, Suicidal*) are also in speculation for the same.

Kamala Das, a well known English poet, who has written about her persona, her life and her experiences, through her poetry, reveals certain traits that are very close to Borderlines and thus, calls for extensive study. Her poetry is marked with sudden and dramatic shifts in self-image, characterized by shifting goals and values. It also portrays in abundance, sudden changes in mood, identity disturbance characterized by markedly and persistently unstable self—image or sense of self. The poetic persona of her poetry may suddenly change from the role of a needy supplicant for help to a righteous avenger of past mistreatment. Although she usually has a self-image that is based on being bad or evil, she at times has feelings that do not exist at all. Such experiences usually occur in the poetic world of Kamala Das where the persona feels lack of a meaningful relationship, nurturing and support. She may show worse performance in unstructured situations.

The term "Borderline" here is restricted to Borderline Personality Traits and does not speak about Borderline Personality Disorders (BPD) as defined by DSM IV. Also, the views here do not propagate something that needs to be fixed. The intention is to study various facets of Das's poetry from psychological perspective with reference to her life, a confessional that she is. Kamala Das writes her autobiography into her every poem. She admits in *My Story*,

> [A]lthough I write with a lot of detachment, I do figure in my writings, unless when [sic] I am writing a short story.[2]

She further maintains that poets:

> cannot close their shops like shopmen and return home. Their shop is their mind and as long as they carry it with them.[3]

This study intends to probe, in the poetic works of Kamala Das, the following borderline traits: Depression, Split-self, Dualism, and Lack of clear sense of identity. The other equally important two traits "Unstable relationships" and "Chronic feelings of emptiness and boredom" are taken up by the author elsewhere.

"Why does love come to me like pain / Again and again and again?"[4] These lines summarize the agony of the persona in finding love for herself and hence portray her frustration in love seeking. This frustration soon transforms into depression and forms an important feature in the poetry of Kamala Das. This feeling is almost all pervasive except for the poems where she talks about her sons or those who portray sensuality. It is common to experience depressed moods or "the blues" at some points in life. Most often, these periods of sadness occur as a result of a life change, either in the form of a personal setback or a loss, such as the death of a loved one. The painful feelings that accompany these periods are usually transitory and should be viewed as inherent aspects of the human experience. This can be true for any person with whatsoever personality trait. However, when feelings persist and result in significant distress depression should be considered a part of one's personality trait. Anisur Rehman in this context says:

> The quest for an emotional liaison and her failure to establish one is the central burden of Kamala's poetry. From the thematic standpoint her poetry originates from a dark end. There are no hopes, struggles and failures...[5]

Depression and mood swings are common features for those with Borderline Personality Trait. Although depression is often thought of being an extreme state of sadness, there is a vast difference between depression and sadness. Sadness is a part of being human—a natural reaction to painful circumstances.

All of us will experience sadness at some point in our lives. Depression, however, is an extended state with many more symptoms than an unhappy mood. The poems of Kamala Das epitomize most powerfully her failures, which lead her to depression. In "The Freaks", she says:

> He talks, turning a sub-stained
> Cheek to me, his mouth, a dark
> Cavern, Where the stalactites of
> Uneven teeth gleam, his right
> Hand on my knee, while our minds
> Are willed to race towards love;
> But, they only wander, tripping
> Idly over puddles of
> Desire. . .[6]

Research says that Borderline Personality Trait (BPT) may be related to genetic, environmental and hormonal influences. The frequency in women is two to three times greater than men. The increased frequency of borderline traits among women may also be a consequence of incestuous experiences of their childhood, which can be the case with Kamala Das. The roots of depression were sown in her childhood, watered during her adolescence and bloomed to be a full-fledged tree when she grew up. One of the factors that could have been the major cause of depression is unavailability of her parents in terms of emotional support. The only option she was left with was her grandmother. Her distressed relationship with her father is shown in "Next to Indira Gandhi".

> Next to Indira Gandhi my father I feared the most
> He was the one who told me when I was five
> That dark children should only wear white
> He was the one who had no time for me[7]

The last line clearly indicates her emotional distance with her father. She further says:

> Climbing down the stair
> He stared past me
> His office problems kept his thoughts away from us

Father, I ask you now without fear
Did you want me
Did you ever want a daughter[8]

In an interview in 1997 she explains the background:

> My father was a patriarch, an autocrat. He roared at us and gave us no intimacy. He wanted always to control us or to send us away. My mother lay on her bed, writing religious poetry, not intervening in any way. I was desperate for love. To punish us, we were sent to boarding schools where we were treated with subtle forms of sadism. When my father could no longer do that, and after I had rheumatic fever, he called our relative Das and asked him to take me off his hands. So I married him.[9]

Study reveals that this chronic or periodic victimization and sometimes brutalization can later result in impaired relationships and mistrust of men, which is found true in relevance to Kamala Das. As a child, longing for love, which she never got from her parents, she takes refuge in the lap of her grandmother.

...My grandmother's, she was
The first I loved, trunks, when opened, after
She died, contained only dolls...[10]

And later in life when she does not find love enough to satiate her endless female hungers, she strays to other men leading to many unsuccessful relationships. Kamala Das's poetry reveals excessive preoccupation with sexuality, sexual promiscuity, inhibitions, deep seated depression and a seriously damaged self-image. The same vein is noticed in Anisur Rehman's interpretation of Kamala Das's poetry.

> Kamala Das's failure to establish an eternal an eternal bond and realise the meaning of existence is at the root of her poems in so far as she invents a set of objects, situations and a chain of events which are the formula of her creative process. She recalls painfully her emotional life and is torn between dual loyalties to the self and no-self.[11]

Das started writing poetry at the age of six. She wrote her first poem about a doll that had lost its head and had to remain headless for eternity.

> I was six and very sentimental. I wrote sad poems about dolls that lost their heads and had to remain headless for eternity. Each poem of mine made my cry. My brother illustrated the verses and wrote faintly political articles.[12]

Sadness is a transient feeling that passes as a person comes to term with his troubles whereas depression can linger for weeks, months or even years. The sad person feels bad, but continues to cope with living. A person with depression may feel overwhelmed and hopeless. Das's poetry seems to be influenced by the latter. She accepts this gracefully in an interview with Kaur that suffering was going to be her raw material if not her creative inspiration.

> Pain and turbulence seem like grand gifts to a real writer. After the heartache and turmoil the first thing that the writer does is to chronicle the event. If joy is the wrap of writing, grief is certainly its woof. (Kaur)[13]

And with the added trauma of a matchless marriage as her stimulus, she wrote her first serious poem while still in her teens:

> Wipe out the paints, unmould the clay;
> Let nothing remain of that yesterday...[14]

In several other instances she confirms her sorrow, grief and pain which ultimately lead her into depression. She herself expresses her gratitude to the poetry for having helping her vent out her misery.

> If I had not learnt to write how would
> I have written away my loneliness
> or grief? Garnering them within my heart
> would have grown heavy as a vault, one that
> only death might open, a release then
> I would not be able to feel or sense.[15]

Writing to her is, therefore, a psychic necessity, an antidote to loneliness and betrayal. Das's poems reveal that her main thrust is towards a more valuable and lasting acquisition—the desire to be possessed by love. Her poem "Lines Addressed to a Devdasi" shows signs of exhaustion:

> Ultimately there comes a time
> When all faces look alike
> All voices sound similar...
> ....
> ......It is then your desires cease
> And a home sickness begins
> And you sit down on the temple steps
> A silent Devdasi, Lovelorn
> And aware of her destiny. . .[16]

The poet sits on the temple steps all spent up and exhausted, almost in a stage of indifference to the worldly objects. Her longing for love, throughout her life is noted by all the critics. Anisur Rehman expresses his views in this regard:

> Craving for that rare gift (love), she is torn within.[17]

Her main concern happens to be suffering and humiliation meted out to all women in general and herself in particular. She found that she is not alone in the ocean of depression and humiliation. Indian women, more or less, are treated in a similar way. Her poem "Nani" draws our attention towards the pathetic condition of Indian women which lead to severe frustration. The poem focuses on a pregnant housemaid hanging herself, an act to which she was driven by shame and moral austerity of the society in which she lived. The spectacle of Nani hanging from a rope is heartrending which raises questions:

> Nani the pregnant maid hanged herself
> In the privy one day. For three long hours
> Until the police came, she was hanging there,
> A clumsy puppet, and when the wind blew
> Turning her gently on the rope. ...[18]

The persona has been a puppet in the hands of fate and the culprit who has subjected her to such humiliation is the society and its moral codes. The frustration deepens with the poem and she ironically says:

> ....it seemed
> To us who were children then, that Nani
> Was doing, to delight us, a comic
> Dance....[19]

Commenting on the hippocratic attitude of the society, she writes:

> ....Each truth
> Ends thus with a query. It is this designed
> Deafness which turns mortality into
> Immortality, the definite into
> The soft indefinite....[20]

The effect of social suppression on women in India has become quite disastrous, and Das's poetry stands testimony to this. She finds women reduced to the status of a body in the world. Her poetry reveals, candidly, the agony, for which, no other than patriarchal hierarchies are responsible.

Another obvious feature of her poetic persona that draws attention is her inner conflict. She constantly struggles with herself and finds difficult to meet the societal expectations. She invariably, switches between split-self and dualism, trying to strike a balance between what she is and what society expects her to be. The term split-self first gained significance for women's poetry, in Flourence Howe's *Introduction to No more Masks*[21]. It brings out an opposition women feel between essential aspects of the self, between what is socially prescribed, between what a woman feels she should be and what she feels, she is. Dualism is the concept that our mind is more than just our brain. This concept entails that our mind has a non-material, spiritual dimension that includes consciousness and possibly an eternal attribute. One way to understand this concept is to consider our self as a container including our physical body and physical brain along with a separate non-physical mind, spirit, or soul. The mind, spirit, or soul is considered the conscious part that manifests itself through the brain in a similar way that picture waves and sound waves manifest themselves through a television set. The picture and sound waves are also non-material just like the mind, spirit, or soul.

The poetry of Kamala Das reflects both; self-split and dualism. She has written a considerable number of poems exploring this duality, the pain and frustrations. She particularly identifies the two selves with the domestic gender role and the artist. The former occupies a safe position accepted and esteemed by society in general and male in particular, while her counterparts haunts the fringes of human intercourse, isolated from men and women alike, and repressed by the women of those psyche she is a part. Irshad Gulam Ahmed talks about two diverse aspects of Kamala's personality:

> When the fictious Kamala stalks the world, perplexing, amusing, shocking, titillating, satirizing and even embarrassing her readers, the autobiographical Kamala prefers to confine herself to her cosy home in a rather puritanical posture, exhibiting exemplary qualities of a mother and wife-a mother not only to her own children but to all youngsters who turn to her for help.[22]

While shooting for the documentary film, *An Introduction*, Kamala Das in conversation with Suresh Kohli said:

> I suppose by writing poetry we are forming a crust over us. Over the essence. The essential self. But even then I think that it is like breaking the back of a cockroach at night. Without knowing people unwittingly crush our backs, crush our egos. They walk around crushing us.[23]

In answer to the question asked by Shobha Warrior, in an interview, "Did those roles you had to play help you or not help you in your creative writing?" she plainly replies, "It helped me. Sometimes consciously, deliberately, I would even adapt a kind of role because I wanted to write about such a person. So I would act out the role before I wrote the story about such a person."[24] There lies a dualism in Kamala Das's writings in English, in which soul is contrasted to body. She seemed to imagine overwhelming this dualism only through death; her poems are filled with yearnings for death, especially to drown in the sea, water being connected in her mind with an all-encompassing universal calmness, formlessness in contrast to the conscious mind and body of the anxious individual. The dualism results from the fall from childhood innocence into the adult realm of sexuality, marriage and life amongst strangers. Rather than a poet of free love, Kamala Das elucidates the disenchantment of sexuality. It can be said that her entire poetic career is a spirited defiance of the coercive commands of the "categorizers". The poem articulates, among other things, the sustained social pressure on the poet to choose a name and accept the socially sanctioned role which becomes almost synonymous with the name:

> Be Ammi, or be Kamala. Or better
> Still, be Madhavikutti. It is time to
> Choose a name, a role...[25]

The poet is Ammi to her husband as well as to her very close friends; Kamala to the readers of her English-language poetry and also to her parents and to other relatives including her grandmother; and Madhavikutti to the readers of her fiction in Malayalam. Not only the three names represent the diverse roles she played in her life but also are the major sources of roles in her drama of selfhood. These names symbolize contradictory roles she played at the same time. And she did it so skillfully that many people, including her grandmother was not aware of the fact that Kamala and Madhavikutti were one and the same person:

> I think I was compelled to choose a name because I did not want to embarrass my conservative family. I knew that I was a misfit within my family. I think I practiced writing as people practice a secret vice. Like boys going to bathroom to smoke. Especially, I did not want to hurt my grandmother who was my favourite human being. And I don't think she knew that I was Madhavikutti till she died.[26]

There are different shades of love in Kamala Das's poetry. In the poem "Love" she expresses her happiness and contentment in love:

> Until I found you,
> I wrote verse, drew pictures,
> And went out with friends
> For walks....Now that I love you,
> Curled like an old mongrel
> My life lies content
> In you....[27]

This poem is clearly without any pricks, without any tensions. There is no craving for the lips meant for others, no instinct of challenge, no streak of complaint, as one usually finds in love poetry .But this kind of mood is only short-lived for Kamala Das, and she soon swings back to her usual grudge and grouse against men. She might even accept the inevitable married life for a girl and its responsibilities, but not without lodging her forceful complaint against the male kind as a whole and hollow marital relationships. This is how we discover her saying in "A Relationship":

> Yes,
> It was my desire that made him male
> And beautiful, so that when at last we
> Met, to believe that once I knew not his
> Form, his quiet touch or the blind kindness
> Of his lips was hard indeed. Betray me?
> My body's wisdom tells and tells again
> And even death nowhere else but here in. My betrayer's
> arms....[28]

The earlier poems of Kamala Das suggest a desire to win true love that is not much beyond blood and flesh. Again and again, in her poetry she asks for love not only from her husband, but also from other men.

> I asked for love, not knowing what else to ask
> For, he drew a youth of sixteen into the
> Bedroom and closed the door.[29]

This is in sharp contrast with her later poems where her love shapes into spirituality and she finds solace only in the arms of lord Krishna. There is endless waiting for the ideal, a dream come true. The poems entitled "Radha", "Radha Krishna", "The Maggots", "Lines Addressed to Devdasi" and "Ganshyam" express her apprehensions in poetical terms. "The Maggots" emphasizes on the futility of sexual union whereas "Substitute" portrays a passive stance of un-involvement and shrinking away from the pressure of past memories.

> At sunset on the river bank, Krishna
> Loved her for the last time and left.
> That night in her husband's arms Radha felt
> So dead that he asked what is wrong
> Do you mind my kisses love, and she said
> No, not at all, but thought, what is
> It to the corpse if the maggots nip?[30]

and

> After that love became a swivel door,
> When one went out, another came in.
> Then I lost the count, for always in my arms
> Was a substitute for a substitute.
> Oh, what is the use, explaining—
> It was a nameless, faceless crowd.[31]

Besides, her poetry also brings out a conflict between what she is and what she wants to be. She feels that there is someone within her, her inner self, which is left unborn.

> ...There is a sea wailing beneath the sea,
> A sky behind the taut drapes of our firmament,
> A rain that rains hard and long within the summer-rain.
> Another lives in me, I fear, a twin left unborn,
> Unnamed, unacknowledged, bitter with defeat,
> And she with her new-mood eyes stabs my face
> And turns me so often, half human,
> Half feline.[32]

Irshad Gulam Ahmed, in this context opines:

> The two Kamalas in the first phase of her poetic career are so dissimilar that they can hardly recognize each other; they might have never met as they represent the two extremes of human values, except for the fact that both are equally intrepid. The fictionalized Kamala is highly controversial whose autobiography begins in the second part of *My Story*. Indeed, the autobiographical Kamala is far from being a zealous feminist crusader. She has nothing against men as will be seen in chapter three. Even then the created Kamala can vociferously repudiate an androcentric cult: "Men are worthless, to trap them / use the cheapest bait of all, but never / Love, which in a woman must mean tears /And a silence in the blood." ("A Losing Battle").[33]

It is evident from the above discussion that Das's poetic persona embraces dissimilar traits existing parallel to each other:

> I believe that each of us must live in two worlds existing close to each other like substance and shadow-one the world visible to us and therefore called real, and the other invisible, existing in the sixth and inaccessible dimension which we fill with fantasies.[34]

Five years later, the poet reaffirms this in an interview to P.P. Raveendran:

> Frankly, a writer deals with a world that is supposed to be real and then a world that is only a shadow of this real world. This second world could even be called an unreal world. But unless we live in these two worlds at the same time, simultaneously enjoying the fruits of each world, I do not think a writer can progress much. The strength that you get from this imaginary world, this shadowy world, this dream world, can be utilized when working in the other world. You can add to the experiences of the other world with this. It's like an alloy. Like adding alloy to make the metal strong. I think that's most necessary. Every writer will have a split personality.[35,36]

The extracts indicate that the idea of the double in das is philosophically grounded and she presents a vision of cosmic duality. This dualism and split-self leads to the hectic search of 'Who am I?' Central to the borderline syndrome is the lack of a core sense of identity. The borderline does not accept her own intelligence, attractiveness, or sensitivity as constant traits she possesses, but rather as comparative qualities to be continually re-earned and re-judged against others. Many critics have spoken about 'doubles' and 'identity search' in the poetry of Kamala Das. Her poems reflect her poetic persona with different character traits. This persona portrays her feelings and she searches her inner self in her persona. The borderline's struggle in establishing a consistent identity is related to a prevailing sense of inauthenticity—a constant sense of faking it. Most of us experience this sensation at various times in our lives, but it is transient and soon overcome by our adaptation to new circumstances. The borderline, however, never reaches that point.

> Life is quite simple now—
> Love, blackmail and sorrow.
> It will be all right when I learn
> To paint my mouth like a clown's
> It will be all right if I put up my hair,
> Stand near my husband to make a proud pair.[37]

Marriage for a woman like Kamala Das becomes a sort of infringement on freedom creating a crisis of identity. This has been true to other Indian women poets like Mamta Kalia, who says:

> After eight years of marriage
> The first time I visited my parents
> They asked "Are you happy, help us"
> It was an absurd question
> And I should have laughed at it
> Instead, I cried
> And in between sobs, I nodded yes. (Poems 78,26)[38]

The cohesion between the particular and the general, the local and the universal detects in her character of the whole humanity, and her humanity is replicated in other women.

> ...I am a sinner,
> I am a saint. I am the beloved and the
> Betrayed. I have no joys which are not yours, no
> Aches which are not yours. I too call myself I.[39]

There are diverse modes in which the alienated self of Das engages in hectic search of herself. Juggling with her identity, she writes:

> ...I was a child, and later they
> Told me I grew, for I became tall, my limbs
> Swelled and one or two places sprouted hair.[40]

Tired of bearing consequences of being a woman, she painfully writes:

> .....I wore a shirt and my
> Brother's trousers, cut my hair short and ignored
> My womanliness. Dress in sarees, be girl,
> Be wife, they said. Be embroider, be cook,
> Be a quarreler with servants. Fit in, Oh,
> Belong, cried the categorizers.[41]

Sharing her experience about her visit to Qatar with her biographer, Weisbord, she says:

> If I'm really a fake, as I expect I am, always wearing a mask, but never really a mask, it is the real me taking part in a masquerade as the real me. The nudity in the eyes is appalling, not of this mask but of my naked mask, this person with tears in my eyes begging for love, please love me, please love me.[42]

It takes Weisbord a little time to comprehend what she means, which she finally interprets as follows:

> She seems to be saying that her "naked mask", her vulnerable openness, is just another mask. Yet when she defines "naked mask" she says "*this* person with tears in *my* eyes." It seems that for her the real and the masked are indivisible.[43]

So much the persona feels torn apart that she considers her real self as a real mask. She is so much into faking and pretending that she is unable to gather her real self. Outwardly playing multiple roles, meticulously, she is completely exhausted and alone from within.

To sum up, Kamala Das is an Indian poet quite conscious of her artistic design and purpose as well as of her responsibility towards her vision. The factors that contributes to her enduring agony are depression and frustration, she encountered throughout her life at various stages. She feels repelled against the existence under the burden of sickening experiences of her later life. She often feels that love is a hollow word as the male-dominated society, shows no understanding of a woman's aspirations. But life is always interesting and it has to be lived.

> . . why should I remember or bear
> That sweet sounding name, pinned to
> Me, a medal, undeservingly
> Gained at moments when, all of
> Me is ablaze with life?

However, it should be very well noted that everyone has characteristic patterns of perceiving and relating to other people and these patterns determine the personality traits of an individual. No two persons can think alike in a situation; similarly no two persons are completely alike in their personality traits. Even with a category of personality traits, you can find number of variations. Like all others Kamala too has a personality, distinct and unusual from others in its own sense. Assuming her as a borderline does not definitely make her stand among the people who are suffering from the acute BPD and require medical aid. Thorough study and systematic research of her prose work in general and poetic work in particular, reveals certain peculiar features which are identical to borderlines. An all-pervasive depression, inevitable dualism, never-ending search for love, and complete alienation; can be traced easily in her poetry. The presence of all these elements in her poetry proves that she had mind-set similar to those of borderlines, though she may not be suffering from BPD.

References

1. S.B. Smith *Diana in Search of herself: Portrait of a Troubled Princess Crown*. Newyork: Signet, 2000. [Print].
2. Kamala Das, *My Story*, New Delhi, Sterling, 1996. [Print].
3. Ibid., p.165.
4. Kamala Das, *Only the Soul Knows How to Sing*. 4th ed. Kottayam: DC Books, 2009. 136. [Print].
5. Anisur Rahman, *Expressive Forms in the Poetry of Kamala Das*. New Delhi: Abhinav Publications, 1981. 8. [Print].
6. Das Kamala, *Only the Soul Knows How to Sing* po. cit., p.59. [Print].
7. Ibid., p.148
8. Ibid.,
9. http://www.martinfrost.ws/htmlfiles/june2009/tribute-kamala-das.html
10. Das, *Only the Soul, op.cit., p.* 113
11. Rahman, Anisur. op.cit [Print].
12. Das, My Story, op. cit., p. 8.
13. Iqbal Kaur. op.cit.,
14. Ibid., p. 94
15. Das, Kamala, *"Anamalai Poems"*, No. III.
16. Guptara, P.S. *The Lotus: An Anthology of Contemporary Indian Religious Poetry in English*, Writers Workshop, 1988, 43
17. Anisur Rahman, *op.cit.,* p.30. [Print].
18. Das, *Only the Soul, op. cit., p.* 95
19. Ibid.
20. Ibid.
21. Flourence Howe, *Introduction to No More Masks*. Perennial, 1993.
22. I.G. Ahmed, *The Poetic Pilgrimage*, New Delhi : Creative Books, 2005. 18. [Print].
23. Suresh Kohli, *An Introduction*, Documentary film on Kamala Das.
24. The Rediff Interview/Kamala Das
25. Das, *Only the Soul,* op.cit., p.119
26. IL 155, 1993, 148
27. Das, *Only the Soul,* op.cit., p.128
28. Ibid., p.128
29. Ibid., p. 123
30. Ibid., p.119
31. Ibid., p.66
32. Ibid., p.43

33. Ahmed, op.cit., p.22
34. Irshad Ahmed in Kaur, op.cit., 1995, 79-81.
35. IL., 155, 1993,150
36. Das, *Only the Soul,* 65
37. Mamta Kalia, *Tribute to Papa and Other Poems*. Calcutta: Writers' Workshop, 1974.
38. Das, *Only the Soul,* op.cit., p.119
39. Ibid.
40. Ibid.
41. Weisbord, Merrily. *The Love Queen of Malabar*. Montreal: McGill-Queen's University Press, 2010. 181. [Print].
42. Ibid.
43. Bruce King. *Modern Poetry in English*. Bombay: OUP, 1987. 151. [Print].

7

The Magic World of Poetry and Poetic Art of Kulbhushan Kushal

—N. K. Neb

Poetry as a form of verbal art has certain qualities that mark its difference from other verbal arts like fiction, prose, drama. The most distinctive feature of poetry is recitation. Whereas fiction and prose are meant for reading, drama is spectacle—oriented; poetry primarily has appeal for the listening faculty. The elements like rhythm, music, melody and harmony have greater significance for poetry than they have for other verbal arts. Apart from this, poetry being closer to human emotions and feelings has comparatively more and immediate impact on the listeners or readers and generates quick response. Consequently, greater importance is awarded to how rather than what has been said. It makes the craft part of a poem more significant than the content. It is perhaps due to this quality of the poetic art that most of the critics have tried to define poetry in terms of its ability to add charm to the ordinary and the prosaic through the use of different devices that make a verbal expression poetic.

The significance awarded to artistic devices in poetry or the poetic art can be easily ascertained from the views expressed by different critics and thinkers. According to Ransom, "The true poetry has no great interest in improving or idealizing the world, which does well enough. It wants to realize the world; to see it better poetry is the kind of knowledge by which we must know what we have arranged that we shall not know otherwise" (Ransom, 2000: 22-23). Similarly, Cleanth Brooks thinks that the purpose of a poet is:

> To give the charm of novelty to things of everyday, and to excite a feeling analogous to the supernatural, by awakening the mind 's attention from the lethargy of custom, and directing it to the loveliness and the wonders of the world before us.
>
> *(Brooks, 1986:96).*

Thus the job of a poet mainly is to explore the startling potential of words to generate responses in the members of the community who share a common language and culture. In the words of M. Sivaramakrishna, "To be true to itself, the poem has to be the community's sharing of the startling potential of words to explode into triggers of consciousness" (Sivaramakrishan, 2001: 24). In order to realize this potential of words a poet no longer uses language in its prosaic form: he rather moves towards the use of meta-types that involves the use of symbols, images, metaphors, rhythm and other devices to capture the experiences in an artistic way. The repeated use of certain devices forms the typical nature of the art of a particular writer. The elements that provide a distinct form to the poetic art of Kualbhushan Kushal form the subject of the present study.

The use of images related to nature forms one of the major poetic devices used in Kushal's poetry. The clusters of images that one finds in these poems tend to make his poetry thinking in images. Their recurrence and the ease with which they appear in his poems mark a constant flow in the form of sequences of images providing particular structural pattern to his poems, for example, in the poem "Haven of Rocks" the images indicate the nature of the world expressed in the stanzas that follow them. The poem begins with these images:

> This is the country of rocks
> In the desolated deserts
> Blossom stones
> Pebbles dance
> In the whirlpool of sands
> The dinosaurs
> Jumping on the rocks
> Dream of green valleys
> Full of flowers
>
> (*Whirlpool of Echoes,* p. 37)

These images turn out to be the signposts to reveal the nature of reality existing in the background.

The immense use of the objects of nature in Kushal's poetry gives the impression that the poet perceives different aspects of life in term of nature. His poems mark his attempt to explain human behaviour, social relationships, nature of life and its complexities so that the immediate surroundings seem to acquire an active role in day-to-day life. He comments on the nightmarish nature of contemporary reality through the image of inverted cycle of seasons. The world informing destabilization of traditional values signified by the cold summers and hot winters marks the distortion of reference in which the desired thing is not spring but winter:

> Fifty cold summers
> Fifty winters hot
> The reluctant autumns accepted
> My invitation, yet asked
> Where shall we go this summer?
> (*Rainbow on Rocks* p. 15)

The extended use of nature imagery using birds, animals, fables and elements of folklore add another dimension to his poetic art. In his poem "Perils Ahead" the image of a parrot, as it appears in the Punjabi folk literature, has been used so dexterously that it suits the situation conveyed and tends to make the poem acquire the potential of a fable having multiple associations. His poetic use of this form of animal imagery seems intended to provide an interesting replica of human situations and it offers these situations as objective correlatives for a better understanding of their implications. How he attempts to provide parallels from the animal world to human situations—like the betrayal of a promise and its resultant frustration and pain—is presented in these lines:

> Thousands fish swarm
> In rainbow nets
> Singing for deliverance
> Now thrown away on land
> (*Rainbow on Rocks* p.13)

The diversity informing the significances attached to the natural objects in Kushal's poetry corresponds to the diversity in life. Therefore the elements of nature like rocks, rainbows, deserts, ocean, seasons, planets, spheres, rivers, trees, glowworms, termites, flowers, leaves, sky earth, moon, stars floods, nightingales, sparrows, parrots, etc., acquire different associations in different contexts. It makes the use of nature imagery in his poetry functional instead of decorative or ornamental. The following lines present an artistic example of functional use of imagery:

> In the thick
> Foliage of associations
> Several moons
> Rise and melt
> Silently mingling their hues
> With the horizon
> In the dungeon dark
> Dazzle host of stars
>
> (*Striking Horizons,* p.29)

The poetic value of these lines is realized in their potential to relate the rise and fall of moon with the changing pattern of human relationships and the way they leave their impact in one's life. This device of making functional use of concrete images seems to serve the poetic purpose pointed out in the following lines: "There is no emotion as such in the poem itself, but the reader, in apprehending the concrete images in the poem, will feel with full force of the identical emotion originally felt by the poet. The poem then is to be objective bridge between the similar emotions, of the poet and his audience" (Chandra, 2000: 28). It marks Kushal's proximity to the romantics as they express the poet's emotions and relay them to the readers through concrete images.

The metaphoric quality of the images used in Kushal's poetry tends to make the utterances poetic. Instead of using imagery as a practical means of thinking, i.e., as a means of placing objects into categories, Kushal uses imagery to reinforce an impression. In the process his poetic utterances tend to be more complex. It is through the specific use of imagery that we find in his poetry, "impressions and experiences combine in peculiar and unexpected ways" (Eliot, 1986: 30). This combination of different elements in an unexpected way forms a major poetic device in his poems. For example, in his poem "Maya", the images add an element of wonder through the unexpected and unusual ways these images have been arranged:

> The days remembered not
> Initiated us to reflection
> Wrapping the rainbows
> In the coloured clusters
> Of brilliant moonshine
> Gently dancing
> On the waves of water
> (*Rainbow on Rocks,* p. 48)

The image of rainbows wrapped in coloured clusters of brilliant moonshine in the waves of water becomes poetic through its quality to evoke a particular impression and register its impact. Apart form this, the image adds a quality of fantasy and romance to heighten its poetic quality. The uncommon use of different elements that constitute this image comes forth with the association of rainbow with moonshine instead of sunlight. Such images used in abundance in Kushal's poetry form a distinguishing feature of his poetic art. The poetic value of these images is realized through the active role of the reader's imagination that these images tend to activate to enable the reader have a feel of the impression of the poetic experience. For example, the following images in two different poems "Transition" and "Twilight" in *Rainbow on Rocks* mark such use of images:

> Twittering sparrows holding
> Rainbows in their beaks
> Smiling pigeons waiting
> For the fairies dark
> Inviting children
>
> Singing 'twinkle, twinkle little star'
> Wondering where they are
> Refuse to retire
> (*Rainbow on Rocks,* p. 76)

And the grey moon
Dancing in a tunnel
And in the fields green
The tired cows
Stars in their eyes
Look towards the sky
Cherishing the twilight
Aware not of the call
Of their master

(*Rainbow on Rocks,* p.77)

The recurrence of such images makes Kushal's poetry difficult for the reader to relate them to certain contexts. Their semantic indeterminacy results from the complexity of the poetic experience that the poet intends to realize through these images. Consequently, his poems tend to become artifacts with peculiar structural characteristics. The nature of his poetic art then comes close to the views expressed by Hawkes: "A poem consists, less of a series of referential and verifiable statements about the real world beyond it, than of the presentation and sophisticated organization of a set of complex experiences in a verbal form" (Hawkes, 1986:152).

A careful use of pauses and the way these pauses have been developed to hold the meaning of certain lines tends to award poetic intensity to the thoughts presented in Kushal 's poems. It makes the recitation of the poems coincide with the occurrence of the thought process. Such poems develop through very short sentences that tend to form a pattern like that of stairs to reach the top. The special feature of this pattern in Kushal 's poetry is that it seems to provide some time and space for the next step to be taken, i.e., for the meaning to be realized. A sense of expectation aroused by the use of short sentences and the way meaning or information is released in the next part results in the rhythmic realization of thoughts, ideas, feelings and emotions carried in the verbal structures. There are different poems that mark the variations of this style. For example, the poem "Dreams Are" progresses in a pattern in which each line seems complete and independent in itself. But the additions of meanings in subsequent lines make it more complex and wonderful:

Dreams are realities
Hampered while chasing
The rainbows across Heaven

Dreams are the songs
Of the birds when captived
In the golden cages
(*Whirlpool of Echoes,* p.22)

The first lines in both the above stanzas have the potential to activate the intellectual zone of the reader to make sense of the words put into a new and different context. Similarly, the poem, 'Poetry is ' has been structured in short sentences that tend to mark different qualitative features of the art of poetry as envisaged by the poet. The other poems in which this structural feature is prominent are, "Read Not My Poems" "Time the Thief", "I Have A Dream", "I Have A Fear", "I Have Another Fear", "A Proposal", "These Are Not The Nights".

A significant aspect of Kushal's poetic art is its proximity to different art forms used to convey multiple meanings in a quick succession of images and sounds. Like cinema and advertisement, a message in his poetry is flashed through a series of images, narratives, anecdotes, literary and mythical allusions and symbols. Their effect is realized in the way they leave sudden sparks that carry the reader from one element to the other. The message thus flashed sometimes marks a sense of incompletion but it has the potential to activate the readers' responses to award certain meaning to realize its significance. The following images presented in quick succession appear in the form of different scenes that carry semantic significances to express multiple perspectives:

And this summer
The hands of autumn
May be too dreary to hold
And with her shall come
Truncated banyans
Naked *neem* trees
Perpetual shower
Of yellow leaves

Falling incrementally
And also the songs of beggars
In the trains
(*Rainbow on Rocks* p.16)

Similarly, references to literary, mythical and historical personalities and incidents in the poems, "Grammar of Peace", "Crafty Craft", "Pooran", "Strange Times", "Barren Successes", "Maya", "Beaches and Breaches", "Back To Elements", in Rainbow on Rocks evoke a host of associations.

This aspect of his poetry indicates the difficulty of manipulating words to communicate his special insights into life informing high degree of complexity. His use of these elements that tend to complicate meaning involves his endeavor to overcome the difficulty of expression by finding a contemporary poetic idiom. In the process, his poetic expressions tend to be difficult for an ordinary reader. However, the complex nature of his poetic utterances turns into almost an imperative when his poetry involves the expression of the variety and complexity informing contemporary life. In T.S. Eliot's words we find a justification for such complex poetic structures:

> We can only say that it appears likely that poets in our civilization, as it exists at present, must be difficult. Our civilization comprehends great variety and complexity and this variety and complexity, playing upon a refined sensibility must produce various and complex results. The poet must become more and more comprehensive, more allusive, indirect in order to force, to dislocate if necessary, language into his meaning. (Eliot, 1951: 289).

In the light of T. S. Eliot's observation the complexity informing Kushal's poetry is symptomatic of the complex nature of contemporary human existence.

Complexity informing Kushal's poetry brings his poetic style closer to what in I.A. Richards's terms can be called the poetry of inclusion. In his *Principles of Literary Criticism*, he asserts that, "there are two ways in which impulses may be organized; by exclusion and by inclusion, by synthesis and by elimination" (Richards, 1959: 249). Although he uses these terms for tragedy but they are applicable to all forms of art. According to him exclusion means the excluding of disparate elements to limit the poem to a specific mood. On the other hand, inclusion; refers to complex poetry that admits heterogeneity and conflicting feelings. A poet introduces every impulse alternative to the explicit impulse expressed in the poems, "By the extensive use of paradox, metaphor, and ambiguity, which while expressing one attitude, simultaneously suggests any number of alternative attitudes" (Chandra, 2000: 31). Some of Kushal's poems that make use of these elements more prominently include, "Beaches and Breaches," "Nightmares", "Girls and Demons", "We Are Ghosts". The following lines can be seen as an example of the use of these elements in Kushal's poetry:

> It's better we search our identities
> And get lost in the bright darkness
> Holding hands of statues
> To the land of liberty
> A curse that man only suffers
> (Song of Silence, p.21)

It shows how the poet has been able to make skilful use of paradox and ambiguity to bring to bear on each word of the poem a system of semantic analysis that reveals complex network of meanings in his poetry. In this way Kushal makes judicious use of images, words and phrases to include a rich variety of meanings into his poems.

As discussed earlier, a poet's attempt to express the impressions realized mark a constant struggle to grapple with the medium. Consequently, the poetic utterances inform their ambivalent nature. Kushal's poetry seems to show this in its development in quite lengthy structures involving a series of images, anecdotes, metaphors, poetic statements, symbols and sound patterns. In the poet's endeavour to capture the impressions in their natural state, the poet seems to make repeated use of these elements. In the process the poetic utterances develop in the form of multiple perspectives focusing sometimes on certain experiences and sometimes involving multiple experiences, ideas and impressions. Therefore, most of his poems spread over several stanzas consisting of multiple images. Sometimes, the development of thought forming a kind of argumentative logic or a framework, instead of marking its limited scope tends to evolve an extended structure. It relates to the feature of his poetry concentrating on multiple perspectives and the use of different elements to reinforce particular thoughts, experiences and feelings. For example, his poem "Perils Ahead" seems to develop in the form of a dialogue between innocent self and the self developed through experience. Here, the poet seems to express the realization that comes after having undergone the experiences warned against. This poem also extends into several stanzas as the poet always seems to make the medium come closer to the experience captured in the poems.

Kushal's other poems that mark complex structural development and extend into several stanzas include, "Beaches and Breaches", "Strange Times", "Rocks", "Vengeance", "Time The Thief", "Time To Celebrate", etc. The poet's attempt to grapple with the divide between the experiences and their expression results in the centrifugal structure of most his longer poems. This structural aspect of his poetry embodies the complexity informing the poetic vision and the nature of the world that finds expression in these poems.

Kushal's style of indirectly suggesting the opposite of what apparently seems the case marks a special feature of his poetic statements. It makes his poetry ironical. His clever use of irony in his poems makes it subtle and effective. Sometimes, the irony involved in a poetic statement is so subtle that the reader is easily taken in and carried away by the apparent and the simple meaning. As there is every danger of one's missing the ironic tinge involved in his poems these poems demand a careful and concentrated study that is likely to unearth new meanings after each subsequent reading. For example, the following lines can be studied as an example of this style:

> These are not the times
> For prayers
> For the lost
> In the whirlpool of goods
>
> (*Rainbow on Rocks* p.88.)

Similarly, there are poems like, "Time to Celebrate", and "Time the Thief" that present combinations of phrases that convey inverted views to reinforce certain ideas and attitudes. In the poem "Time to Celebrate" the words 'to celebrate' associated with 'betrayals' 'burning springs', 'sweet regrets', 'faces of masks ' and the poetic assertion. 'These are the times to sing songs of despair', 'And to repent for successes', apparently seem to have comic overtones but they form sarcastic comments on the present nature of human affairs. In fact, it is the poet's way of saying things with a tongue in cheek style.

However, there are certain poems that reinforce certain ideas and experiences directly. Such poems tend to follow a centripetal structural development. These poems are comparatively much short and involve straight forward expression of certain experiences and ideas through poetic rendering. The beauty of such poems in *Shrinking Horizons* lies in their presentation of unfamiliar world of thought through catchy statements given in very short sentences. Sometimes the ideas organized in a dramatic way become a special feature of Kushal's poetic art. His poems like "Adventure", "Cunning Craft" in *Shrinking Horizons* and "Pooran", "Neck to Neck" "Cunning Craft" in *Rainbow on Rocks* present examples of this art. These poems embody an integrity that provides a deeper pleasure with each new reading. The poetic presentation of philosophical perspectives and striking views makes his poetic creations different from the poetry of statements only. The striking nature of these elements evokes strange experiences and provides food for thought. This feature of his poetic art adds freshness to his poetry. His poems "Time", "Communication", "Summers Then", "Let Us Play Again", "That Dog" involve the presentation of different perspectives on certain concepts like 'time' 'communication' and human existence face to face with ultimate extinction. The views contained in small but pointed words and expressions have the potential to haunt the reader. This quality of his poetry makes certain lines memorable and ultimately these lines carry the potential to become quotable quotes: 'The raw is fine', 'ripeness-a smile, before the decay', 'We count our failures, wiser we grow', 'our successes show, how foolish we are now'. 'No rest within, no respite without' the mind a haunted house, 'Heart—a garden'.

The rhetorical devices and use of alliteration forms a significant aspect of Kushal's poetic art. It enhances the recitation value and rhythmic appeal of his poetic utterances. Apart from this, the use of rhetorical questions functions to emphasize a particular nature of the experience realized in different poems. In *Shrinking Horizons* the very first poem of the collection "Cunning Craft" marks the implied awareness of the reader about the cunning craft that has transformed the natural flow of life. The repeated use of question words like; who, whose, why, what is a device to quiz the reader in a way that marks poetic persona's imploring the reader to see through the game of the forces that have caused disjunctions in the social fabric. The last lines of the poem not only form a comment on the state of affairs but also imply an appeal to the people to relocate the earlier order:

> Who has snapped
> The ties of blood
> Why alien is the land
> Why hostile the sky
> Why alien the stars?
> (*Shrinking Horizons,* p.26)

The rhetorical questions here tend to set a probe into the present state of affairs and reinforce the relevance of the order that in its changed state now informs snapped ties of blood, alien and hostile nature of the land and the sky respectively. Similarly, the recitative value of these poems is realized through the use of short sentences and phrases that often carry an action, an idea or an object within their fold, for example 'After a long discussion they decided to touch the sun' (*Shrinking Horizons,* p.41). And the use of pretty short sentences using two or three words help recite the words in a way that approximates them to the feelings, experiences and the activities realized through them: For example, see the following sentences that occur in different poems:

Hungry chaos now
Is devouring shores
Kissing homes domes
(*Shrinking Horizons,* p.40).

The turbulent ocean,
Thirsty images
Search for water
(*Shrinking Horizons,* p.38)

In all seasons
Broken promises
Chase us.
(*Shrinking Horizons,* p.48)

The use of contrast in the form of paradoxical statements and placement of opposites in a specific order runs throughout Kushal's poetry. Sometimes paradox contained in certain poetic statements embodies a probe that activates the creative imagination of the reader. For example:

Tiresome is the journey
More tiresome is the rest
(*Shrinking Horizons,* p.54)

How poor the rich
How rich the poor
(*Shrinking Horizons,* p.33)

The use of contradictions has also been employed to express the topsy-turvy nature of the world impacted by a misplaced sense of values pointed out in the following lines:

Time has stolen
Meaning from words
Search them in
The caves of silence
(*Whirlpool of Echoes,* p.51)

Thou will eat
Your neighbour with respect
Though will deceive
Your brothers with love

With love alone
You will violate
The solemn vows
(*Whirlpool of Echoes,* p.40)

Such statements highlight the irony informing human existence. The use of such expressions displaces their understanding to award them poetic intensity. Instead of using certain elements in their accepted form the poet adds the element of wonder through a different arrangement. For example:

On the lips dances
Silence grim
(*Shrinking Horizons,* p. 28)

Green deserts,
Thirsty waves,
Profuse rain
Drenched the earth drier
(*Shrinking Horizons,* pp.34, 45)

Another element that recurs in Kushal's poetry is the awarding of different meanings to certain expressions by placing them in new contexts. Usually the poet uses the opposite words to heighten the changed context. It results in the formation of wonderful combinations that tend to jolt the readers. For example, the poem "Time to Celebrate" is replete with different expressions carrying opposite meanings:

Cursed blessings
Burning springs
Soft betrayals,
Hard promises
Faces of masks
(*Whirlpool of Echoes,* p.11)

Similarly, the expressions associated with specific significances mark a displacement of meaning in sentences like:

These are the times
To parade failures

And to repent for successes
And these are the times
To celebrate
The death of our friends
(*Whirlpool of Echoes,* p.13)

And the expression 'Faces are intimate strangers' in the poem "Dance of Masks".

The objective use of poetic persona forms one of the major constituents of Kushal's poetic art. The voice that governs and determines the poetic expression not only sets the tone of the poetic utterance but also tends to determine the nature of the poetic discourse and its relation with the assumed readers. Whereas the use of the pronouns 'I' or 'We' involve a process of the identification of speaker, their absence in a poetic structure marks the creation of the text as an objective form, rendering a particular shape to the artistic creation. Such kind of poetry tends to free itself from the dangers of being related and thus limited to the personality of the poet. Of course, the poet, as the governing consciousness of the work of art is not absent but it makes the divide between the person who writes and the adopted voice clear and visible. This aspect of Kushal's poetry foregrounds the text and the personality of the poet remains relegated to the background. In his poetry the way words, phrases, symbols, images interact becomes more important and the reader is involved in an interactive game by responding to the arrangement of these elements as per his/her own framework of understanding. The different elements of a poem then play the role of a stimuli that activates the responses and thought processes of the reader. As a result of this the poetic voice in these poems involves a kind of, persuasion, invitation and an attempt to call the target reader to realize and examine what seems to be strikingly different and wonderful yet it is closely related with human existence at large. As the use of 'I' or 'we' to involve the people or the audience is indirectly made the success of the poet depends on the ways the poet evolves to initiate this process. Sometimes it involves the introduction of the elements of wonder, the repetition of same words and phrases, sound patterns, subtle variations of meanings, displacement of myth. All these elements facilitate the kind of rhetoric the poet uses as a part of his poetic craft.

The use of mythical allusions forms a significant feature of Kushal's poetry. The mythical allusions are used by him to evoke certain contexts against which the present experiences and incidents are placed to create different meanings. Instead of awarding the myths a new meaning that some poets often attempt, Kushal uses them to heighten the evil nature of contemporary life governed by self interest ignoring moral values and human concerns. The poet himself is aware of this element in his poetry, "There is a latent energy in myths historical icons, mythical figures and this energy has been used to make the poet's point. It is a technique used for making the reader experience evil" (Kushal, Interview). It shows the conscious use of myth that the poet makes for specific ends. In his poem the references to mythical incidents are suggestive of the evil prevailing in contemporary life.

Another feature of the use of myth and historical icons in Kushal's poetry is that these elements bring out the poet's stance towards particular situations, experiences, ideas and incidents. Apart from using myth he uses 'reversal technique' to heighten the poetic effect. In his use of this technique, the reverse of the generally accepted views is projected in a way that awards the poems a comic touch. In the process, the poet's rejection of certain attitudes and ideas is introduced in a very subtle way. For example, in the poem "Dreams", he says:

Dreams are our friends
Sleeping in our minds
Plotting against us
Praying for themselves
(*Whirlpool of Echoes,* p.23)

And in his poem "Prayers", the poet talks about the mechanical nature of the religious ceremonies in this way:

My prayers have shown
Resilience supreme

Their texture has assumed
The tone and colour of circumstances
Bright they are during the day
And dark at night
I've packaged them well
For God to buy
(*Whirlpool of Echoes,* p.47-48)

Instead of concentrating on a single idea, mood or experience, Kushal's poetic utterances involve the presentation of various elements in a single unit. It results in clusters of thematic implications and makes a sense of diffusion of the content. Such nature of his poetry highlights the elastic feature of his poetic art. It tends to become an unedited overflow of thoughts, ideas and impressions that seem to spill over the limits of formal structure. This may indicate the urgency of expression that certain poetic experiences require but at the same time they indicate a lack of control so far as the formal structure is concerned. He seems to be more concerned with the expression than with the craft part of his poetry. In other words, the sincerity of his objectives does not seem to be marked in the pedantic cloak of his style. It brings his style close to Indian oral tradition informing multiple digressions. The reader has to grasp the shifts and changes of the ideas and moods expressed through a conscious effort to ascertain their complete implications. For example, the poems "Raw deals", "Girls and Demons", "Ghosts We Are", "Twilight" in *Rainbow of Rocks* and 'Darkness' 'The Hand' 'Haven of Rocks' in '*Whirlpool of Echoes*' highlight this feature of Kushal' poetic style.

The foregoing study of the poetic art of Kulbhushan Kushal reveals how he too shares a number of poetic elements with other modern Indian English poets pointed out by Amarnath Prasad in these words, "The modern poets like A.K.Ramanujan, Kamala Das, Jayant Mahapatra, Nissim Ezekieil, P.Lal, Shiv K.Kumar, Pritish Nandy, O.P. Bhatnagar, to name only a few, bade goodbye to the early traditional images and symbols and put in their place some harsh and solid images of day to day reality which are full of complexities and ambiguities; they are also replete with ironies,paradoxes, oxymoron and sometimes the deliberate distortions of some certain rules and regulations of morphology and syntax so as to properly conform to the feelings of the characters and situations" (Prasad Amarnath, 2009:1). Their poetic art is obviously different from the poets interested in simple expression of thoughts without putting heavy demands on the reader's faculties to unearth meaning. Kushal's poetic craft like that of the poets mentioned above helps make his poems significant artistic voices that tend to involve the reader in the process of experiencing the magic world of poetry.

Works Cited

Brooks, Cleanth (1986). "Language of Paradox", *Contemporary Literary Criticism: Modernism through Post-structuralism* ed. Robert Con Davis. New York & London.

Chandra, N.D.R. (2000). *Literary Theory and the New Critics*. Delhi: Prestige.

Eliot, T. S. (1951). *Selected Essays*. London: Faber & Faber.

____ . (1986). "Tradition and Individual Talent" in *Contemporary Literary Criticism: Modernism through Post-structuralism* ed. Robert Con Davis. New York & London.

Hawkes, Terence (1986). *Structuralism and Semiotics* London: Methuen.

Kushal, Kulbhushan (2007). Interview with Dr. Sudesh Sharma.

___ (1989). *Shriking Horizons*. Jalandhar: Nirman Publications.

___ (2005). *Rainbow on Rocks*. Jalandhar: Nirman Publications.

___ (2006). *Whirlpool of Echoes*.

___ Jalandhar: Nirman Publications.

___ (2008). *Songs of Silence*. Jalandhar: Nirman Publications.

Prasad, Amarnath (2007) "Harmonizing Poetic Truth and Beauty: A Study of Five Major Poems of Indian Poetry in English", in Binod Mishra ed. *Rainbow Redemption: Bearings in Indian English Poetry*. New Delhi: Adhyayan Publishers & Distributors.

Ransom, John Crowe, quoted in *Twentieth Century Literary Criticism Bijay* Kumar Das, Delhi: Atlantic Publishers and Distributors, Third ed. 1998.

Richards, I.A. (1924). *Principles of Literary Criticism* London: Routledge and Kegan Paul, rpt. 1959.

Sivaramakrishna, M. (2001) "Variety No Hierarchy," in Rama Nair ed. *Trends and Techniques in Contemporary Indian—English Poetry* Delhi: Prestige, 2001.

8

An Analysis of the Poetry of Toru Dutt with Special Reference to Her "Sita"

—Anindita Chatterjee

Indian literary history is divided into two phases whereas one consists of expression of identity emerging from a deep sense of tradition which was written primarily during the colonial rule; the other consists of a representation of a consciousness that emerged from a confrontation between tradition and modernity during the post colonial period. Macaulay had propagated the idea of educating the Indians in English to facilitate administration and governance. Several progressive families of the contemporary society accepted these modern principles although some resisted them as a threat to the conventional national identity. Among the early practitioners of English verse Michael Madhusudan Dutt and Henry Vivian Derozio are considered to be the most noted names in the history of English poetry. Toru Dutt, Manmohan Ghose and Sarojini Naidu followed thereafter.

Harihar Das in *Life and Letters of Toru Dutt* describes Toru Dutt as a rare genius for her capacity to imbibe foreign languages. "In all her too brief life she mastered Sanskrit and wrote in French and English with a grace, a facility, and an individual distinction which has given her rank among the authentic voices of Western Literature"(Das, vii). Her poetry is characterised by sensitive descriptions, lyricism and vigour and they revolve around themes of loneliness, longing, patriotism, frustration, nostalgia, dejection, illusions, exile and captivity. She struck a genuinely Indian note in her verse and was the first Indian woman to reveal the spirit and essence of her homeland to the West. Skilfully crafted, her poetry reflects a passionate commitment of theme, character, and setting.

Toru Dutt was a product of nineteenth century Bengal Renaissance. She belonged to a family of newly converted Christians. Christianity was introduced in Bengal primarily through the upper caste Hindu elites who were impressed by the liberal principles and the theory of western education that was popularized in the institutions established by the British authorities. The introduction of the printing press by Rev. William Carey at Srirampore, to propagate Gospels in Indian language intensified the euphoria for the new religion. The Dutt family of Rambagan, was one of the very first few families to imbibe the new faith.

Toru Dutt's family was baptized in 1862 when she was six years old, but the new religion never alienated her from her traditional roots. She sought inspiration for her creativity from the Hindu epics and myths.

Toru Dutt inherited the literary genius that was inherent in her family. It was a family of noted historians and poets—Romesh Chunder Dutt, Govin Chunder Dutt, Hur Chunder Dutt, Greece Chunder Dutt, Omesh Chunder Dutt were some of the noted intellectuals of the age. Her father was a great influence in her life. It was he who instilled in young Dutt a deep passion for the ancient tradition that served as source and inspiration to her creativity. She herself acknowledged her father's role in determining the course of her life—"Without Papa I should never have known good poetry from bad, but he used to take such pains with us ... When we were quite little ones... I wonder what I should have been without my father, nothing very enviable or desirable, I know" (Das, 222).

Toru Dutt's poetic output was brief for her literary career was truncated by her untimely death. Despite the brevity of its volume, it remains a 'real gem' (Dwivedi, 27) because of its worth and merit and it has enabled her to carve out a permanent place for herself in the history of Indian English literature.

Toru Dutt's life was fraught with many tragedies. It was the personal experience of pain that she translated into her verse. Her poetry was tinged with an acute sense of loss, anguish, longing and nostalgia. Her poetry also reveals a fusion of romantic and classical elements. K.D. Verma claimed that early Indian women poets like Toru Dutt and Sarojini Naidu were like *Romantic singing Birds of India* providing 'sufficient provocation to experiment afresh' (Verma, 3). They had laid the foundations and set new standards as well as helped in preserving what was vital in the tradition of the nation. Besides its intense romantic longing and nostalgia her poetry also brings out her deep interest in myths and *puranas*.

A Sheaf Gleaned in French Fields (1876), a collection of nearly one hundred translations of French poets, was the only work which Toru Dutt could see published during her lifetime. A novella in French entitled *Le Journal de Mademoiselle d' Arvers* (1879) was published posthumously. It was the first French fiction written by an Indian. Of the 165 poems published in *The Sheaf* eight were by Aru Dutt although the title page did not mention her name. These poems were enthusiastically received in England and India, and soon went into three editions. "The most significant aspect of Dutt's literary career was her use of the rich Indian heritage of myth and folklore" (Paranjape 11). However Toru Dutt is best remembered for her posthumous publication of *Ancient Ballads and Legends of Hindustan* (1882). Her ballads highlight her narrative skills. Edmund Gosse reviewed her poems in *The Examiner* in August 1876. Her fame chiefly rests upon her ballads. H.A.L. Fisher is right when he claims that it was her sheer genius that enabled her to earn a place for herself and a right to be "enrolled in the great fellowship of English poets" (Das, vii). She writes of the tropical Eastern enchantment as well as of the western delights with equal forte.

Toru Dutt drew her inspiration from the popular stories from the *Ramayana, Mahabharata* and the *Puranas.* Seven poems based on mythical and legendary themes and nine ballads are included in the volume. She drew upon folklores and popular tales from the past. She was indebted to her mother for her inspiration. It was her mother's evening chants that acquainted her with the traditional lays. They touched her sensitive soul and inspired her to creativity. In her poem "The Legend of Dhruva", included in the collection, Dutt relates the story of prince Dhruva who abjured power for the attainment of spiritual knowledge. The poem "Prahlad" shows how faith enables one to win over all forms of hostility in the world. In this poem the poet vividly depicts a young boy's fearless devotion to Gods despite the cruelty and hostility of his father. The poem finally concludes with a hope that God never deserts his true believer. The poem "Lakshman" recounts a conversation between Sita and Lakshman where Sita urges Lakshman to go and find Rama for she is disturbed by Marichis deceptive cry in the voice of Rama. Lakhman reluctantly reminds her that Rama had asked him not to leave Sita alone and unprotected. Sita interprets Lakshman's reluctance as cowardice and selfishness and finally persuades Lakshman to go, unconsciously ushering in her own doom. Lakshman is depicted as an ideal brother, an epitome of chivalry and courage. The poem "Savitri" deals with the love of Savitri for her husband Satyavan that wins over the force of death. The poem conjures up a picture of an ideal Indian wife selfless in her devotion to her husband. In the poem "Jogadhya Uma", Uma is affectionately described as a young girl that corresponds to a part of the Indian cultural tradition where the goddess is seen as a family member, a married woman who comes home with her family from her in-laws every autumn. The story derives its origin from a folklore that was recounted to the young poet by her family nurse Suchee. These poems evoke an aura of the old world of simplicity and innocence. The poet herself proclaimed:

> Absurd may be the tale I tell,
> Ill suited to the marching times,
> I loved the lips from which it fell,
> So let it stand among my rhymes.
> "Jogadhya Uma",
> *(Ancient Ballads and Legends of Hindustan)*

Toru Dutt's poems are concerned with the simple human emotions. They portray various shades of the feminine form, in most cases reinstating the virtues of sacrifice and surrender, which have been glorified by patriarchal order as ideal feminine behaviour.

She was the harbinger of a new era of Indian writing in English. She is often identified as the Keats of Indo Anglican literature. She had a brief life and died of consumption. It is the tragedy of her life that marks her poem with a romantic tinge. Her poetry shows a fusion of the East and the West and brings out her deep indebtedness to her Motherland and its inherent tradition. She was an Indian at heart despite being educated in the West. Her poetry is characterized by intensity of expression and sincerity of feelings that make her one of the pioneers of Indian poets in English. Her short life and untimely death adds a romantic and poignant perspective to her creativity. In the words of K.R. Srinivasa Iyengar, "Like Emily Bronte it is a note of what 'might have been' that is integral to our assessment of Toru Dutt's life and creativity which both fascinate and depresses us simultaneously." (Iyengar, 55)

Toru Dutt is remembered most for her *Ancient Ballads and Legends of Hindusthan*, a posthumous collection of her poems which deals with familiar legends and myths of India, which she sought to popularize in the Western world of thought and ideas. Making extensive use of Indian fables, legends and folk lore in her verses she sought to familiarize and acquaint the Western world with the stories that were a part of Indian lore and folk culture. Her treatment of the myths and legends 'reveals on the whole, an instinctive understanding of the spirit underlying them, though as a recent Christian convert living in a half-Anglicised atmosphere at home, she occasionally betrays certain inadequacies, "yet, we cannot doubt, that for a young girl it was a daunting task to write about her land, her faith and her people in the newly acquired language" (Naik, 41). Dutt combined prosodic mastery and English mellifluousness with the Indian subject matter and an Indian sensibility, Indianising the European form and Europeanising the Indian voice in equal measure, "an accomplishment which she replicated in prose in her unfinished English novel *Bianca* (1879)" (Roberts, 269).

The mythical poems like "Sita" and "Savitri" included in the collection deal with the archetypes of Indian womanhood, whereas lyrics like "Dhruvo" and "Prahlad" are concerned with the unfailing power of human faith. The poem "Sita" presents a picture of love, warmth and affection. The poem depicts a picture of a domestic bliss with a mother recounting a tale to her three children. The poem has autobiographical elements embedded within it. The poet conjures up a vision of her own childhood through the poem and through the image of Sita and her children in forest she goes on to recollect the image of her own mother who used to read the stories of the Indian epics to her three children. In this poem the poet remembers the tragic tale of Sita and how the three siblings wept in pain when their mother recounted her painful story to them. The poet also finds subtle similarity between Sita's children, Luv and Kush who lived with their mother in exile and themselves. Secluded from the royal comfort, the mother and her two children lived in a dense, dark forest far removed from the din and bustle of courtly life. The children grew up in close proximity of nature under the loving guardian ship of their mother. The poem recounts a moment of togetherness when the mother shares her grief with her children. The young poet felt an instinctive sympathy for the gentle and suffering figure of Sita.

Toru Dutt was always fascinated and touched by the poignant tale of Sita's life. As a young girl, she identified with her misery, trauma and suffering.

In a letter to her French friend Clarissa Bader, Toru Dutt wrote

> Can there be a more touching and lovable heroine than Sita?
> I do not think so. When I hear my mother chant, in the evening,
> the old lays of the country, I almost always weep. The plaint
> of Sita, when banished for the second time, she wanders
> alone in the vast forest, despair and horror filling her soul, is so

> pathetic that I believe there is no one who could hear it without shedding tears.
>
> (qtd in Iyengar, 71)

In the short lyric included in the *Ancient Ballads,* "Sita" is conceived as an ordinary woman devoid of her divine enigma. Dutt's "Sita" is a short poem included in *Ancient Legends and Ballads of Hindusthan* that reflects upon Sita's agony and her "unmerited suffering at the hands of Rama". (Dwivedi, 36)

The poems "Sita" and "Savitiri" depict the ideal prototypes of Indian femininity and womanhood, and through the representation of mythical and epic characters, Dutt shows women in suffering, persevering and self-sacrificing roles, thereby representing an Indian culture that she was familiar with. The young poet felt that these 'deathless' legendary stories would provide her with the fitting creative resource that would enable her "to give expression to her maturing poetic powers". (Iyengar, 65)

"Mythology in India is not just an academic or historical subject; it is a vital and living topic of contemporary relevance" (Lal and Gokhale, xiv). Valmiki's *Ramayana*, Kalidasa's *Raghuvamsha* present Sita as a brave dutiful ideal wife, who does everything to preserve the order of the patriarchal universe. Valmiki's *Ramayana* does not allow much space to Sita for the heroic poem celebrates patriarchal virtues of chivalry, loyalty, honour and courage and women are conceived as sacrificing, obliging and accommodating entities. "Sita appears in 26 sargs out of 645, accounting for barely 10 percent of the Valmiki *Ramayana*" (Lal and Gokhale, 4). It was only at the end of the epic that Sita asserted her independent will and indicated her anguish by departing from the mortal world after being asked to take the second test of fire to prove her chastity. Her silent protest against her injustice has rendered dignity and heroism to her character. Although she emerges as the ideal wife in the epic, Rama cannot be identified as an ideal husband, for he fails to fulfil his matrial vows, where he had pledged by fire to protect his wife from all perils. It was Rama himself who urged his wife to prove her chastity despite being aware of her complete innocence.

It has been observed that Dutt's treatment of women is mostly conventional and like her contemporary thinkers she too often idolized her women figures, and emphasized on their divinity, thus in a way, unconsciously reinforcing the conventional gender roles structured by patriarchy. It has been a long standing convention of patriarchy to perceive women as venerable beings, thereby dehumanizing them, for goddesses and divine figures are after all lifeless entities. Shashi Deshpande had once sarcastically remarked, "For quite a while I believed—a belief that came from all around ne—that men's lives are more important, more significant. And therefore, that serious writing is done by men and is about men. That women's writing, like their lives somehow lacks weight and substance" (Deshpande, 107). Unlike the later women poets of India like Kamala Das, who ventured on a quest for selfhood and identity, seeking a room of their own, Dutt's poetry, can be seen more as an attempt to disseminate knowledge about India's legends, myths, folklore and historical origins to the Western world. It is true that in her poetry, we often come across women who are depicted more as victims, enduring, passive, uncomplaining and self-denying characters, but it cannot be doubted that she endeavours to portray the real human face and deconstruct the real woman behind the façade of divinity. Despite the fact that the representation of image of the woman in literary forms has undergone a substantial change over the last few decades, yet it cannot be denied that it was through her poetry that the Western world first got to see the Indian woman and hear 'her' story.

The image of the ideal woman as conceived by patriarchal Indian society is one who follows her father's orders before marriage, abides by the laws imposed by her husband and her in laws after her marriage, and one who listens to her children when they become adults. Since the time of Manu it has been believed that a woman must be devoted and dedicated to her husband and she must not protest or defy him under any circumstances. In short it was implied that a woman would not have any will or individuality of her own. Though Mary Wollstonecraft had come up with her *Vindication of the Rights of Woman* in 1792 claiming that femininity was only an artificial construct, a structural imposition of patriarchy to assert their own authority, yet in India the prevalent norm till the nineteenth century was that a woman's ideal space was her kitchen, and her primary duty was to serve her husband and ensure his prosperity and progress. Pam Morris in a study interlinking literature and feminism claimed that "creative forms of writing can offer special insight into human experience and sharpen our perception of social reality. Literary text may therefore provide a more powerful understanding of the ways in which society works to the disadvantage of woman". The strong emotional impact of imaginative writing can help to engender indignation at gender discrimination and hence lead to an eventual abolition of it. "Positive images of female experience", according to Morris, "can be used to raise women's self esteem and lend authority to their political demands". (Morris 29)

In Toru Dutt's poem "Sita" it is evident that Indian women contributed immensely towards the strengthening of the already existing oral tradition. A woman is portrayed as an important repository of folklore wisdom and culture. Sexual stereotyping can be considered to be perpetrated through tradition and culture which is quite successfully decoded in Toru Dutt's "Savitri". It is in this context that Elaine Showalter's perceptive differentiation of feminist consciousness into three separate phases—the feminine phase of internalization, the feminist phase of revolt and the female phase of self discovery becomes relevant. She points out that in the Indian context "there is no such historical linearity, what is witnessed here is the simultaneous existence of all 3. It is in this direction that Toru in her poetry has made an attempt to raise explicit questions about re assessment formulating a consciousness that aims at asserting one's pride within and outside the country at the global arena. She deconstructs the supremacy of man as the ultimate repository of 'knowledge', 'light' and instead re-examines these positive virtues in a woman like 'Savitiri' conceived hundreds of years ago in our rich cultural tradition (Naikar, 6). "Toru Dutt, a Hindu convert to Christianity made poetry a vehicle of asserting women's rights to re-define her place in society that was appropriated by the patriarchal world" (Naikar, 1).

Dutt does not merely translate the legends of Hindustan from the *Ramayana* and the *Mahabharata* but tries to establish a place of esteem for Indian women in the patriarchal society. She constitutes a vision of emancipated womanhood in her *Ancient Ballads and Legends of Hindustan*. The Indian woman in her poetry is manifested as a Third World Intellectual confronting the distortions and disfigurations of the past to emerge as the most progressive emancipated intellectual woman. Empowerment through knowledge is examined as a Virtue in her women characters and doing so, she goes beyond the restrictive regimentation of time and place to discover the power of women's discourse through legend of Savitri. (Naikar, 7)

Sita, according to traditional conventions, embodies the image of an ideal Indian wife and even till this date her image is worshipped with reverence and veneration across the country. She is represented as the good, pure, submissive and obedient wife. When her husband Rama asked her to take the test by fire Sita had willingly obliged. Rama agreed to take back Sita after he was convinced of her innocence and chastity, but it did not terminate Sita's woes forever. It was after they had lived in Ayodhya for few years that Rama heard people still doubting Sita's innocence. In order to prove himself as a righteous king, he decided to banish Sita from the kingdom for he sought to eradicate gossip and scandal from his kingdom. He was forced to sacrifice his personal feelings before his political responsibility. Despite Sita's purity, Rama rejected her twice and doubted her fidelity. Sita silently endured her destiny and without even questioning her husband's motive or actions once she decided to leave her husband's home to find shelter and refuge in forest. Her decision to leave her husband's abode and bringing up her children on her own as a single abandoned mother in Valmiki's hermitage was an act of silent rebellion in itself. It is at the end of the epic that the usually passive and silent Sita finally emerges as a strong woman with a will of her own.

Sita, Savitri, Lakshmi, Uma still serve as powerful cultural icons for Indian women and it is their self sacrifice that is emphasized as virtues worthy of emulation. Ian Mackean, in *The Essentials of Literature in English Post-1914* claims that since mythical times, the dominant feminine prototype in India is that of the chaste, patient, enduring and self-denying wife, Sita. The mythical and legendary figures such as Savitri, Draupadi and Gandhari have exemplified virtues of patience, perseverance, tolerance and sacrifice over the ages. It is in their patient acceptance of the conventional roles as dutiful wives that history remembers them as ideals of womanhood.

At the end of the poem Sita emerges as a human form. The poem is enriched with deep pathos, personal feelings and human sentiments and in her diction, content and style Dutt resembles the Romantic and Victorian school of British poets.

Though Rama is seen as an emblem of divinity and perfection in Indian sub-continent and worshipped as one of the primary divine figures of Hinduism, yet his treatment of his wife has often been subjected to criticism. The epic *Ramayana* records how Rama had asked his chaste and pure wife to undertake an *agnipariksha* or test by the fire to prove her chastity to the world. Based on hearsay rumours he had ordered that his wife would have to undergo the trial and prove her innocence to world and show them that her purity had not been violated or maligned during the period in which she had been confined in Ravana's Lanka. Sita remained unscathed in the fire, although her innocence was proved to the world but it sundered the husband and the wife forever. Sita left the comforts and luxury of her husband's abode and went to live as a recluse in the hermitage of Valmiki. The legend has several other versions and interpretations as well; there are some religious historians who believe that Sita was exiled and banished by Rama for a second time after he asked her to undertake the test by the penal fire, whereas some other argue that it was Sita who herself decided to leave the royal splendour of Ayodhya with her two sons, for she was shattered by the public humiliation and the disgrace that she was subjected to in the hands of her husband, who was hailed as a form of the divinity by the world.

Both the Indian epics bring out similar tales of public mortification of women, in *Mahabharata,* Draupadi was assaulted in the royal court, in the presence of her 'husbands' and it was Lord Krishna who came to her rescue. Sita too was subjected to a similar emotional torment. Both in the case of Draupadi as well as Sita, it was their respective husbands who were instrumental to their ordeal.

Toru Dutt begins her poem with a picturesque description of Valmiki's *ashram* or hermitage, where Sita had taken refuge with her two children Lav and Kush. Much like Tennyson's lyrics Toru Dutt's poem too begins with an element of pictorial description which serves as a framework for the poet to recount and explore the mythical legend thereafter. The depiction of the nature is abruptly interrupted in the tenth line with the introduction of the elegiac note which comes as a sudden aberration. Sita's life too had undergone such a drastic transition. Being born as a princess and brought up with love and care by Janaka, and married to a prince thereafter, Sita's life was always marked with pain, torment and anguish. She was forced to leave the royal life immediately after her marriage and followed her husband as he decided to live the life of a recluse in forest for fourteen years, to fulfill his father's pledge. It was a period of intense agony for Sita, who was captured by Ravana the demonic king of Lanka. She was eventually rescued by her husband who fought against Ravana and thereby secured the victory of good over evil. It was after they returned to Ayodhya, and Rama was reinstated in power that there began another series of trial for Sita. In order to satisfy the odd curiosity of his subjects Rama ordered Sita to prove her innocence and purity to the world. Based on hearsay rumours, he decided to banish his wife, thereafter. The husband and the wife were estranged both literally as well as psychologically. Dutt's poem "Sita" begins at this point, where Sita had left her husband's home to find shelter for herself and her children in the hermitage of Valmiki. The poet describes the hermitage as a land of pastoral innocence

> A dense, dense forest, where no sunbeam pries,
> And in its centre a cleared spot,—there bloom

> Gigantic flowers on creepers that embrace
> Tall trees; there, in a quiet lucid lake
> The white swans; there, "whirring from the brake,"
> The peacock springs; there, herds of wild deer race;
> There, patches gleam with yellow waving grain;
> There, blue smoke from strange altars rises light,
> But who is this fair lady? Not in vain
> She weeps,—for lo!
>
> (Toru Dutt, "Sita")

Dutt thereafter goes on to reflect upon the epic tale of Sita's misfortune and evoke sympathies for her through Sita's tale of misery and eternal suffering she subtly refers to the thousand un recounted tortures and torments that a woman is subjected to in a male dominated world both in the public as well as private sphere of life. Sita had pledged her whole life for her husband's sake and had retained her faith on him living in hope for years that he would recover her from her confinement; yet, ironically enough the same man who had rescued her had also subjected her to severe mortification and agony. Rama, despite being the champion of justice and truth forgot the vows he had taken as her husband during her marriage to protect his wife till death. He sought to test her integrity despite knowing that his wife Sita was devoid of any tint of blemish. Dutt presents Sita as a human entity and not as a divine being and recounts her misery at being banished and betrayed by the same man whom she loved more than her own life. She depicts Sita's plight with a vivid intensity and how she responds to it like any other ordinary woman who had been subjected to humiliation and betrayal.

In the poem "Sita" Toru Dutt describes how Sita as a mother recounts her own tale of misery to her children who empathise with her anguish and are touched by her grief.

> At ever tear she sheds
> Tears from three pairs of young eyes fall amain,
> And bowed in sorrow are the three young heads
>
> (Toru Dutt, "Sita")

The picture of the grief stricken Sita touches our heart. The poet thereafter goes on to mention how the picture of Sita sharing her grief with her children is also reminiscent of her childhood when she along with her brothers Abju and Aru would cry together listening to the tale of Sita recounted to them by their mother during the evenings.

> And bowed in sorrow are the three young heads.
> It is an old, old story, and the lay
> Which has evoked sad Sita from the past
> Is by a mother sung...

According to Iyengar the poem is also a "tribute to Toru's mother genius for story-telling, and the last two lines are a poignant elegy on the early death of her brothers' who had died much before their prime." (Iyengar, 71)

> When shall those children by their mother's side
> Gather, ah me! As erst at eventide?

The brief lyric "Sita" strikes us with its note of integrity and tragedy. Dutt presents Sita as an ordinary woman devoid of any divine glory. There is no glorification of pain, but rather a subtle condemnation of the injustice that she had been subjected to as a woman. Although Dutt has often been criticized for her depiction of Indian women as paradigms of perfection and endurance, yet in "Sita", we come across a young girl trying to depict another woman's tale of distress to the world% she is neither a goddess nor any deity; she is just another Indian girl like Toru. Although the young poet does not delve in detail about Sita's life or her loss, yet the poem is significant for its sensitive rendering of Sita and its evocation of the spirit of humanity and compassion in its assessment of a woman's suffering in a patriarchal world.

Works Cited

Banerjee, Benoy Kumar and Kaustav Bakshi, *Studies in Indian Poetry in English*, Calcutta: Booksway, 2008.

Chakraborti Santosh, *Four Indo-Anglian Poets*, Calcutta: Dhakeswari Library, 1987.

Das, Harihar. *The Life and Letters of Toru Dutt*, With a foreword by H.A.L Fisher, London: Oxford University Press, 1921.

Deshpande, Sashi "Of Course, of Anxieties," *Indian Literature*, 9.5, 1996.

Dutt, Toru, *Ancient Ballads and Legends of Hindustan*, with an Introduction by Edmund Gosse, London: Kegan Paul, 1882.

Dwivedi, A. N. *Papers on Indian Writing in English*, New Delhi: Atlantic Publishers, 2001.

Gokak, V.K. eds. *The Golden Treasury of Indo-Anglian Poetry 1828-1965*, selected and edited by New Delhi: Sahitya Akademi, 1970, 97-98.

Iyengar, Srinivasa K. R, *Indian Writing in English*, New Delhi: Sterling Publishers Private Limited, 1962.

Lal Malashri and Namita Gokhale, *In Search of Sita: Revisiting Mythology* New Delhi: Penguin, 2009.

Lokuge, Chandani ed. *Toru Dutt Collected Prose and Poetry*, (New Delhi: Oxford University Press, 2006.

Mackean, Ian ed. *The Essentials of Literature in English Post-1914*, London: Hodder Arnold, 2005.

Morris, Pam *Literature and Feminism: An Introduction*, Oxford: Blackwell, 1993.

Naik, M.K. *A History of Indian English Literature*, New Delhi, Sahitya Akademi, 1982.

Naikar Basavaraj ed. *Indian English Literature*, Volume 7, New Delhi: Atlantic, 2007.

Paranjape, Makrand *Indian Poetry in English:* New Delhi: Macmillan India, 2000.

Prasad, Hari Mohan and Chakradhar Prasad Singh. *Indian Poetry in English.* New Delhi: Sterling Publishers.

Roberts Neil, ed. *A Companion to Twentieth Century Poetry*, London: Blackwell, 2001.

Verma, K.D. *The Indian Imagination: Critical Essays on Indian Writing in English*. New Delhi: Palgrave, 2000.

9

A Displaced Generation: Re-Reading Kamala Das's *Treatment of Old Age*

—Amit Bhattacharya

Forgive me, mother,
that I left you
a life-long widow
old alone.
It was to kill or die
and you got me anyway;
The blood congeals at lover's touch.
The guts dissolve in shit.
I was never young.
Now I'm old, alone.
In dreams
I hack you.

(*Eunice De Souza*)

A woman's frame, a long life, and the changing times have ensured that Kamala Das has had to bear witness to and put up with the abominable treatment meted out to the *ageing* and the *aged* by a *productivity*-driven and *youth*-oriented society. Sociologists have used the term 'ageism' to define this 'discrimination against people on grounds of age' (Giddens: 2001, 683). Society, today, is perceived to operate on the basis of 'age-sets' or 'age-grades'. According to John Scott and Gordon Marshall, these 'broad age-bands' indicate the 'social status', 'assigned and permitted roles', and 'activities' of individuals or groups belonging to them (Scott and Marshall: 1994, 8). Transitions from one of such grades into the next are always marked by rites of passage, changes in societal expectations and perceptions, and changes in both physical and mental abilities.

These changes associated with the phenomenon of ageing lead to 'age-stratification', a term defined as a 'system of inequalities' linked to 'age-sets', whereby both the young and the old are treated as 'relatively incompetent' and 'excluded' from 'much social life' (Scott and Marshall: 1994, 8). In fact, the physiological process of ageing has important socio-cultural ramifications. Since 'age' is not only a 'biological inevitability' but also a 'cultural category', its meaning, significance, and traits are seen to vary with time and across cultures (Scott and Marshall: 1994, 9). In our industrialized and capitalist system, the retirement from external production at a certain age means that the aged are viewed as unproductive and a burden. The concept of the nuclear family entails a perceived 'uselessness' and 'undesirability' of the elderly. In the case of women, the fact of ageing with its attendant certainty of the menopause, leads to a further physical impairment. Besides, in most cases, older women's financial dependence on their children makes them vulnerable to neglect and abandonment.

Ethel Shanas et al. have criticized the acquiescent functionalism under whose influence society is often seen to legitimate ageism by excluding the elderly from the labour market and other significant social roles (Shanas et al.: 1968, 26). In such a society, therefore, the advancing years entail a consequent loss of 'productivity', both financial and reproductive. In this context, Julie McMullin has suggested, "The productive and reproductive lives of the younger people are the ideal against which older people are judged" (McMullin in Arber and Ginn: 1995, 32). As a result, the aged are often found wanting on these scores.

In many of her poems and prose articles, Kamala Das has tackled the issue of ageing and its consequent degradation as well as discrimination that lead the aged to the accursed fate of 'structured dependency'. I.G. Ahmed, in this connection, observes, "As a Third World Feminist Das exposes the agony of alienation of the aged [...]" (Ahmed: 2005, 143). It is quite revealing that poems written mainly in and after her mid-forties (the average age of the menopause) reflect this concern of the poet. In poems such as the "Anamalai Poems", "A Short Trip", "At Chiangi Airport", "Stock Taking", "A Widow's Lament", "Middle Age", "Home is a Concept", "My Sons", "Effusions" etc. the poet presents a rather bleak picture of individuals who find themselves progressively marginalized by their dear ones because of their age. In the present paper, therefore, efforts will be made to re-read many such poems with a view to showing how the poet deals with the trauma and turbulence associated with this inevitable physical process, and the attitude of this productivity-driven and money-minded society towards 'ageing' and the 'aged'.

In fact, alienation, ill-health, nostalgia, and a love-hate relationship with death constitute their thematic range. These poems can be seen as truly 'autobiographical' as the 'mask' is finally abandoned, merging the man who suffers with the mind which creates. The subdued melancholy, characteristic of them, results from the ingratitude of children and youngsters who ruthlessly abandon their parents and the elderly, since the aged can no longer be of any use to them.

If one of the factors responsible for this progressive marginalization happens to be the failing strength and ability of the aged, then the other factor certainly turns out to be the increasing self-reliance and self dependence of the young ones. In the familial context, this fact is clearly brought out in a poem like "Middle Age". In fact, "Middle Age" gives us a poignant description of a mother who is too old to day-dream and too young perhaps to 'find / comfort of meaning' in old memories (Anamalai Poems XVI, *Literature and Criticism* 157). Her children who were once dependant on and attached to her now become self-dependant and assert their personal opinions with an utter unconcern for her feelings. I.N. Agrawal, in this context, has commented, "Middle Age is a poem of illusion and disenchantment. It is a poem about a middle-aged mother—all mothers in general—whose children have gown up and now they don't need her for the daily task of life or for her guidance" (Agrawal: 1984, 47).

In keeping with Agrawal's opinion mentioned above, the poem begins by showing a perceptible change in the attitude of the children towards the woman-speaker who happens to be a mother as well:

> Middle age is when your children are no longer
> Friends but critics, stern of face and severe with their tongue
> It's the time when like pupae they burst their cocoons and
> Emerge in harsh adult glory, and they no longer
> Need you expect for serving tea and for pressing
> Clothes, [...]
>
> (*Symphony*, 26)

The fact that the mother's entry into her middle age coincides with the children's entry into their youth means that the generation gap begins to widen. As a result, her children who were once 'friends' become 'critics' as revealed by their stern 'faces' and harsh words. The bursting of cocoons and the emergence of the children in harsh adult glory pushed the mother to the precincts of the family. Having grown out of needs and out of arms, the children make her almost redundant to their needs, asking of her only to serve them tea or press their clothes.

This sudden demotion of the mother and diminution of her usefulness are, however, very difficult to accept, since the mother's needs for her children rather then diminishing in fact increases with her greying hair:

> [....] but you need them all the same, and badly too, so
> That when left alone, you touch their books and things, and
> Weep a little secretly....
>
> (*Symphony,* 26)

The mother's marginal status is clearly revealed by her secret tears while touching the children's 'books and things' at their absence. Harish Raizada, in this context, calls attention to the mother's loss of her identity as a 'feeling woman' in the eyes of her children and their treatment of her as a mere commodity of their utility (Raizada in Prasad: 1983, 124).

As if to prove the ever-widening generation gap between the mother and her son, whereby the views of the older generation seem preposterous to the younger ones, we now get to hear a fierce rebuttal of the mother's life-philosophy by her son:

> Middle age is when your son to whom you sent,
> Once open a time, the squirrels' invitation to their
> Jungle-feast, writing in golden ink and posting
> It at night, turns round in disgust, crying, you have lived
> In a dream world all your life, it's time to wake up, Mother,
> You are no longer so young you know.
>
> (*Symphony*, 26)

The son's argument that the mother has lived all her life in a dream that she should wake up from those dreams now and that she is no longer so young as to day dream reinforce his undeniable ageism. He seems to forget the fact that his own youth and authority will not last forever either. Moreover, his rude reminder to his mother that she is not the young woman any more seems unduly harsh.

It seems that the poet's motive in writing this poem is to prepare ageing mothers like her to face the banalities of the inevitable 'middle age'. Thus, as K.V. Surendran points out, "'Middle Age' is a poem which surveys the little unnoticed pangs of mothers who are already on the 'wrong side of the forties'" (Surendran in Mittapalli and Piciucco: 2000, 133).

If "Middle Age" shows us the poet's concern with the fate of the ageing mothers, then "Home is a Concept" gives us Das's take on the condition of the aged fathers. That the fathers described in this poem are a little bit more advanced in years is shown by their desperate attempts to 'find / comfort of meaning' in old memories (Anamalai Poems XVI, *Literature and Criticism* 157).

Among all the poems of Kamala Das on the subject of old age, "Home is a Concept" has a special place, because in this poem the poet-speaker remains extra-digetic, sympathizing or rather empathizing with the aged male-figures described in the poem. The mental picture that the poet helps us conjure up is that of a busy airport with its luggage-toting air-travelers waiting for aeroplanes. For practical reasons, they are required to tote their 'luggage' even if it feels 'heavy'. Similarly, for emotional reasons, they are bound to bear the burden of their past (e.g. photographs of laughing children) even if the only reward they can expect is 'pain':

> The unwanted wait here and there for aeroplanes
> clutching at heavy briefcases that hold
> the papers to be read at seminars,
> passports, visas and photographs of laughing
> children. The unwanted carry heavy bags
> and overcoats but the heaviest luggage
> they tote is pain. [...]
>
> (*BKD* 117)

Evidently, the poet is writing about ageing persons whom she has termed 'the unwanted'. They have to bear this pain because they want to cling to 'photographs of their laughing children'. But, their children no longer want them; for children grow into adults and 'grow out of needs' ("Composition").

In the next section of the poem, the poet presents 'home' not as a physical entity but as a concept (love) or in terms of its inmates or family members (a group prepared to love). In fact, the aged are seen to be craving only for love but to no avail:

> [...] If home is a concept
> they shall not know it, if home is a group
> prepared to love, the traveller has not known that
> group and never shall. [...]
>
> (*BKD* 117)

It is the inability of the travellers to know the concepts of home and homey that has caused them the 'pain'. As a result, their worldly accomplishments like seminar papers, passports, and visas all seem utterly meaningless to them.

In order to hide this pain and their feeling of nullity, these aged persons try in vain to engage in loud talk and excessive work:

> [...] The unwanted speak in
> strident voices. Silence holds terrors for them.
> When they speak of the need for a Centre
> to promote Commonwealth Literature or of
> the Nuclear Holocaust they are merely
> crying out to you, love me, I am not so
> different from the ones seem to love.
>
> (*BKD* 117)

The strident voice adopted by these men is only a means of self-deception, because their loud talks on divergent subjects like Commonwealth Literature and the Nuclear Holocaust are mere empty words, concealing their only-too-human need to be loved. Just like "An Introduction", this poem too ends with the speaker's tentative attempt at pointing up human similarity and human solidarity, because just like the fact 'I too call myself I' ("An Introduction", (*SC* 60), here too the speaker suggests, 'they are merely / crying out to you, love me, I am not so / different from the ones you seem to love'. The marginalization of the aged with an utter disregard for their previous centrality within the family betrays the ingratitude of 'children' whose laughing photographs still accompany and haunt them. That the laughing children are captured in photographs, and then therefore, taken out of the stream of time can justify their durability as a sentient image of the past whose real-life growth in and with time these aged persons have failed to come to terms with.

Retaining the setting of the airport and yet returning to her characteristic singular narrative ('I'/'Me'), "At Chiangi Airport" acts as a companion piece of the pervious poem. The poem begins and ends with the desire as well as the desirability of 'forgetting', and yet the middle part of the poem betrays the speaker's inability to do the same. The alternative title of this poem, "In Transit at Chiangi", highlights the temporary story that the speaker must have had at the airport (Das in Paniker: 2004, 51-52). Moreover, it includes the suggestions of 'in transit' and 'transit', indicating thereby the act of being transported from one place to another and the transition or passage from a 'fifty and two' year old life to 'death's lustrous chambers'.

The poem begins at Singapore with the speaker's auto-suggestions of 'travelling light' and of 'forgetting' (presumably her past). But, the fact that she is unable to do so having been burdened by memory is made clear just a few lines later in the poem:

> [...] Each evening I had
> asked the reception-desk, any message for me,
> any mail? I had watched the younger ones pick up
> their mail, had heard them swagger up the stairs
> humming
> pop tunes. The old have no mail. A displaced generation
> must find its comfort in tea; fifty and two is
> not a nice age to be. [...]
>
> (*BKD* 114)

In this excerpt, the aged speaker gives vent to her feelings of loneliness and abandonment. It is obvious that the speaker belongs to this 'displaced generation', which is why 'each evening' 'she has to ask for 'any message' or 'any mail'. She is left only to watch the younger ones pick up their mail. Hence the rueful realization, 'fifty and two is / not a nice age to be'.

A few things should be clarified in this context if we are to fathom out the speaker's mental state. Reviewed from her ultimate realization about the seamy side of being old, her decision/desire to 'travel light' seems to have been determined by her unwanted status. The absence of 'any mail' or 'any message' for her proves this contention beyond any reasonable doubt. However, her act of asking the reception desk for the non-existent mail or message, and that too 'each evening', points up her own 'urge for communion and reintrigration' that I.G. Ahmed has alluded to (Ahmed: 2005, 143). Her lack of the coveted mails and the young ones' stack of them not only place them (the speaker and the young ones) at the two extremes of alienation and acceptance, it also alerts the sensitive poet to the same fate that awaits those 'young ones' in future. Thus, her agony is not only self-centred but also tinged with her sympathies for the young ones. In fact, she cannot forget that the 'displaced generation' of which she is a present member and to which by implication the young ones will have to enter 'must find its comfort in tea'. Das here seems to second Osip Mandelstamm in looking back on days gone by:

> The buds will swell again,
> And the sprouts will burst.
> But your spine has been shattered,
> My beautiful, pitiful age.
> And you look back, cruel and weak,
> With a senseless smile,
> like a beast that was once supple,
> at the tracks of your own paws.
> ("My Age". *Mandelstamm in Bold,* 1970, 146)

Just like "Middle Age", "My Sons" is another of Kamala Das's poems that describes the peripheral existence of the aged in general and the aged mother in particular. Needless to say, the aged mother described here belongs to the 'displaced generation' ("At Chiangi Airport"), and has tried unsuccessfully to 'find' and 'know' home as 'a group prepared to love' ("Home is a Concept"). Though the title of the poem suggests a possible description of her sons, it is chiefly about the mother-figure with occasional and topical allusions to her children.

The poem begins with a rueful statement from the poet-speaker about the non-existence or at any rate the non-availability of love as an ennobling emotion even in spite of her sincere attempts at finding and praising the same:

> No, there is nothing like love. I used up
> My blood as ink to praise its worth, [...]
> (*OSKHS* 47)

By mentioning her 'use' of 'blood' as 'ink' to praise the 'worth of love' the speaker subtly hints at the act of poetic creation. This literary act is later on used to implicate the act of procreation or writing the 'unborn generation' on the book of life. The hurry of that unborn generation to see the light of the day resulted in anger at the mother's delay. But, since procreation is a joint responsibility, the would-be father too was hauled up for that delay:

> [...] it was
> The unborn generation rattling in
> My pen, angry at my delay, and his.
> (*OSKHS* 47)

The mention of the husband-figure rather the father-figure in this context reminds the mother of him. The fact that he is no more and no more is the smell of his skin and his words deeply sadden the speaker.

From the remembrance of things past, she is brought back to the world of the present by the perceived transformation of the once-unborn generation into her own adult sons:

> [...] My sons are old enough to take
> Their own women, old enough to forget
> The lullabies I sang and the prayers
> Recited near their beds when they were ill.
> (*OSKHS* 47)

Since her sons have now grown out of needs and out of arms to have taken their own women, they have managed to forget the love and anxiety with which their mother had reared them up. This fact, along with the earlier exclamation that no body remembers him (her husband) or the father of these sons, highlights the marginalization of the aged in and by a youth-oriented society. In fact, the same idea is expressed by Das (Suraiya) in one of her columns "Geriatrics, Geriatrics", "The Old are losers all the time" (*PC* 39). The speaker goes on to describe her sons in ironic and insinuative terms as 'users of vulgar words and of jeans' and as creatures impotent to enjoy the pleasures of the flesh with the women of their tribe. But, life has tutored the mother sufficiently enough to make her realize the inevitable transience of their enjoyment. So, she remembers to caution her sons of the imminent arrival of another generation that may similarly marginalize them in the future:

> Users of vulgar words and of jeans that
> Chafe desire to a hot flame, they swing
> Round and round with the females of their tribe.

> Yet another generation awaits
> At the closed doors behind their faded jeans...
> (*OSKHS* 47)

While in "Middle Age" the emphasis was on preparing the ageing mothers to face their inevitable fate of neglect and mockery, in "My Sons" the poet-speaker focuses on cautioning the younger generation about the inevitability of their own ageing . In this respect, it can be read as a virtual extension of "At Chiangi Airport" where 'fifty and two' is considered 'not a nice age to be', as much for the aged speaker as for the 'swagger'-ing 'young ones' who can very easily be likened to her sons.

The "Anamalai Poems" also tell us the sad story of a 'not-so-nice age' of 'fifty and two' from the perspective of lived experience. In fact, along with the gender question the Anamalai Poems also deal with the issue of 'ageing' as well as the resultant marginalization. Since these poems have a woman-persona, the issues of gender and ageing are seen to overlap in them. As discussed earlier in the present study, this is especially true for women whose advancing years entail a loss of productivity and value, at once financial and reproductive.

Even though throughout the "Anamalai Poems" we bear witness to the woman-speaker's increasing disillusionment with family and domesticity, it is in the latter group of the "Anamalai Poems" (nos. XII to XVII) that we get to see Das's sustained treatment of the question of age.

In the thirteenth poem of the series, the woman-persona lays bare her marginal status as an aged mother at the hands of her unfeeling grown up children. Feeling the chill of neglect and desirous of getting the warmth of human love, the woman-speaker enters the room where her grown up children are seated. The use of the word 'sidle' to describe the woman-speaker's entry into the room betrays her feelings of uncertainty and apprehension. Assailed by the same doubt, she does 'unobtrusively' 'settle' herself 'a distance away'. That she has rightly taken such precautions becomes clear, since her children take no notice of her:

The talk goes on
The banter and the laugh
But the language seems to me so alien so strange
(*Literature and Criticism* 156)

The fact that the 'talk', the 'banter' and the 'laugh' are continued without a pause greatly alienates the mother whose feeling of 'strange'-ness makes her uncertain about her biological connections (as a mother) with her impudent children:

Did my womb really spawn these raucous crows
I ask myself amazed
Did I grant them this strident voice
The indignity of their stare
The cunning jest?
(*Literature and Criticism* 156)

In fact, their 'strident voice', the 'indignity of their stare' and the 'cunning jest' dehumanize them in her eyes, making them mere 'raucous crows'.

The mother's realization that her only gifts to the world have been 'these raucous crows', when she has received much joy and happiness from it, makes her ashamed of herself. But, beneath this surface feeling of shame, runs a strong undercurrent of sorrow, because the aged mother cannot totally suppress her own need for 'the warmth of human love' that these children could easily have given her.

The fourteenth poem of the "Anamalai Poems" clearly shows up what may befall an aged mother in the eventuality of her being neglected by her children:

Yes, this humble me without a doubt
The empty mailbag, the silent phone
And my lying around for the past
Several days like a parcel left unclaimed.
(*Literature and Criticism* 157)

What humbles the speaker is the lack of concern shown to her by her children. Evidently, she too is a representative of the 'displaced generation' who in an ageist society is fated to lie around for 'several days' like a 'parcel left unclaimed'. The 'empty mailbag' and the 'silent phone' clearly reveal to the speaker 'What love was worth / In the end' ("A Request", *D* 5).

The experience of 'lying around' like 'a parcel left unclaimed' teaches the aged speaker the necessity as well as the desirability of vacating 'the earthly seat' and leaving in her own good time. It is this realization that finds poetic expression in the fifteenth poem of the series:

> For after all I am a mere guest although
> The decanters are still half full and the long
> Candles still burn on, not for a moment must
> I overstay; other guests are expected
> Yes, I must vacate my earthly seat and leave.
> (*Literature and Criticism* 157)

This realization of the speaker is accentuated by the perception that the decanters are already half empty and the candles 'burn on' only because they are 'long'. She, being a mere guest, naturally remembers the possibility of other guests' arriving. The fact that both she, as a guest, and the other would-be guests are under the obligation to leave sooner or later makes her self-conscious and sad about the fateful hour.

The sixteenth poem of the sequence shuns the philosophical aspects of ageing and death to dwell upon the practical problems of the ageing woman-speaker:

> The insects have a better time than I do now
> They exult so in the winter sun. I sit behind
> The window pane, the black shawl hiding my greying hair
> Too old to daydream and too young perhaps to find
> Comfort of meaning in old memories.
> (*Literature and Criticism* 157)

Her inability to 'exalt' in 'the winter sun' and the compulsion to 'sit behind' the 'window panes', covering her 'grey hair' (and perhaps warding off the chill) in the 'black shawl', betray her advancing years. But, her 'middle age' poses the intractable problem of being 'Too old to daydream' and 'too young perhaps to find / Comfort or meaning in old memories'.

The last poem of the group presents the speaker's loneliness which becomes so acute as to warrant the donning of 'fear' as her nightgown (companion at night):

> And if fear is my nightgown tonight
> What of it? I still welcome the change.
> It is not as cold to my skin as
> What I wore on countless nights the blue
> Wrap of loneliness. Yes if fear is
> My nightgown tonight I shall welcome the change.
> (*Literature and Criticism* 157)

Bereft of both the warmth of the 'winter sun' and the warmth of 'human love', her 'skin' has become so 'cold' that even being frightened seems a welcome change to her than being lonely.

The Anamalai poems record the depressed feelings of a disturbed psyche with the characteristic candour and the minimum amount of literary frills. Das's perception of her ageing self, the lukewarm response of her grown up children, and the sensitive awareness of her impending death to their ageing mother make the "Anamalai Poems" a true document of her marginality due to age.

What was an awareness of her impending death in the Anamalai Poems, gave way to a grim experience of her husband's death in "Stock Taking". In fact, it is her husband's death coupled with the onset of her own old age and ill health that gives her an added incentive to take the 'stock' of her own life this far.

What was implied in "My Sons" in the exclamation about the fates of oblivion suffered by 'him' (the speaker's husband), is made explicit in the poem "Stock Taking". As the title suggests, it is the time when the speaker needs and wants to 'take stock of all' and this need has been accentuated by her inability to get over her bereavement. In fact, one factor usually associated with the experience of *ageing* is the awareness of mortality. This awareness acts in two ways to dampen the spirit of the aged (here the woman-speaker)—by snatching away a loved one as also by making her/him aware of the approaching end. The resultant senses of loss and loneliness cause a depression which, for want of a better term, may be called 'natural marginalization'.

The poet-speaker begins with a vivid account of her husband's death that has resulted in her utter unconcern with any 'promise of immortal love':

> Do not beguile me with a promise
> of immortal love
> for, I have seen the glaze in a dying
> husband's eye and have lost faith in all
> Do not promise great moments
> of self-realization
> or serener incarnations
> I have seen terror twist
> my husband's face and have heard
> the awesome rattle of his final breath
> Do not talk to me of beauties
> still to be envisaged, for I have
> seen the waxy pallor of a dead man's
> skin and I do not care now
> to see more.
>
> (*OSKHS* 120)

The memory of 'the glaze in a dying / husband's eye', his 'terror'-twisted face, 'the awesome rattle of his final breath', and 'the waxy pallor of a dead man's skin' have turned her cynical about any 'serener incarnations' of love and beauty. In fact, the death of her husband has opened her eyes to the inevitability of physical decay, whereby 'beauties / still to be envisaged' are also destined to end in the 'awesome rattle' of the 'last breath'.

The above realization forces the speaker to lose any interest in the wisdom of the scriptures or in the peace of the philosophers. Both the enjoyment of the pleasures of sex and the sense of fulfilment inherent in child-care have proved inadequate in neutralizing her thanatonic consciousness:

> Do not thrust upon me
> the scriptures compiled by sages
> wise and celibate
> or pacifying philosophies.
> I have held a man

between my legs and have
brought forth goodnatured sons
If there is a God somewhere
despite the distance he kept
between himself and me
please heed my request today
I need a lull in this living
a pause to take stock of all.
(*OSKHS* 120)

The speaker's sense and sensibility ultimately induce a prayer to the God if any. That she is sceptical about His existence is proved by the decapitalizing of the letter 'h' in 'he' and 'himself'. In spite of the providential indifference she has previously experienced, she begs of 'God' to grant her 'a lull in this living', 'a pause to take stock of all'. The implication may be a death wish as a possible escape from the tyrannies of the flesh.

The death of Das's husband revealed to her the 'tyrannies of the flesh' and the overswaying power of 'sad mortality'. Divested of the care and protection (even if overbearing) of her husband and fed up with the 'cold-platters of faces / heaped with mushy sympathy', the widow is left only to lament her fate. "A Widow's Lament" records an old woman's rough passage from a life of domestic centrality to that of senile superfluity. In fact, it is a dossier that outlines women's marginal status in the patriarchal set-up. The poem begins with an extended question of the now-widowed speaker, regarding her present status and future prospects:

Is the soul too,
now autumned,
rusted in the awful recollection
of spilt blood,
readying itself for the fall?
(*OSKHS* 125)

Her doubts regarding the soul seem strikingly original, going as it does, against the Hindu concept of the eternal soul:

na jâyate mriyate vâ kadâcin
nâ 'yam bhûtvâ bhavitâ vâ na bhûyahò

ajo nityahò siâsivato 'yam purânòo
na hanyate hanyamâne siarire

> (He is never born, nor does he die at any time, nor having [once] come to be will he again cease to be. He is unborn, eternal, permanent and primeval. He is not slain when the body is slain.)
>
> (*The Bhagavad Gita,* ch. II. sloka. 20 1993, 107)

The word 'rusted' with its undeniably physical association brings in the added import of decay. The awful recollection of spilt blood with its elemental association with rust and iron may hint at a post-menopausal existence of the speaker who has no other preoccupation than 'readying' herself for the 'fall' (death). The lamenting widow who can gain her identity only in relation to a now-dead male (her husband) has so long led a subservient and dependent life as a wife. As a natural corollary to wifehood, she had also been made a mother. In her dual roles as wife and mother she was at least granted a useful existence even though she had to pay the heavy price of tearing to shreds the tarot cards of her fate to attain this 'bliss'. In fact, the woman-speaker had to subordinate herself to the needs and moods of her husband and sons. After the death of her husband and the growth into adulthood of her sons, she loses even the prop of domestic importance; for she finds herself in the doubly-precarious positions of both a widow and an abandoned mother. Her realization of this loss snatches away from her even the purpose of existence in 'this' 'someone else's world'. Mushy sympathy and cold platters of faces that remain her only provisions can cause fear and trembling; for there is sadly no prospect of any God's putting forth 'a wrinkled hand to wipe my brow'. The wolves of worry and loneliness are not going to spare her, since with the death or departure of her male relatives the old woman has to walk the 'high way' 'alone' and 'naked' (unprotected and hapless) as a 'babe'.

The old woman's rough passage from the life of domestic centrality to that of senile superfluity is neatly encapsulated in her act of walking 'the high way alone'. This journey motif is deftly continued in the poem "A Short Trip". The nuclear family, an invention of an ungrateful age, and the old-age home, the socio-economically imposed substitute for home—these factors not only aggravate the marginalization of the aged but cause in them a deep sense of dejection. Kamala Das's poem "A Short Trip" encapsulates the psycho-spatial polarity between the centrality of youth and home, and the marginality of 'age' and the old age home. It is indeed a 'short trip' from youth to age and from home to old-age home. But, the psychological 'trip' that one has to take in a bid to arrive at the latter from the former is certainly quite long and arduous; for it is the trip of experience and realization.

At the beginning of the poem, the woman-speaker who in the ninth line of the poem expresses her gendered identity by using the feminine pronoun 'her' equates a 'short trip' from 'home' presumably to an old-age home with 'a kind of death'. The recent reality of domestic importance and love and the present realization of brutal displacement at the hands of her ungrateful offsprings seem to the woman-speaker infinitely dissimilar:

> Even a short trip from home is
> a kind of death for one who till recent
> times believed that one reaped only what one
> had sown, and the discovery that one
> might reap what another had sown was sad,
> and jolting, as though while plucking flowers
> one gathered with them a squirming snake. [...]
> (*OSKHS* 105)

In fact, the poet-speaker's earlier belief that one 'reaped only what one / had sown' had given her hope of receiving a humane treatment from her offsprings, because she had showed only love and affection on them. But, her unpleasant discovery that one 'might reap what another had sown' ensures an eventual othering of the aged even though it is based upon an 'illogical hatred'. The expectation of flowers and the reality of the squirming snake adequately encapsulate what the aged expect out of life and what they get.

If the displacement of the aged mother-figure from the centre of domesticity is tantamount to 'some kind of death' for her, it also connotes a kind of change and severance of ties with the past. Though the young offsprings in their foolish conceit dish out hatred to the aged, this hatred is grounded in illogicality and, therefore, destined to be self-defeating:

> [...] Yes
> even a trip is a kind of death and
> the traveller by her brief absence lifts
> from others left behind the domestic
> inhibitions that plague human beings
> who have learnt to hate illogically
> although both the hated and the hater
> cannot ever hope to explain why.
> (*OSKHS* 105)

The reality of a home where the offsprings have become impatient with or indifferent to the aged mother ("Middle Age"), as contrasted with the reality of an old age home to which the aged mother is shifted against her will ("A Short Trip"), presents the confused and aggrieved poet-speaker with the dilemma of choice. The only possible resolution of this 'dilemma', therefore, is to seek a 'lull in this living' ("Stock Taking") or vacation of her 'earthly seat' ("Anamalai Poem XV").

Arthur Rimbaud had held poets responsible not only for humanity but also for animals (Rimbaud in Ellmann and Feidleson: 1965, 204). Following in full Rimbaud's advice Kamala Das too shows her artistic concerns for both human beings and animals. Poems like "The Cart Horse" and "Old Cattle" point up the similarities that mark and mar the aged as much in the human world as among the animals.

As suggested by the title, "The Cart Horse" is a poem about animals domesticated and overworked to do others' bidding. The 'arduous' roads and the 'too heavy' burden of the old cart horse make its gallop 'jagged'. But, this mention of the cart horse's plight is made by the poet-speaker to implicate her own condition in old age:

> Of late my words have worn
> Thin, my speech resembles
> The jagged gallop of

A cart horse that needs to
Be reshod and perhaps
Given rest, for, poor thing
Its roads were arduous
And its burden always
Too heavy. [...]
(*CP* 62)

The fact that 'Of late' her 'words' have worn 'Thin' and her 'speech' resembles an old cart horse's 'jagged gallop' glance backwards at a purple patch gone by during which the speaker had been in total control of her writing and speech. P.P. Raveendran in this connection has observed, "In [...] "The Cart Horse" the image of a tired horse is used to suggest both physical weakness and poetic failure" (P.P. Raveendran in Das: 1991, XV). To recall Shelley in this context, the 'heavy weight of hours' seems to have 'chained and bowed' the once-free poet-speaker and brought on the loathsome old age the consequent dissipation of the persona's poetic powers ("Ode to the West Wind". P.B. Shelley: 1994, 362).

At this juncture of the poem, the vehicle of the comparison, namely, the old cart horse is brought to the foreground to point out the sad plight awaiting the aged in the animal world. Since the unlucky old cart horses are 'taken out' and 'shot' dead in an utter disregard of past services faithfully rendered, to the poet those horses that die in harness seem 'lucky':

[...] An old horse,
If lucky, dies on road,
Flopping on its side with
Pink foam spurting from its
Twisted jaw and four of
Yellow front teeth showing
The not so lucky are
Taken out and shot, [...]
(*CP* 62)

This foregrounding of the cart horse by showing the marginal status of the aged animal also reveals the poet-speaker's subaltern voice. As a result, even physical annihilation seems preferable to creative impotence.

The old horses being starved or under-fed become 'decrepit' and sometimes wake up from their senile stupor to 'neigh, / loud in hunger'. The strategic use of three separate lexical items (i.e. 'old', 'decrepit', and 'senile') from the same semantic field serves to play up the wretched condition of the age-worn cart horses whose hunger may at once reflect a lack of and then therefore a craving for food; for the 'parents of the rich' who are relegated to a life of retirement and destined to remain without their children and with paid keepers, this 'hunger' may be for the non-existence of filial affections:

> [...] for,
> The old and decrepit
> Waking at times from their
> Senile slumber, neigh, loud
> In hunger, and parents
> Of the rich who sit with
> Their keepers on benches
> Beside the sea wall, with
> Cataract on their minds
> Tremble at this sound, for
> No reason the old ones
> Purse their mouths and tremble.
> (*CP* 62)

These old men can, therefore, empathize with the old cart horses whose loud 'neigh'-s make them 'purse their mouths' (in disapproval) and 'tremble' (for fear of being similarly abandoned in future). In the final analysis, the fact that the aged ones (i.e. the poet-speaker, the old cart horses, and the parents of the rich) had once wielded authority or been useful and potent, aggravates their marginal status. As P.P. Raveendran has opined, "In old age there is no poetry; there is no communication; there is no present. Only the past seems to have any meaning for the old" (P.P. Raveendran in Das: 1991, XVI).

As in "The Cart Horse", the ruthless societal attitude towards the domesticated animals is revealed in "Old Cattle" as well. How perception of similarity may lead to empathy is shown afresh in this poem. The "Old Cattle" of the title have grown old in human service and yet at old age receive no sympathy and compassion from their owners. On the contrary, they are taken to the slaughter house to continue their service to and feeding off human beings through and after their death.

In fact, the beginning of the poem reveals how the poet-speaker saw aged cattle being taken to the slaughter house when she was being taken home after a heart-attack. K. Radha has pointed out that this incident took place when she was being taken home from a hospital near Calicut, after receiving treatment for her heart trouble (Radha: 1986, 54). The vermillion brand on their shoulders as well as their thin haunches greatly upset the sensitive poet who is further disturbed by seeing their innocent reaction of chewing at the 'shrubs' or gazing around:

> When I was being taken home from the city's nursing home three weeks
> after a heart attack I saw near the mountain passes the aged cattle
> being driven to the slaughter-house. I saw their thin haunches and
> the vermilion brand on their shoulders. Some of them paused to chew
> at the shrubs and to gaze around. [...]
>
> (*CP* 66)

Having suffered a heart attack that had taken her to the verge of death, the aged poet can easily empathize with these hapless creatures. This feeling of sadness instigates her to think of getting down from the car and join these poor and death-bound animals. Ultimately, however, she realizes the basic similarity between the old cattle and herself (an aged woman), since as the old cattle are being taken to the slaughter house she too is being taken home where the children's indifference and irritation will ensure a veritable slaughter of the sensitive poet:

> [...] I wanted to, for one short moment,
> get down from the car and join them.
> Human beings are never branded with a hot iron. They are merely sent
> home with their electrocardiographs and sedatives.
>
> (*CP* 66)

If their 'thin haunches' stood for the decrepitude of the old cattle, then, in case of the aged poet, her electrocardiograph and prescribed sedatives are seen to perform the same function. Like the 'vermillion brand' on the shoulders of the old cattle, these marks of disease and infirmity ('electrocardiograph' and 'sedatives') have signalled her impending death also.

A witness as well as a victim to the process of ageing in her dual specificity as both 'human' and 'woman', Kamala Das reveals the physical, the psychological and the social aspects associated with this virtual 'tragedy of life'. In "Lines Addressed to a Husband", she discovers the reality of her 'ageing flesh'. In "Middle Age", she is reminded by her sons of 'a new found ugliness'. In "Home is a Concept", by observing the pitiable condition of the aged 'traveller', she realizes the futility of seeking love as and for the aged. The Chiangi airport makes her aware of her generational 'displacement' that leads to the agony of alienation. Looking at her aged mother she shudders at the real possibility that her 'childhood fear' of losing her mother to death will come true sooner rather than later ("My Mother at Sixty Six", *BKD* 148). The death of her husband and the departure of her sons fcr 'other homes' and 'other loves' leave her alone and under compulsion to fend for herself ("A Widow's Lament"). Thus, she reaches the seventh age of woman, aware of the loss of her past importance, remembering youth as a photograph ("Youth is a Photograph"), and readying herself like the autumn leaves for the 'fall' ("Autumn Leaves" *BKD*, 75).

Works Cited

Agrawal, I.N. "The Language and the Limits of the Self in the Poetry of Kamala Das." *A Literary Spectrum*. Bareilly: Prakash Book Depot, 1984. 41-48.

Ahmed, I.G. *Kamala Das: The Poetic Pilgrimage*. New Delhi: Creative Books, 2005.

Mandelstamm, Osip. 'My Age'. In *The Penguin Book of Socialist Verse*. Selected by Bold, Alan. Harmondsworth: Penguin, 1970. 146.

Das, Kamala. 'Anamalai Poems' (XII-XVII). *Literature and Criticism*. Vol. 2, no. 1 April, 2002. 156-157.

___ *The Best of Kamala Das*. (abbr. to *BKD*) Kozhikode: Bodhi Publishing House, 1991.

___ *Collected Poems*. Vol.1. (abbr. to *CP*) Trivandrum. Navakerela Printers, 1984.

___ *The Descendants*. (abbr. to *D*) Calcutta: Writer's Workshop, 1967.

___ 'In Transit at Chiangi'. In *Modern Indian Poetry in English*. (Ed.) Paniker, K. Ayyappa. New Delhi: Sahitya Akademi, 2004. 51-52.

___ 'Middle Age'. *Symphony*. Calicut: University of Calicut, 1995. 26.

___ *Only The Soul Knows How To Sing: A Selection From Kamala Das*. (abbr. to *OSKHS*) Kottayam: DC Books, 1996.

___ *Summer in Calcutta*. (abbr. to *SC*). New Delhi: Everest Press, 1965.

Suraiya, Dr. Kamala (formerly Das, Kamala.) *The Path of the Columnist*. (abbr. to *PC*) Calicut: Olive Publications, 2000. Giddens, Anthony. *Sociology*. Oxford: Blackwell, 2001.

McMullin, Julie. "Theorizing Age and Gender Relations". In *Connecting Gender and Ageing: A Sociological Approach*. (Eds.) Arbar, Sara and Ginn, Jay. Buckingham: Open University Press, 1995. 30-41.

The Bhagavatgita. Radhakrishnan, S. (*trans*.) New Delhi: HarperCollins, 1993.

Raizada, Harish. "The Confessional Note in the Poetry of Kamala Das." In *Indian Poetry in English*. (Ed.) Prasad, Hari Mohan. Aurangabad: Parimal Prakashan, 1983. 113-135.

Raveendran, P.P. "The Ideology of Intimacy." In Das, Kamala. *The Best of Kamala Das*. (abbr. to *BKD*) Kozhikode: Bodhi Publishing House, 1991. ix-xvii.

Rimbaud, Arthur. Letter to Georges Izambard and Paul Demeny [1871]. In *The Modern Tradition: Backgrounds of Modern Literature*. (Eds.) Ellmann, Richard, and Feidleson, (Jr) Charles. New York: Oxford University Press, 1965. 202-205.

Scott, John and Marshall, Gordon. (eds.) *Oxford Dictionary of* Sociology. Oxford and New York: Oxford University Press, 1994.

Shanas, Ethel. Townsend, Teter. Wedderburn, Dorothy. Friis, Henning. Milhoz, Poul. And Stehouwer, Jan. *Old People in Three Industrial Societies*. New York: Atherton Press, 1968.

Shelly, P.B. 'Ode to the West Wind'. In *The Works of P.B. Shelley*. Hertfordshire (U.K): Wordsworth Poetry Library, 1994.

Surendran, K.V. "Suffering and Humiliation in Kamala Das's Poetry". In *Kamala Das: A Critical Spectrum*. (Eds.) Mittapalli, Rajeswar and Piciucco, Pier Paol. New Delhi: Atlantic Publishers, 2000. 130-139.

10

A General Review of Prevalent Themes of Kamala Das's Poetry and Her Poetic Stance

—Chavan Sandip

Kamala Das, recognized as one of India's foremost poets, has to her credit prose and poetical writings in which she highlights the plight of Indian women caught in the morass of effete conventions—social and familial. But at the first instance they portray her own joys and sorrows, happiness and agony that she herself experienced in different situations of her life. She is a sensitive soul recording in her poetry and novels all the intimations of wrong and turbulence that she feels she underwent through her life. What distinguishes her writings is her ability to transform her personal experiences into something general, to give a universal colouring to her personal sufferings. Through the presentation of her own experiences in her famous autobiography, *My Story,* in most of her poems and even essays and through the various situations depicted in her short stories,

> she has highlighted the various images and roles of an Indian woman, as a wife, a mother, a daughter, a mistress and even as a prostitute. She has focused her attention on the problems faced by a woman in a male-governed social set-up, the categorized roles assigned to her, the prejudiced attitude of man towards woman, the status and identity of a female child, the treatment of woman mainly as a sexual object, and the new concepts and problems arising for her in the wake of changing socio-cultural and economic scenario.[1]

As a matter of fact she empathizes with the numerous Indian women who daily suffer unspeakable tribulations, who are the victims of the same socio-familial set-up against which she herself takes the cudgel. She identifies herself with 'every woman who seeks love,' finds oneness with every woman who spends life in misery and bondage, sexual, familial and social, and participates in all the experiences of the woman in her life of sufferings.

In a brilliantly evocative poem—"An Introduction"—she maps out the effete social mores which seek to keep the woman in a perpetual bondage of conventions. The woman is asked to place herself in the stereotyped gender roles of mother, wife and daughter and forget her identity outside the known parameters of existence:

> Dress in sarees, be girl,
> Be wife, they said. Be embroiderer, be cook,
> Be a quarreller with servants. Fit in, Oh,
> Belong, cried the categorizers.

The point is that she wants to rebel against this injunction for docility and hence she even puts on an androgynic appearance:

> I wore a shirt and my
> Brother's trousers, cut my hair short and ignored
> My womanliness.

Some of Kamala Das's poems will no doubt find a natural and honourable place in any future international anthology of contemporary women poets. And though she deals with the 'conflict between passivity and rebellion against the male-oriented universe,' her poetry is in the final analysis an acknowledgement and a celebration of the beauty and courage of being a woman.

Kamala Das is essentially a poet of the modern Indian woman's ambivalence, giving expression to it more nakedly than any other Indian woman poet with the possible exception of Amrita Pritam in Panjabi. The reason for this is that Das seems to have a good deal of the conventional woman in her make-up, so that not only can she speak of the common woman and her basic need for love and security with inside knowledge, but cannot help, in addition, expressing an ambivalence proceeding from her own duality, proceeding from, that is, the combination in herself of a need for domestic security and the desire for an independence, an independence consistent with a non-domestic mode of living. Married at the age of fifteen, and finding herself tied, as she tells us time and time again, to a hollow relationship which she could not untie, Kamala Das' story, despite its sensationalism which is sometimes heightened by the directness of her manner, makes poignant reading and in essence strikes one as representative of a not so uncommon social phenomenon in India. When she celebrates love outside marriage, she is not really recommending permissiveness, but voicing her constant search for a relationship which gives both love and security and which should have been hers right at the start.

"The Old Playhouse" and "The Stone Age" deal with the reality of the situation in which love is offered by another man rather than the husband. In the latter, the husband is seen as an "old fat spider" that weaves "webs of bewilderment" around the woman-persona and builds the dead, stony, dull wall of domesticity, smugness, passivity, and turns her into "a bird of stone, a granite dove." He is the perpetual irritant, an unwelcome intruder into the privacy of her mind: "With loud talk you bruise my premorning sleep,/You stick a finger into my dreaming eye." Other men haunt her mind, and "sink/Like white suns in the swell of my Dravidian blood." When the husband leaves, she drives along the sea and climbs "the forty noisy steps to knock at another's door." At this point, the act of defiance having taken place, the deed done, freedom asserted, and the dull cocoon of domesticity assaulted, the lines suddenly become alive with the energy of questioning, and the theme of winning and losing, of reckoning, asserts itself:

> . . . Ask me, everybody, ask me
> What he sees in me, ask me why he is called a lion,
> A libertine, ask me the flavour of his
> Mouth, ask me why his hand sways like a hooded snake

Before it clasps my pubis. Ask me why like
A great tree, felled, he stumps against my breasts,
And sleeps. Ask me why life is short and love is
Shorter still, ask me what is bliss and what its price....

Concern with disease, illness, decay, and death is at the centre of "After the Illness," but what emerges from her reflections on the brevity of love is the mysterious force that keeps the lover filled with the thoughts of her survival. Apparently inspired by Kamala Das's recovery from a serious illness, the poem is concerned with the theme of survival: not merely of "the weary body settling into accustomed grooves", but of her lover's love in spite of the fact that in her:

. . . There was
Not much flesh left for the flesh to hunger, the
blood had
Weakened too much to lust, and the skin, without
health's
Anointments, was numb and unyearning.

Filled with the thought of what was perhaps a miraculous survival, she finds herself wondering as to what sustained his love for her: "What lusted then/For him, was it perhaps the deeply hidden soul?" It is characteristic of Kamala Das not to attempt to resolve the dilemma beyond the limits inherent in the very nature of the experience envisaged in the poem. To say this is not simply to point out the element of realism in her portrayal of her moods, but to underline her approach to experience which makes such realism, if that is the right word for the borderline between the beauty of sexual love and that of spiritual love, possible. She seems to suggest that perhaps the two are inseparable, but that she finds it difficult to experience this wholeness, this sense of completeness without a shadow of doubt and uncertainty.

In "The Suicide" published in *The Descendants* and reprinted in *The Old Playhouse and Other Poems,* Kamala Das narrates her childhood memory of swimming in "a pale-green pond" in her house in Malabar until she was reminded by her grandmother that she "was much too big to play/Naked in the pond." Since then, "... the only movement I really know/Is swimming," and the lover is like water or "a pale-green pond glimmering in the sun" in whom "I swim all broken with longing." The analogy between the lover and water is a vehicle of the poet's symbolic swimming in the forever changing and elusive realities of life. In its sexual connotations, the image can be compared to the nude swim in a poem of the same name by Anne Sexton:

> I lay on it as on a divan
> I lay on it just like
> Matisse's *Red Odalisque.*
> Water was my strange flower
> One must picture a woman
> without a toga or a scarf
> on a couch as deep as a tomb.

Indeed, one might link Kamala Das not only with Sylvia Plath, but with Anne Sexton who "is a truer example of the confessional mode." There is an appreciable commonalty of interests between the two poets as can be indicated here by referring to Anne Sexton's volume of poems *Love Poems,* and in particular to her poems such as "Little Girl, My String Bean, My Lovely Woman," "In Celebration of My Uterus," "For My Lover, Returning to His Wife". And if one is led to write about Kamala Das's poems in psychoanalytical terms, it is not only because, as she herself indicates, she "must let my mind striptease" and "must extrude autobiography," but also because her poems, like Anne Sexton's, seem to be precipitated by the need to solve her personal problems through a kind of self-imposed therapy, though the significance of both these poets extends beyond the mere psychological basis. Emphasising the validity of poet's preoccupation with her own self she opines that, "A poet's raw material is not stone or clay; it is her personality."[2] However, like American poet Sylvia Plath, the predicament of her inner self manifests itself in her poetry because she also believes: "One's real world is not what is outside him. It is the immeasurable world inside him that is real. Only the one who has decided to travel inwards, will realise that his route has no end." [3]

Kamala Das is a poet of aesthetic sense and her poems make us, through words which never seem to stop their coming as well as the theme of emotional inadequacy and ambivalence, breathless and disturbed rather than content. But within her limitations, she composes poetry which is brilliantly and lovingly true and spontaneous. By her confessional and personal feelings, she resembles more Nissim Ezekiel, Dom Moraes and other contemporary poets. Confessional poetry is basically the end product, and unconscious act of creation and one can feel upon our pulses, as personality and emotions, the two dragons of the classicists, constitute its essential core. However, one has reasons to believe that Kamala Das's suffering is not a poetic fallacy but a truth realised in its bare form, and the poetic process reveals the constant striving of artists to arrive at a harmony of the human particulars and widely acceptable symbols. Highly subjective experiences, if not properly assimilated, are liable to slip below the level of personal memoirs, but Kamala Das's mind goes one step further and forbears with hard achieved balance the pains of living and the suffering of creation. It is finally the feat of the artist that gives coherent poetic mould to the intensely personal experiences of the poet. But in the case of Kamala Das her concern for the self following the comment of Virginia Woolf is applicable:

> The triumph is the triumph of style. For it is only by knowing how to write that you make use in literature of yourself; that self, while it is essential to literature is also its most dangerous antagonist. Never to be yourself and yet always—that is the problem.[4]

It is in her love poems that she articulates her feminine sensibility: her hankering and passion for love, the denial, the frustration, desperation and even fancy for adultery. In "An Introduction" she gives a brief picture of the history of her love:

> I met a man, loved him. Call
> Him not by any name, he is every man
> Who wants a woman, just as I am every
> Woman who seeks love. In him [...] the hungry haste

Of rivers, in me [...] the ocean's tireless
Waiting.

In her autobiography, *My Story,* she portrays the longing for love of a sensitive girl of fifteen who dreams of love as "a beautiful anguish" (12), fondly imagining life to be "so young, so happy, so full of promise" (57), but is thrust to the reality of marriage with a lustful man who "without warning [...] fell on me, surprising me by the extreme brutality of the attack" (79). There is an obvious echo of this traumatic sex experience and a sort of loveless husband-wife relationship in a number of poems that Kamala Das wrote. "The Stone Age" records the casual treatment of her husband with her in the most explicit and unabashed manner:

Fond husband, ancient settier in the mind,
Old fat spider, weaving webs of bewilderment,
Be kind. You turn me into a bird of stone, a granite
Dove, you build round me a shabby room,
And stroke my pitted face absent-mindedly while
You read. With loud talk you bruise my pre-morning
sleep,
You stick a finger into my dreaming eye.

In "The Old Playhouse", we learn that love is perhaps no more than a way of learning about one's self, that its reward is an insight not into another's being, but really into one's own. One seeks in love the completion of one's own personality:

. . . love is Narcissus at the water's edge, haunted
By its own lonely face, and yet it must seek at last
An end, a pure, total freedom, it must will the mirror
To shatter and the kind night to erase the water.

The poem is addressed presumably to the husband, and protests against the constraint of the married life: the fever of domesticity, the routine of lust, artificial comfort, and male domination. "You" is presumably the husband who wants to tame the swallow, "to hold her/In the long summer of your love" and restrict her ". . . urge to fly, and the endless/Pathways of the sky." She comes to him because she wanted to learn what she was, to realize her true self. But instead she loses her freedom, and, dwarfed by his egotism, she is emptied of all her natural mirth and clarity of thinking:

> You were pleased
> With my body's response, its weather, its usual shallow
> Convulsions.
> You dribbled spittle into my mouth, you poured
> Yourself into every nook and cranny, you embalmed
> My poor lust with your bitter-sweet juices.
> You called me wife, I was taught to break saccharine into
> your tea and
> To offer at the right moment the vitamins.
> Cowering Beneath your monstrous ego I ate the magic loaf
> and
> Became a dwarf. I lost my will and reason, to all your
> Questions I mumbled incoherent replies.

Yet there is a sense in which Kamala Das feels the need to find such a freedom imposed on her not by choice but by the circumstances which breed the fever of domesticity. In "The Millionaires (*sic*) at Marine Drive" the warmth which her grandmother, who died eighteen years ago, gave her still haunts the persona for no man has been able to give her such a love. The more recent shift in Kamala Das's love-theme is from the glorification of sexual love, of the man who fills her emptiness with a child, though she returns to it again and again, to a general dissatisfaction with the male character. It is perhaps consistent with the matrilinear tradition to which she traces her ancestry and with her general criticism of men for their failure to give her tenderness and warmth, that the only figure whom she presents as ideal is her great-grandmother:

> ... all through the sun-singing
> Day, all through the moon-wailing night, think
> Of her, of the warmth that she took away.
> And, contrasted with her,
> ... all the hands
> The great brown thieving hands groped beneath my
> Clothes, their fire was that of an arsonist's,
> Warmth was not their aim, they burnt my cities Down.

Kamala Das actually subverts the myth of conventional Indian marriage by exposing the hollowness of a loveless relationship in which the wife is nothing but a sex symbol. In the poem mentioned above, she writes with the anguish of a hurt soul:

> Through peep-holes, the neighbours watch, they watch me come
> And go like rain. Ask me, everybody, ask me
> What he sees in me, ask me why he is called a lion,
> A libertine, ask me why his hand sways like a hooded snake
> Before it clasps my pubis. Ask me why like
> A great tree, felled, he slumps against my breasts,
> And sleeps.

She is not to give herself up to the sex hunger of her husband blindly; on the other hand she hungers for love as every woman does and articulates this hunger in her poetry. "She is in the main a poet of love, of love from the woman's point of view. To her centre is not blind worship of the husband but the consummation of love."[5]

Sex bondage is the most repressive and unless the woman is roused to rebellion against this bondage—loveless sex as demanded by unfeeling husbands—there is no hope for the Indian woman's emancipation. What she advocates poetically as an antidote to a loveless home is also repeated in an interview with Shobha Warrie. In a poem titled "Substitute", she bitterly and rather cynically records how her loveless marital status led to adultery:

> After that love became a swivel-door,
> When one went out, another came in.

In an interview with Shobha Warrier she repeated the same sentiment, "I always wanted love, and if you don't get it within your home, you stray a little."[6] Now the question is whether Das's bold advocacy of adultery smacks of a nymphomaniac rebellion. The fact is that born into the matrilineal system of inheritance and succession, she was nurtured with an inherent spirit of independence. In the following passage from *Summer in Calcutta,* one gets a glimpse of this spirit:

> I shall some day leave, leave the cocoon
> You built around me with morning tea,
> Love-words flung from doorways and of course
> Your tired lust. I shall some day take
> Wings, fly around [...].

While she speaks of the monotony and tiresome bind of a hollow married life, she also "speaks here as a 'liberated' woman, who resents 'the cocoon' built around her and desires to flit about without any restrictions. The fairer sex receives a better deal from this sensitive poetess, who airs out its grievances and sufferings in a striking fashion."[7] Similarly in the call for adultery, one notices a mischievous glint of irony in her eye for in the following extract from a poem called "A Man is a Season" she enunciates how by a clever machination her husband thrust her into paramours' arms only to show that he is 'eternity' to whom she wants to revert ultimately:

> A man is a season,
> You are eternity.
> To teach me this, you let me toss my youth like coins
> In various hands, you let me mate with shadows,
> You let me sing in empty shrines, you let your wife
> Seek ecstasy in others' arms....
> ... Perhaps I lost my way, perhaps
> I went astray. How would a blind wife trace her lost I
> Husband, how would a deaf wife hear her husband call?

Kamala Das in the same scornful vein expresses her problem through one of her characters in *A Doll for the Child Prostitute.* "Falling in Love", says Ayee, a character in the novel, "is a dangerous thing. It is like tying oneself with a rope."[8] Moreover, the terror of sex, its attraction and repulsion are vehemently expressed in the poem "Gino":

> You will perish from his kiss, he said, as one must
> surely die, when bitten by a krait who fills

> The bloodstream with its accursed essence. I was
> quiet
> For once, my tongue had failed in my mouth.

Thus there is a marked degree of discontent in Kamala Das's work which explains its double-edge of rebelliousness and tenderness. Although the freedom which she has acquired is a Janus-faced gift, it is valuable. It has given her an individuality, a gusto, a courage, and above all poetry, although deep down there are also the dark whispers of mortality, intimations of the truth that our "loneliness is eternal" and that "We are born with great hollows that need to be filled, for us to feel to complete." This does not however make her look for comfort in philosophy, or find protection in a falsified image of life like Denise Levertov's hypocrite women because:

> . . . how seldom we speak
> of our own doubts, while dubiously
> we mother man in his doubt!

Courage and honesty are the strength of Kamala Das's character and her poetry; and the courage lies in not only being able to admit that one has aged, when one has, but in also being able to assert in the face of it that in the final analysis one has no regrets to add that one has lived beautifully in this beautiful world, and that one can,

> . . . look at my maker if at all that is possible with no
> apology for my past exuberances, no extenuations, for
> deep inside I know well that I have lived beautifully in
> this beautiful world . . .

Such an assertion is not a matter of mere hindsight, though hindsight is a necessary gift to an imaginative sense of one's growth, but a flowering and a patterning of the anti-cipations, the hints, and guesses contained in "I Shall Some Day" from *Summer in Calcutta* which is reprinted in *The Old Playhouse and Other Poems:*

> I shall some day leave, leave the cocoon
> You built around me with morning tea,

Love-words flung from doorways and of course
Your tired lust. I shall some day take
Wings, fly around, as often petals
Do when free in air, and you dear one,
Just the sad remnant of a root, must
Lie behind, sans pride, on double-beds
And grieve. But, I shall some day return, losing
Nearly all, hurt by wind, sun and rain,
Too hurt by fierce happiness to want
A further jaunt or a further spell
Of freedom, and I shall some day see
My world, de-fleshed, de-veined, de-blooded,
Just a skeletal thing, then shut my
Eyes and take refuge, if nowhere else,
Here in your nest of familiar scorn . . .

What distinguishes her among the women poets of India is her bold frankness in articulating sexual urges and feelings. She is the most renowned Indian woman poet of the confessional mode and easily places herself in the company of Sylvia Plath and Anne Sexton. The following extract from "Forest Fire" shows her in the frankest and yet most confessional mood which makes her a class apart:

Of late I have begun to feel a hunger
To take in with greed, like a forest-fire that
Consumes, and, with each killing gains a wilder,
Brighter charm, all that comes my way [...]
My eyes lick at you like flames, my nerves
Consume; and, when I finish with you, in the
Pram, near the tree and, on the park bench, I spit
Out small heaps of ash, nothing else.

She may not command the intellectual vigour of the two poets of the confessional mode mentioned above, but "she does not lag behind in lyrical outburst of unpremeditated thoughts and feelings and in emotional intensity. In truth, she is more aware of the pathos in the life of a common woman playing a very passive role in our tradition-bound society than some of these women poets highlighting a different cultural and moral ethos".[9]

She finds a devotional means of self-fulfilment and elevation to the role of the victor by invoking the Mira Bai and Radha-Krishna myths. Just as Mira merges in the ultimate consciousness, God, and Radha surrenders herself in a blissful union with Lord Krishna, the eternal lover, so Kamala too merges with the eternal lover and thus escapes the travails of an unhappy love life:

> Everything in me
> Is melting, even the hardness at the core.
> O Krishna, I am melting, melting, melting
> Nothing remains but
> You [...].
>
> ("Radha")

Whether this is panacea for the long-suffering marginalized Indian woman is another matter.

Kamala Das's poems lean on the cluster of associations and emotional implication with the past especially in relation to some ideal or dream. After all, these poems simultaneously recall the past and rehearse the present. The pangs of suffering as well as the hope of restoration are suggested through formal structure, comprising rich ambiguities and subtle ironies. She is really a goldfish in a well-lit bowl, revealing herself in all transparency and beauty. According to Kamala Das:

> Large areas of my ignorance had been obliterated by the lessons I had learnt from life and 1 wanted my readers to know of it. I had realised by then that the writer has none to love her but the readers. She would have proved herself to be a mere embarrassment to the members of her family, for she is like a goldfish in a well-lit bowl whose movements are never kept concealed.[10]

Moreover, a critical evaluation of Kamala Das invariably invites her comparison with many contemporary Indian and foreign poets. She is unique in herself and broodes over the problem of women to highlight the erotic ties of man-woman relationship. Therefore, Bruce King perceptively remarks:

> Das's themes go beyond stereotyped longings and complaints. Even her feelings of loneliness and disappointment are part of a larger-than-life personality, obsessive in its awareness of its self, yet creating a drama of selfhood.[11]

Sometimes in her poetry, she becomes very serious like Sylvia Plath and Emily Dickinson, and sometimes Keatsean analogy can be found. Unlike the poetry of Sylvia Plath, the poetry of Kamala Das culminates in aestheticism, eroticism and ethos. One can find no where such kind of poetic excellence as in her in the whole range of Indian poetry in English.

References

1. Tejinder Kaur. Images of Indian Women in Kamala Das's *'Padmavati, the Harlot and Other Stories'*, in *Literary Voice*, February 2000. p.11
2. Kamala Das, *My Stoty*, New Delhi: Sterling Publishers. 1988; rpt. 1991. p. 157.
3. *Ibid.*, p. 109.
4. Virginia Woolf, *The Modern Essay*, *The Common Reader*, London. 1962. p. 275.
5. Bijay Kumar Das, *Critical Essays on Post-colonial Literature*. 2001. p. 42.
6. Shobha Warrier, *The Rediff Interview / Kamala Das.*" Rediff on the Net. 1996. Online. Internet.
7. A. N. Dwivedi, *Kamala Das and Her poetry* Delhi: Doaba House, 1983. p. 21.
8. Kamala Das, *A Doll for the Child Prostitute*, New Delhi, 1977. p. 52.
9. A. N. Dwivedi, A. N. *op.cit.,*
10. Kamala Das, *My Stoty, op.cit.,*
11. Bruce King, *Modem Indian Poetry in English*. New Delhi: O.U.P., 1987, p. 147.

11

Sexuality as an Expression of Emancipation in Selected Women Protagonists of Vijay Tendulkar

—Deepali Rajshekhar Patil

> Most of the feminine traits that psychometrics have revealed can be easily explained in sociological terms. So woman is less dominant because that is what society requires of her, more emotional because her thoughts and education have been directed to the heart rather than the head, more conservative because hearth and home do not change much and do not (like the competitive world of business and public affairs) require the capacity for change as a condition of survival[1].

Cutting through the edge of moral behavior designed for them Tendulkar's female protagonists set us thinking. They cannot be confined to the social and moral obligations that are imposed by the conventional patterns of upbringing as mentioned by Eva Figes. Certainly it would be an interesting endeavour to investigate Tendulkar's selected heroines whose radicalism is clearly perceptible in their non-conformism. Their independent nature not only initiates them to violation of ethical codes but nevertheless makes them endearing to the readers and spectators alike. One is often led to marvel at the dramatic genius and mettle of Tendulkar who created a gallery of women characters that challenged the man-woman hegemony, indulged in adultery and yet retained their hypnotic effect to arouse sympathy and understanding.

There is, as Robert Lifton points out in his essay "Woman as Knower", a "sudden emergence in often exaggerated form of psychological tendencies previously suppressed by social customs".[2] He believes that this "release phenomenon" produces a proliferation of the deviant types.

The underlying connotation prevalent in Tendulkar's plays to be discussed is that a woman can find a meaningful existence and refuge from disaster only through her union with man. This in turn once again makes her subservient to the male dominated society.

In *Silence! The Court is in Session*, Leela Benare's sexual overtures trigger off a series of recriminations, so that she is publicly ostracized for her immorality and the stigma of infanticide causes immeasurable pain. It needs to be fully comprehended that her alleged seduction of men and her amorous advances towards Ponkshe, Rokade and Samant denote a much serious situation. An easy target for Mrs. Kashikar and others, her zeal and exuberance springs from her need to find security and support in the society. Every man turning his back upon her makes her all the more gullible. In her feeble attempts to lure the men to marry her and save herself from public disgrace, she offers her only asset, her physical charm and consequently belittles herself. Her turmoil is intensely felt as she emphatically declares:

> These are the mortal remains of some cultured men of the twentieth century. See their faces—how ferocious they look! Their lips are full of lovely worn-out phrases! And their bellies are full of unsatisfied desires.[3] (117)

In a rebellious spirit she challenges the hegemony of man-woman relationship but her attempts are thwarted by her own kind. She is unsuccessful in subverting the vertical relationship of man and woman. Mrs. Kashikar becomes an accomplice with the men to fling harsh insinuations and serious charges against her. Assuredly her way of expressing her sense of freedom through sexuality is in itself self-deprecatory but given the circumstances, deserted by her lover she seems to be left with no other alternative but to entice someone to marry her. Even her past spells out her ignominious relationship with her maternal uncle who reaps physical pleasures but denies marrying her. She receives another blow in her illegitimate relationship with Prof Damle, a married man who forsakes her after impregnating her. Benare becomes the butt of social ridicule as both her illicit affairs mark her indifferent yet pleasure seeking attitude. Both the relationships she develops are doomed to failure, one unveils incest whereas the other promiscuity. Benare is compelled to find a suitable marriage partner who will accept her and provide her illegitimate child a 'father's name'. What she desires is not inappropriate but the path she chooses to tread is unjustifiable under any given pretext.

Samik Bandyopadhyay credits the play, *Silence! The Court is in Session,* as:

> The first significant modern Indian play in any language to centre on woman as protagonist and victim that locates its heroine Benare not at an acquiescent receiving end, but at a point of conflict where as aggressive-transgressor of the sexual mores of her community, she challenges the executors or power in absentia. It is part of Tendulkar's dramatic strategy that Benare's immediate persecutors in the play are as powerless as she, and all their exertions to cut Benare down to size are more their striving after power than a real exercise of power.[4]

These subtle manoeuvres that re-define the asymmetrical power structures are at work in the play.

Tendulkar's own remarks are quite illuminating:

> As a social being I am against all exploitation and I passionately feel that all exploitation must end. As a writer I feel fascinated by the violent exploited-exploiter relationship and obsessively delve deep into it instead of taking a position against it. That takes me to a point where I feel that this relationship is eternal, a fact of life however cruel, and will never end.
>
> Not that I relish this thought while it grips me but I cannot shake it off.[5]

This thematic obsession with sprightly females who display the courage to retaliate with full force against injustice continued in later plays also. In *Sakharam Binder*, Champa is depicted as a sensuous woman who exercises command over Sakharam's household. Though she seemingly detests 'man-woman stuff' she voluntarily goes off in the afternoons to meet Dawood. Her willful indulgence in carnal pleasures exhibits her liberal ideas that in turn emphasize her conception of self-assertion. As Shanta Gokhale opines, "Champa is more like the socially despised temptress, the other woman. She is lazy, doesn't give evidence of understanding that, as a woman, she must be subservient, she appears not to respect men, Sakharam, her present patron included"[6] (36).

The very fact that Champa controls Sakharam, the defamed womanizer in her own ways and outwits him by developing relations with his bosom friend testifies to her independent nature and mutinous spirit. She is quite practical and stronger compared to her other female counterparts. After deserting her husband, Champa is offered shelter by Sakharam, to satisfy his 'itch'. When Laxmi is threatened by an adversary and submissively yields her right over Sakharam to Champa, she is determined, "I'm on my own"(181) and to Laxmi's enquiry of getting along with him, she cleverly retorts, "Your Sakharam, he really takes his money's worth out of a woman. I've managed to last out here. What else can I do? Go out in streets? Face half a dozen animals every day! Easier to put up with this one"[7] (181).

Champa gains sympathy because she suffers the most because of her voluptuous body and is finally killed. Champa is perhaps the only character to be discussed here who is a desirous woman, her contradictory nature is truly baffling, on one hand she loathes physical relationship on the other hand vehemently condemns Sakharam for turning impotent in Laxmi's presence and finally chooses to find solace in Dawood's company.

Champa mercilessly thrashes her own husband in the presence of Dawood and Sakharam who are stupefied with her violent outbursts and her offensiveness. She not only challenges the patriarchal norms through her lasciviousness but she cajoles the victim who turns into a perpetrator and retaliates with double force.

In *Gidhade* (Vultures) the play that entails blood-curdling violence the only redeeming figures are Rama and Rajaninath. Rama's yearning for motherhood compels her to step beyond the threshold and seek sexual gratification from her brother in law. She tries to set free the shackles of morality only to attain the celestial joy of motherhood. Her bold step is evidently a condemnable offence but her crime is mitigated by her pure intentions.

Rajaninath's opening soliloquy brings out her longing for a child:

> For twenty-two long years. All her hopes, her expectations
> Were scorched, uprooted where they grew.
> But she only knew
> One longing,
> Only one. Embraced it to her
> Tightly, as one might one's life.
> Gathered up all her body, her being,
> Grain by grain.
> Threw off her chains in her need.
> The need to swell with fruit.
> A soft fulfillment.
> Each womb-bearing woman's right by birth.[8]

It is not her sexual urge but maternal instinct that initiates her into the abominable act. Rama is a silent sufferer who witnesses the inhuman, horrifying acts of violence perpetrated by her husband and his family. Her conjugation with Rajaninath, the only pure soul besides her in the play, is the single redeeming act in the series of spine-chilling brutality.

Rama's anguish is clearly evident when she frantically explodes:

> It's not even my fault! This womb's healthy and sound, I swear it! I was born to become a mother. This soil's rich, it's hungry. But the seed won't take root. If the seed's soaked in poison, if its weak, feeble, lifeless, devoid of

> virtue—then why blame the soil? And if still the soil should cherish that seed—should with god as its witness make efforts—beyond life itself—to guard that seed, to nourish it".[9]

Rama's character appeals to the heart, her woes are heart rending as they are the unspoken cries of a woman who longs to be a 'mother'. Her end is not much different than other women who aim to cross the limits for reasons of their own. When she finally is gifted with some moments of glory in her pregnancy, her mirth is short-lived, as she has to succumb to her husband's capriciousness and suspicion. The ending shows her husband taking her away from the vulturesque house, with Rama turned into stone, unfeeling and benumbed. She has remained a barren form that follows Ramakant into a dismal future that breathes annihilation.

In Tendulkar's *Baby,* the eponymous heroine is molested and forced to accept illicit relationship with Shivapa after she is left forlorn in the world. Her brother Raghav being sentenced to jail, Baby is compelled to accept the atrocious conditions of Shivapa, the conman to survive. Perhaps in any other play, the complete undoing of the heroine would have been the tragic ending of the story line. But the author is interested in portraying the other side of reality and transcending the conventional norms. Baby is certainly an endearing character who tries to cling to life despite least hope for change and bears no grudges for her lot. She not only demeans herself to remain under the protective care of Shivapa, but also willingly consents to his strange demands, parading like a coquette, behaving like a pet dog and slavishly obeying him. Baby's plight becomes all the more intense and pathetic when she gesticulates like a faithful dog and pleases Shivapa with gestures that he demands. Her cloistered world is temporarily disturbed with the return of Raghav. The tragedy of the siblings is truly striking as none can venture to escape the predestined fate. It is the distinct Indian ethos evoked by Tendulkar that demands a discomfited realization of the patriarchal set-up where greater power is vested at the hands of men though they are misfits in the world. His dilemma is more acute for his actual imprisonment has ensnared him in fears. His suffocation is more intense as he helplessly witnesses the sorrow of his sister, her brutal exploitation but is too feeble, impotent to alter her pitiable condition. His emotional and psychological turbulence incapacitate him to act second time as Baby's rescuer, instead he becomes a puppet in the hands of Shivapa. Shivapa, the goon, not only despoils Baby, but also extracts physical pleasures ranging on inhuman perversity and demands financial assistance from her for his sick wife. Baby is drawn in more sympathetic colors particularly because she is purely commodified by Shivapa and even Raghav, who is weak to lift the cloud of suffering that shrouds her world. Incidentally Baby works incessantly to satisfy the demands of these men who are dependent on her—one who physically rapes her and the other who emotionally drains her. Neither of the men who pose as her saviors is able to offer solace to her or even alleviate her sufferings. Baby sticks to Shivapa to save herself from public recrimination, with the awareness that becoming his mistress is the only means of escape from suicide or prostitution. She invites Karve with the hope of fulfilling her fantasies of passionate love. She agrees to keep Raghav with her despite her embarrassment as he would provide some help in her household chores. All these hopes and wishes are frustrated as these men lack the moral courage and strength that she desires and the situation demands.

Baby's predicament is even more disquieting because she is fully conscious of her oppression, wishes to liberate herself from the bondage but finds no way out. Even her momentary romantic escapade with Karve is cursed by the arrival of Shivapa, who seems to be the wicked hand that ruthlessly rules her world.

Baby rises like a phoenix from the quagmire of evil, she is defiant, does not succumb to the circumstances. She fervently proclaims her philosophy, "Suicide is cowardly. No matter how difficult, we mustn't give up hope; we must keep making the effort. Life is a battle, Raghav!, later she voices her genuine feelings, "One who struggles can't afford to despair".[10] She joins the film industry as an extra to sustain herself against all odds.

Her indulgence in sexual overtures towards Karve phenomenally reveals two aspects of her sexuality. She exploits her sexual potentials firstly for her survival and secondly secure love and affection. Her licentious behaviour does not show a characteristic pattern but conversely depicts the oscillation between reality and idealism. Her promiscuity is thrust upon her initially but later she exploits it as a means to gain freedom from the unwanted relationship. Each move towards a positive relationship is coincided by a step beyond her suffocating, cloistered world.

Another play, *Chiranjeev Soubhagyakanshini,* previously entitled *Anji* which is yet to be translated into English, sketches Anjali Bhide's journey from innocence to maturity. She seems to be one of the boldest heroines stage ever witnessed. In a peculiar way she recollects and rejoices every moment of her rape for she looks at it as a process of awakening. The momentary interaction leads her into a consciousness of womanhood. In Tendulkar's *Chiranjeev Soubhagyakankshini* once again the ethical norms are challenged by the desires and wish fulfilment of Anjali Bhide, the central character. It verges on the psychological problem of schizophrenia and Anji's rape by the schizophrenic Shekhar Bhagwat, who baffles Anji and mesmerizes her with his quick temperamental changes. In a very strictly codified and culture specific context, Anjali who has passed the marital age like most of the earlier women (Benare who is always concerned about the loss of their youth) is searching for a suitable life partner. She finds her virginal fastidiousness desecrated by Shekhar who assumes the role of his own brother intermittently and speaks different languages and switches roles between an NRI and a Bengali Babu. Anjali however does not protest over her rape or lose self control like Benare, neither is she totally disintegrated like Blanche but reckons it as a kind of self awakening. She finds herself a completely changed woman after the strange interlude.

> Heroine: The first experience ever in the life of twenty nine years. Giving the pain of death and a sense of wonder something unwanted and yet something that should not end[11].

Later when the narrator learns what disaster has befallen, he utters the word "Sorry". She unexpectedly raises her voice and questions him,

> What's there to be sorry about? It was the only experience to be preserved, are you unhappy about it? Otherwise perhaps—that pleasure or happiness would never have come to me. I could never earn it. I was denying it scared of my father. But for that single moment at least I lived. The real sorrow is that I could not live that fleeting moment properly. It ended as it came; but yet it came. At least once it had come! [12]

Unexpectedly, Anjali's reaction to the pitiless and vicious deed is indeed shocking. Instead of being repelled by the ugliness of the experience, she is enthralled by the sheer physicality of the act which would have otherwise never come her way. In a way, Anjali unabashedly not only accepts the occurrence without complaint but cherishes the memory of the momentary pleasure she gained through the bitter-sweet experience. She, then shares a peculiar kinship with Benare who is partially responsible for the moral outrage due to their sexual wantonness. Anjali also needs to be blamed for she herself walks into the trap laid by Shekhar, possibly fully aware of the repercussions but in exhibiting completely unexpected reaction, shows her unconventionality as also challenges the orthodox norms of man-woman relationship.

It is significant to probe the demoralizing act as it could present the complexities of the issue at this juncture. Griffin in her study, "Rape: All American Crime", points out "the male psyche persists in believing that, protestations and struggles to the contrary deep inside her mysterious feminine soul, the female victim has wished for her own fate. The theory that women like being raped extends itself by deduction into the proposition that most or much of rape is provoked by the victim. But this too is a myth".[13] Although the facts reveal that women like Benare, Champa, and Rama in a way contribute to their tragic experiences, their lament or outcry cannot expiate their irrevocable acts, it must be admitted that their promiscuity is an appeal for emotional support and social security, a dependence on male support in a thoroughly patriarchal set up.

Another shade of sexuality is manifested in the portrayal of homosexuality. *A Friends' Story* (Mitrachi Goshta) was probably the first play that opened up issues of sexuality that were prohibited on the stage. It directly dealt with lesbianism. Sumitra's attempts to seek the company of Nama through the mediation of Bapu bespeak of her abnormal craving and desire. Tendulkar's play singularly devotes itself to the quintessence of homosexuality. His selection of the theme certainly shows his deliberate probe into the psycho-sexual realm and his attempt to bring to forefront issues that lay hidden under the dark underbelly of the civilized world. The play was inspired by a real life incident. Mitra seeks love from her own kind and objects Nama's relationship with Dalvi. Sumitra audaciously declares, "I like her with my whole being, Bapu! I've lost my heart to her. I just can't forget her" [14].

The infatuation which Mitra has for another girl ends in a major crisis, finally unable to get the desired satisfaction, Mitra commits suicide. Instead of an endorsement of Mitra's desire for sex and the social acceptance of lesbianism or Nama's indifference to this identification, we have the dramatic rendering of their respective attitudes. The finale, in particular does not offer any proffered solutions, but juxtaposes rather than resolves the divergent perspectives on the subject of women's sexual and social roles.

It is through characters like Benare, Champa, Rama, Baby, Anji and Mitra that the subtleties and complexities of man woman relationship are questioned. One needs to take N.S. Dharan's statement of gynocentric plays of Tendulkar with a pinch of salt. Although it is obvious that these plays revolve around the woman who is central to the drama, she is certainly not nuclear to the relationships rather she is marginalized.

In fact these women attempt to seek attention, re-assert themselves and seek liberty through their wilful indulgence in sex. Eric Fromm's understanding of promiscuous behaviour explains that women desperately hop from one love to another in search of intensity and excitement that the new relationship brings.

> The consequence is one seeks love with a new person with a new stranger. Again the stranger is transformed into an 'intimate' person, again the experience of falling in love is exhilarating and intense, and again it slowly becomes less and less intense and ends in the wish for a new conquest, a new love—always with the illusion that the new love will be different from the earlier ones. These illusions are greatly helped by the deceptive character of sexual desire.[15]

The new conquest is always a boost to the woman's vanity. Further, her preoccupation leaves no time to brood over the pathetic state of her emotional life that is in tethers. This clearly helps to comprehend Benare, Champa or Baby's intimacies with strangers. Paradoxically physical charm becomes a cause of their undoing and also an asset for realization of their identity as an individual. Female sexuality becomes a double-edged word; if it contributes to abuse and molestation, conversely it arms the woman to exploit men for their purposes. "We cannot merely concentrate on those moments in which women rebel or assert themselves, without understanding what they are rebelling against and to what dramatic and historical effect", [16] observes Helene Keysser.

The moral scruples of these emancipated women are signs of repentance for their immodesty; rather they reveal an urge for stability in life and contentment. During their ordeal unfortunately they become easy targets for social criticism and disgrace. But it needs to be understood that the moral depravity of a woman cannot be singularized unless there is a man who contributes to her ignominious state. Very often, the patriarchal set up of the society that easily condemn the women and make her the prime accused fail to ascribe the men guilty, who are absolved of their crime. An unpardonable offence that ensnares a woman and imposes harsh penitence should equally punish the concerned male members of the society and affirm justice. If Anji and Champa are infatuated to the lingering passion, Baby and Laxmi accept their lot and turn to promiscuity as the only solace in their deserted lives, whereas Benare and Rama harbor maternal instincts and are willing to shield their motherhood against all the odds. In such peculiar circumstances 'consummation' is the only act of creation in the relentless process of destruction and disintegration. Sexuality comes as an emancipatory force. They have the strength and inordinate sexual power like nymphomaniacs to draw the men to themselves. Their magnetic sexuality converts assertive men to tamed, submissive, docile existence. The patriarchal power structure or male monarchy is inversed by the female dominance chiefly exercising the authority through their libidinal energy. In such women the erotic love becomes a symbol of virile energy, almost a masculine force that usurps the male-world and divests them of power, rendering them impotent. They articulate their desires; reap physical pleasures, completely indifferent to the conventional social norms which they intentionally trample upon.

If both men and women as the subjects of society respect its moral order, moral degradation would be checked. Very often these women are treated as commodities to be used for gratification and discarded. If Benare would have received the support of Prof. Damle, Rama and Champa's love reciprocated by their husbands, Baby and Anji would have found a suitable match perhaps things would have been completely different. Unfortunately with no other alternative left, these women resort to the last option available to them and try to set things right. None of these women however try to give up their lives except Mitra who is caught in an irreconcilable situation and commits suicide.

'Honour,' 'shame,' 'control' seem to be the epithets that are synonymous with womanhood. In a glaring contrast this 'new avatar' of women blasted the social norms of conduct. As Swapan Kumar Banerjee rightly mentions:" They embraced hardship in following their conscience often in defiance of the dictates of male society".[17] Blatantly embracing their desires, they seem to usurp the male dominion by their remorseless sexual freedom. Their moral offence is unforgivable, it cannot be mitigated by the circumstantial pressures, yet it is an infallible manifestation of their newly acquired sense of individual liberty. Failure is predestined in the relationships that Leela Benare and Rama yearn for. Where Benare is forced to lure men to conceal her moral crime, Rama is compelled to step beyond the limits of marriage to veil her husband's impotence. On the other hand, Champa and Anjali are driven astray by their untamed desires. Baby is dragged into atrocious conditions and Mitra is born with abnormal desires. Incidentally these women deny to be cowed down by the peculiar circumstances and display their seditious nature. Though they are corrupted and defamed by men they trusted, they defy the laws of subjugation by their extremism.

The indomitable will of Benare, Rama, Champa, Anjali, Baby and Mitra bespeaks of their insolent nature that has tasted the air of emancipation but it is attained by paying a heavy price. Benare is left forlorn to face the consequences of being a maiden mother; Rama has to return to her loveless, hapless marriage with a childless womb. Champa is brutally killed by the suspicious Sakharam; Anjali is bereft, baffled unable to cope with the reality of the schizophrenic Shekhar. Baby is treacherously tossed about by life as a homeless wretch, still shouldering the responsibility of hopeless brother. Mitra has to settle scores with her uncompromising lesbianism by committing suicide. Certainly none of these women, who aspire to cross the stranglehold of patriarchy, are rewarded with success.These victimized women project themselves as provocateurs but are predetermined to failure for they choose to swim against the current. Their moral failure is tragic and striking as their physical charms also are inadequate to fulfil their longing for a lasting relationship. In a feeble attempt to overcome victimization their battle is lost even before it is fought.

Such peculiar and complex characters as presented to the stage by Tendulkar are significant endowment to the discourse on gender, because they personify several principles largely unaddressed by the prevalent dramatists. Tendulkar used theatre as a social force by raising questions to the legitimacy of the prevalent social systems and structures. The emergence of the 'new woman', an epitome of distinct personality shaped by education and awareness of her rights took charge of the theatre. Tendulkar's heroines represent the 'new woman', the phrase coined by Sarah Grand in *The American Review* in 1894: "The New Woman became many things to many people, but for all she stood bold, free and capable of thinking and acting for herself. The retiring dimpled virgin, decorative and obedient, was brushed aside by the modern girl who read, knew and understood and refused to sit quietly in a corner".[18] Such women are something other than what society has ordained for them and they are objects of desire as well as desiring subjects. They eschewed their traditional roles of dutiful daughters and acquiescent wives and seized the roles of protagonists. The charisma of such a desire vandalizes the norms of feminine behaviour and disrupts the customary notions of decorum. These women succeed in their quest at least to some extent by seeking sexual gratification through the interchangeability of male-partners. They are destined to occupy the superior position in a sexual power equation and in the process they seize the masculine prerogative of a conventional social structure. Their negotiation with power through their sexuality is juxtaposed with their compromising morality.

To conclude, sexuality is seen as an expression of freedom but such acts cannot be justified under any moral or social pretexts. Such women are abused and castigated for being swayed by passions. It would be preposterous to offer any sweeping generalizations because each woman is trapped in a different situation. Nevertheless each is a product of patriarchy and positively stipulates rethinking and relocation of relationships at personal and social level. Indeed all these women are courageous and fortified with their physical charm, hope to change their world. They claim proper understanding, consideration and sympathy from the world at large. These women appeal to the heart by their vivacity, enthusiasm and zeal for life.

References

1. Eva Figes, *The Case for Women in Revolt: Patriarchal Attitudes*. Greenwich: Fawcett, 1970, p.10.
2. Robert Lifton, "Woman as Knower" in Janeway, Elizabeth. *Man's World, Woman's Place: A Study in Social Mythology*. New York: William Morrow, 1971, p.119.

3. Vijay Tendulkar, *Silence! The Court is in Session, The Vultures.* Trans. Priya Adarkar, A *Friend's Story* Trans. Gouri Ramnarayan in *Collected Plays in Translation.* New Delhi: Oxford University Press, 2003, p.117.
4. Samik Bandopadhyay, 'Introduction' in *Collected Plays in Translation.* New Delhi: Oxford University Press, 2003, p. xiv.
5. Vijay Tendulkar, "Where is the Tradition?" *Frontline*, 25 September, 1992.
6. Shanta Gokhale, "Tendulkar on his own Terms" in Madge, V.M. ed. *Vijay Tendulkar's Plays.* Delhi: Pencraft International, 2007.
7. Vijay Tendulkar, *Sakharam Binder.* Trans. Kumud Mehta and Shanta Gokhale. In *Collected Plays in Translation.* New Delhi: Oxford University Press, 2003, p. 181.
8. Vijay Tendulkar, *The Vultures.* Trans. Priya Adarkar, In *Collected Plays in Translation.* New Delhi: Oxford University Press, 2003
9. Ibid., 241.
10. Vijay Tendulkar, *Baby*. Sathe, Makarand. *Vijay Tendulkar, Omnibus*. Gurgaon: Arvind Kumar Publishers, 2007, p. 187.
11. Vijay Tendulkar, *Chiranjeev Soubhagyakanshini.* Mumbai: Popular, 1992, p.92.
12. Ibid., 92-93.
13. Alice Griffin, "Rape: All American Crime" in Freeman, Jo. ed. *Women: A Feminist Perspective*. New York: Mayfield, 1975.
14. Vijay Tendulkar, A *Friend's Story,* Trans. Gouri Ramnarayan in *Collected Plays in Translation*. New Delhi: Oxford University Press, 2003.
15. Eric Fromm, *The Art of Loving.* London: Unwin, 1978, p.49.
16. Helen Keysser, Ed. *Feminist Theatre and Theory.* London: Macmillan, 1996, p. 56.
17. Swapan Kumar Banerjee, *Feminism in Modern English Drama: 1892-1914.* New Delhi: Atlantic Publishers, 2006.
18. Quoted in Kersley, Gillian's *Darling Madame.* London: Virago, 1983, p. 77.

12

Ritwik Ghatak's "The Rack/The Torment": A Close Reading

—A.J. Sebastian

Ritwik Ghatak (1925-76) a Bengali Indian filmmaker and script-writer, had experienced the ravages of partition and refugee crisis in the wake of Bangladesh Liberation War, which had its impact on his works. In "The Rack/The Torment," in the form of a fantasy with unconnected series of scenes, he presents a dream play on the torment experienced by several characters who have committed suicides.

The setting for the play is that of a meadow with a lonely leafless *babla* (acacia) tree representing a cursed and barren land. Some thorny bushes with scattered thorny cactus are found, adding to the wasteland with stinking stagnant water around. The smog rising from the pool fills the surrounding with a decaying stench. The *babla* tree trembles at the thunderstorm. In the demonic atmosphere, a dark figure comes running from beyond. It is a wailing housewife with a half-burnt countenance. Her saree is half-burnt.

The title is derived from her agonizing cry, "O God! What torment, O!" (Ghatak 135). Suddenly a fifteen-year-old boy appears from somewhere and begins to interact with the woman. He appears soiled and dirty, his head and face smeared with blood. Stretching his arms and yawning, he greets her as a newcomer to the valley of death. She introduces herself as Shefali Bandopadhyay from Kalinghat station. She is in utter dismay. The boy is Khokan who came there in recent times. He reminds her that she is dead and has come there after she killed herself. "Don't you know? Those who kill themselves come her. You burnt yourself?" (136). She burnt herself to death for not being able to sustain her family of five children with a paltry salary of Rs.80 her husband earned as stationmaster at Kalighat. Immersed in starvation and utter poverty with kids dying every now and then, she decided to end her life. It happened that they had no food one morning. When her son Nutu, who loved food, came crying for food, in a rage she struck him on the head. The boy fell down dead. Losing her senses, she struck all her screaming children. In utter despair, she doused herself with a tin of kerosene and set herself ablaze. The opening scene draws attention to women committing suicide. The number of Indian women killing themselves is far higher than in other parts of the world. Housewives form 21 per cent of women who commit suicide due to lack of love and respect at home, dowry harassment, mental torture at the hands of in-laws, abandonment and sexual abuse. On the other hand men are driven over the edge mostly because of financial and health related reasons ("Why Indians commit suicide." http://nitawriter. wordpress.com).

After listening to the woman's torment, the boy wants her to listen to his own story as a beggar. "Listen to the tale of my torment. Did you know I had a mother too. A sister as well. We all came from East Pakistan. We all begged. They got nothing. I earned a little by begging....Then I did. Starvation... sheer starvation.... I too cried... that time... the rail coaches clanked... engine whistled.... I jumped.... They screeched and halted... so I am here" (137-8). When she questions him further about how he felt after all that happened, he can only utter that he got more hardened due to the racking feeling after having been separated from his mother and sister. When asked about her feelings, she shows her annoyance, telling him that she has forgotten them for ever. Observing Shefali's suppressed pain the boy observes: "You'll be on the rack all the more. You and they. Nothing is erased from the mind. Mind cannot forget" (138). He reaches out and touches her heart and the woman begins to feel a new sensation. He calls it the new kind of disease after death. The housewife begins to be emotionally moved when she hears her childrens' cry and longs to go back to earth. She regrets that she burnt herself to death. The boy reiterates that none of them can escape from their torment in the land of the dead. The housewife calling the boy to sit close to her, asks him what she ought to do. He points out to the red sky and tells her that it is blood red since lots of torments have been heaped together. Pointing out beyond the wetland he says: "...you might see the edge of the red sky. The blue one peeps out... I keep gazing...below, perhaps, in one corner, there's the earth, where we live; in happiness, in sorrow" (139).

The housewife longs to gaze at the sky and keeps walking. In a choked voice when the boy calls her mother, she is shocked and says, "I am no mother. No mother. Can't be a mother" (140). She thinks it to be her son Nutu whom she had struck and killed. As she is engrossed in her reverie, a white-haired old man approaches saying that he has crossed the window. He counts three floors he had climbed to jump to his death. With tears in his eyes he sits on a hump. Bhola, a labourer in his mid-twenties, approaches him singing a song. The old man, Purna tells him not to sing out so loud. He reminds the old man that he sheds tears thinking of his grandson. The boy tells the old man that he is sick, thinking of his grandson. He also tells the housewife, that the old man is his grandpa who worked in a post office. He committed suicide jumping from the fourth floor of his house. She introduces herself to Purna as a poor Bengali woman who was tormented by her poverty with five children and husband earning a paltry sum of Rs.80. The old man questions her why she chose to burn herself to death. She fumbles as she knew no other methods to end her misery. He queries why she didn't try to drown herself, jump off or get run-over. She thought of it when she observed many who strolled in the streets and suffered quietly on the rack like herself. They died and no one took notice of them. He agreed with her as he himself in despair jumped off the fourth floor. Moving towards death didn't make him remember what happened.

Purna: It's easy—the road seems to rise. Your determination increases. The windows were moving away. Then many ...don't remember quite what happened... I don't have a few ribs—all broken.

Housewife: If you burn, you know, it smells. The flames...

Boy: Rise in twists and turns. A dance, isn't it?

Housewife: Yes. And terrifying pain. At first you feel like running and screaming... then when the flames embrace, you feel peace and a certain numbness. You remember such details of the past—so many things (141).

The housewife suddenly remembers her happy childhood when her father used to set her on his shoulders whenever she cried. The old man begins to recount the story of Bhola who worked in a jute mill and used to vomit blood since he inhaled jute fibre. Bhola couldn't endure it any more. He tied a stone on his neck, tied his legs and threw himself into the river. But he is not at peace after death. They all discuss how they can get peace of mind. The discussion leads to Purna utterring: "...To end torment one needs to kill oneself: that's what we told the world. You, I, Bhola, Peon, Khoka—all of us let the world know; all who seek relief from the rack—children of burnt mothers—kill yourself, be an enemy to life. No more struggle—peace is certain" (143). The woman remonstrates saying that she never wanted her children to die. She only ran away to find peace being suffocated in life. But the old man accuses her of having run away finding solution in self-destruction and all blessings are gone as all will be destroyed.

Meeting a peon, Purna is told he is on his way to Bholada. The peon claims to have read a lot and quotes Newton who said that each and every action has got an equal and opposite reaction. But in the case of the housewife, her death brought about only the opposite effect.

Purna: ...Hasn't the opposite taken place?

Peon: Who will die?

Purna: Our future, those who are alive. Those who are on the rack.

Peon: Yes. They too are toying with this idea, I know. At this moment imagine just how many are thinking that to end torment, this is the only way out. It is a strange thought. So many, at so many

> different places are thinking the same thing. And we with much effort showed them this way (144).

The peon acknowledges his own torment that led to his suicide. He was forced to die as he wasn't allowed to study. Working as a peon of Presidency College, he cleared his matriculation with personal effort. Though he got admission to college, they prevented him from pursuing his studies. He longed to know the mysteries of the world. His thirst for knowledge made him read through a thin book that spoke of the history of mankind as class struggle. The old man questions why he had to end his life in his search for more and more of knowledge.

The discussion is interrupted by sudden rumbling of thunder and lightning. They all lie flat on the ground. A madman in his loin clothes comes running from the wetlands and stands on the hump. He waves his hands and gives direction like a traffic police. The boy whispers to the housewife that he is a man alive. The madman asks them why they are all there. The conversation is one of irony of life and death.

Madman: Who are you all?

Boy: We are all dead. You aren't.

Madman: No, none can kill me. You could say a mad man is worse than the dead—...

Peon: His soul is dead. His mind is dead. His body is alive, but under huge pressure his soul had committed suicide.

Purna: Since we are dead, we cannot speak about the torments that have racked us. He is alive, yet dead. Cannot speak a consistent word, isn't it?

Madman: Yes I can. You might ask what can a madman say? But I sit beside Hedua tank everyday. Go now and you'll find my body asleep on the pavement under a shade...

...

Housewife: O dear! Where do you live?

Madman: I don't know. I know nothing. Even if I know, I won't speak. Why should I? Then you'll call my own man mad (146-7).

The housewife has her sympathies for his great pain. However, the peon takes shelter in quoting from Tagore and Rolland saying that "the dark night ends... Its almighty peace. All sleep, my hurt mind. Sleep, my bloodied feet. You have toiled a lot. The way was difficult; it was dangerous; yet in spite of the obstacles, the way was gorgeous" (147). The boy tells the woman that he feels a black veil behind him from which some words trickle, but they don't go away. The mad man claims that he is lucky since he cannot think long. "I forget and I don't want to think. Mother, its great pain in the head to think" (148). The madman says that he came for a holiday and he has to go back to control traffic in Calcutta.

Bhola insists that the peon listens to his side of the story. He vomited blood working in the jute mill. In his poverty he went around for a year without food. Finally, he hanged himself. His only thought is now of his wife, father and son, fearing lest they would all end likewise. He could have committed dacoity or looting, but he didn't engage in such activities since he couldn't afford to buy a good knife for the purpose. In sheer despair he took his life.

The housewife wonders what would become of her kith and kin. Would they also end their lives burning themselves? Purna admonishes them all not to die even in the midst of hunger. The boy wonders why there is no remedy for their torments. The madman suddenly starts singing: "I walk alone in this world, who will show me the way" (150).

Bhola suddenly shouts and calls everyone to assemble in the middle of the wasteland. He asks them all to introspect on the reason why they are there.

Bhola: Listen. Try to find an answer.

Purna: Why suddenly have you started all this?

Peon: Bhola, what has happened to you?

Bhola: I have started thinking. I am thinking.

Housewife: What's the feeling in your eyes? ...

Purna: Tell me son. What is it you want to say?...

Bhola: Old man, when did you ever think of dying?

Purna: When I could not carry on the burden alone ...

Peon: The torture I had to face made me so angry—

Bhola: So you hanged yourself. What did you do, sister?

Housewife: Set fire to myself when alone in the room......

Boy: You know Bholada. Jumped before a train—

Bhola: And I! Tied a stone round the neck and jumped into the river—while alone—...

Madman: Don't be angry. I walked alone in this world...

Bhola: Enough... now be quiet. That's the root of evil. We all walk alone on the earth....

Purna: Things are becoming clearer to me. We all made that mistake. We need to unite. But what's the use of knowing now?

Housewife: Why? Our sons are there on earth. Let them unite and live.

Bhola: Sure.

Housewife: Will they really live? Be relieved from pain?...Why did we have to understand it here? How will the earth come to know of our realisation? (150-51).

The housewife requests the madman to go back to earth as he can't think. She asks him to burn down all their torments. They would do the thinking for him. He has to give only his physical body as it is still alive to carry a message to the earth. He agrees, though he is also tormented in pain. Pointing to the blue sky, Bhola tells the madman to go to the earth to warn everyone waiting with torments in their hearts. The housewife's message to those on earth is that they shouldn't commit suicide burning themselves. Her strain is taken up by the others as well. The boy conveys his view that people on earth should get united whatever be their destines. Bhola and the peon affirm with the same spirit saying "Why be on the rack any more?... Hiding tears, staying among all, yet alone... Just come together all men...There are lots of pain. The world is full of pain. So much has accumulated. So much of burning at heart. Bring them all together. When all is put together—fling the fire ball" (151). Their seeking the assistance of the madman is like the story of the rich man and Lazarus in the parables of Jesus (Luke 16:19-31). "... and in Hades, being in torment, he lifted up his eyes and saw Abraham far off and Lazarus in his bosom. And he called out, 'Father Abraham, have mercy upon me, and send Lazarus to dip the end of his finger in water and cool my tongue; for I am in anguish in this flame" (Luke 16:24-25). When his petition was denied, the rich man requested Father Abraham to let Lazarus go and warn those in his father's home. But his plea was of no avail due to the great chasm created between them and their attitudes.

All of them, in their angst and torment, wish to warn those on earth to be out of the rack by being united together as a community. Each of them refer to their isolated and lonely lives that brought them to the brink of despair and suicide. Except for the madman, everyone being sane, are punished with death of their physical bodies. But, the madman, having an unsound mind, his body doesn't die. Hence he is able to return to earth as the emissary of the dead. The dramatist focusing on the absurdities of life and death, ends it on a didactic note. The only solution is to break free from isolated and tormented lives by joining hands in unity and brotherhood.

Works Cited

Ghatak, Ritwik. "Ghatak's "The Rack/The Torment." *Indian Literature*, Sahitya Akademi's Bi-monthly Journal, Sept-Oct. 1997, Vol. XL, No.5. 135-181.

The Holy Bible, Revised Standard Version. London: Catholic Trust Society. 1966 (All Biblical references taken from this edition).

Why Indians commit suicide." http://nitawriter.wordpress.com/2007/05/14/why-indians-commit-suicide

13

Caste, Gender and Sexuality: Reflection on Tendulkar's *Ghasiram Kotwal*

—Anita Singh & Shyam Babu

Theatre/drama in India has been an indispensable part of cultural life. Theatrical shows together with epic relations, songs, and folk tales comprise the principal media of communication. Besides its many technical limitations, drama still has remained a powerful tool of communication and discourse, and it is in this context that it is a viable medium of discussion of such theoretical, social concepts like caste, gender and sexuality. Theatre being one of the most prolific and conspicuous generic sites of struggle and contestation, Indian drama (here used as alternative with theatre) after independence has become more trenchant and successfully interrogated the man made boundaries of nation, culture, gender, sexuality, and of course of language. All the vanguards of modern Indian drama writing in regional languages, for instance, Mohan Rakesh, Habib Tanvir, Badal Sircar, Girish Karnad and certainly Vijay Tendulkar among others have raised the issues like gender, caste, social deformity, political corruption and anomaly in its myriad shades and colours. Modern Indian drama not only reflects over the spectrum of such issues but also refract with the sense of urgency to define and address such pressing problems.

In postcolonial literatures or studies caste, gender and sexuality have been the focal issues for most of the literary scholars likewise for the theatre critics. This has also been significant for them from the both perspectives: as a literary personality and as the intellectual academician. Thus such a study gets twofold significations by its inherent nature of academic engagement and as a site of social functioning. Post-independence Indian drama so to speak has successfully raised the issues of nation, culture, gender, sexuality by forging the amalgamation of several Indian indigenous folk elements with western *avant-garde* dramatic techniques and reach beyond any narrow conceptions of dramaturgy. They do not also adhere to any one particular fashion of performance which undoubtedly reflects the imprint of their originality and deep rootedness to Indian cultural soil. Interestingly enough all modern theatre persons started experimenting with vernacular languages to formulate a new theatre idiom in the early 1950's and 1960's with the same kind of urge and compulsion. This fashion to unlearn alien tactics and return to those intrinsic to one's own culture has been one of the key urges of postcolonial playwrights. To authenticate this broader project of 'national' theatre they made many experiments in their dramaturgy. In this regard the phase of the 1960's stands as high time of bold experimentation, rejection and formulations in the realm of dramatic writings which have proved a stepping stone for the succeeding generation of the playwrights, theatre goers, and theatre artists. Needlees to say their plays are testimonials for political, social, cultural, and psychological complexity and chaos Indian was confronting with at that time. And here it is apt to suggest that it is drama among all genres of Indian writing emerged as the most viable medium to counteract the whole Western mode of narrative or colonial 'canon'. So their anti-establishment, discursive, and self-critiquing mode of engagement not only counteracted the Western and other illusory dramaturgies but also exposed the high held notion of Indian history, myths, and tales. In this context Tendulkar's *Ghasiram Kotwal* invites our attention with its several issues among which caste, gender and sexuality occupy a central concern.

I

The present study is intended to explore the highly debated issues: 'caste, gender and sexuality' in Tendulkar's *magnum-*

opus play *Ghasiram Kotwal.* Here theatre/drama will be discussed as the literary trope of such tenacious issues as caste, and gender and sexuality in the circle of contemporary literary discourse. The play will be discussed from the threefold perspectives, i.e. caste, gender and sexuality to, explore the polisemy nature of this play-text and hence an attempt has been made to establish theatre as a more cogent medium of discourse and problematization of such issues. However, the emphasis will be laid on at the manner in which the gendered identities and sexuality also bear markings of caste identity. So the thrust is on making one think and examine how there is a certain perceptible repercussion between caste, gender and sexuality. The trajectory between 'desire' and 'sexuality' with 'power' and 'domination' in the text provides it poststructuralist flavour and initiative for the theatrical writing as the space of such a cultural study. Needless to say these all essential categories share such features as 'violence', 'subjugation', 'marginalization' and 'power' in their taxonomy in *Kotwal.*

It is better to start off from gender point because gender study incorporates in its curcumference the notions of domination, construction of identity, sexuality. Interestingly if one discusses gender from the caste point of view in the instant of time one will get reminded of brand of 'double colonization' which has been customarily used defining Third World women (Asian and African women) as they were colonized by native male and colonizer at the same time. In Indian caste based social system the condition of low caste woman is the same but the context is different. Precisely gender construction indispensably is the outcome of social indoctrination unlike the biological phenomenon as Simon de Beauvoir has ascertained decades ago. Gender involves the social function in which it constitutes the identity. This process is well defined by Judith Butler: "gender attributes and acts (are) the various ways in which a body shows or produces its cultural signification" (Butler 1990, Jagger, *Judith Butler: Sexual Politics* 27). How characterization has been gendered will be touched upon in the analysis.

Likewise caste which earlier used to be thought of as an ancient fact of Hindu life is still prevalent in Indian society and like gender itself, is social construction—a ideological indoctrination or as Bhimrao Ambedker has pertinently reiterated, 'state of mind'. One implications of argument is also implied that caste and gender identities are constructed through relations of power (economic and intellectual) in Indian society to keep a certain group impoverished for getting the job done and which is also applicable to certain degree genderization of women. These discriminations in the play have been projected through particular figures of a particular period of a particular dominion.

Historically speaking caste system or casteism in India goes back to *Varna Ashram* system (a system of work division on the basis of birth not ability or work skills and to some extent colour or skin based behaviour and hence the term *Varna* which means colour). It has been the focal issue of writing and discourse in Indian philosophy and culture. From the post-*Vedic* period[1] and Buddhism up to the medieval *Bhakti* movement, casteism has been in central position in terms of philosophical discussion and devotional composition. The initiative of abolition of casteism though starts from the poetry of medieval saints like Kabir, Rahim, Raidas among others itself but it got momentum only in the colonial period. By the intervention of European cultural and anthropological thinkers and most prominently after the discourse of Dr. B.R. Ambedker and political formative initiatives of M.K.Gandhi[2].

In postcolonial India in the early 1970's and 80's 'Dalit discourse' emerged as the literature of protest, resistance and untold sufferings of marginalized people works of many writers such as: Sharankumar Limbale, Datta Bhagat, Kaval Bharati, Balmiki, Vinodini among others. This dalit discourse is the alter ego of 'subaltern studies' which is the key area of research of postcolonial literary discourse in general though there is no *dalit* or low caste character in the mentioned play as such. However, the very sense of being of a particular caste, i.e., Brahmin, highest in terms of hierarchy motivates an ordinary man Ghasi whose humiliation that he was no longer Brahmin grew so deep that he went up to extent of selling his own beloved daughter. Certainly, this incident raises the caste issue or casteism as a motivation of the play.

Having disclosed the historical incident in the degenerated form, though not overtly, it is said that caste-politics of the political leaders and ascendency of Brahmins in politics have been exposed and aimed at by Tendulkar in the most effective manner. The play was dubbed as an anti-Brahminical and defamation of historical figure likes Nana Phadnavis. The caste motif of the play interestingly also bears the implicit mythical analogy of the origin of theatre itself. As general notion prevailed in India that drama was the low caste's profession though with exception of archetypical theatre person Bharata.[3]

II

Play text *Ghasiram Kotwal* illustrates these issues with all complexities and subtleties. Briefly, the play is set in eighteenth century Poona and traces out the rise and fall of Ghasiram, an ordinary Brahmin from Kanauj, amidst the existing debauchery and corruption in the power structures under Nana Phadnavis, Peshwa's (Baji Rao II) Chancellor in Pune. Its recurring motif is how men in power create ideologies to serve their purposes, and later destroy them when they have served their purpose. Therefore, it recounts a power game played out in terms of caste ascendency in politics.

The problem in the play arises when a Brahmin, Ghasiram due to poverty is forced to migrate from Kanauj to Poona city with the wife and daughter Lalita Gauri in search of fortune. Finding no option left he joins Gulabi, the famous courtesan of Poona for the daily needs, and acts as the assistant of the prostitute and thus has to choose the profession of dance for livelihood while his wife to serves as the maid in the houses. One day as Nana is dancing with Gulabi he hunts his ankle and without any delay Ghasi gives his support and massage till is he relieved of the pain. Nana departs happily and gives his necklace out of gratitude. This reward jolts Gulabi very much and when he does not hand over the necklace to her she has him thrashed by her escorts. In course of time when he hears about a royal feast thrown in honour of Brahmins of Poona by the Peshwa, he too goes there and askes for the same honour and respect like others Brahmins. Here is hereupon he is convicted as a thief and cheat in the holy city. Having been ill treated by Brahmins and thrashed by the police he takes a vow to avenge once he gets the post of the *Kotwal* of Poona. So he makes out a plan to bargain his own daughter for that post as Nana is mesmerized by Gauri's physical beauty. He found in Nana a strong, powerful statesman who can give power as he is a sexually driven man and a womanizer too. Thus he decided to play a game of 'sex and power' with Nana who appoints him as the *Kotwal* of Poona for getting Gauri and satisfying his sexual need. However, this game of power does not end here, rather it starts where we come across the manipulations of power from the hands of the more powerful Nana to the less powerful Ghasiram. This chain of power relations is interwoven in the complex structure of personal and public gains. For his personal gains Nana hands over the state power and when enforced by the state snatches the same power to curve his ascendency as the latter is no longer useful for the former. Nana gladly murmurs:

> NANA: Go, Ghashya, old bastard. We made you. We made Kotwal. Raise hell if you wish. But you don't know the ways of this Nana. [...] your manner will be more arrogant than that of the Chitpavan Brahmans. You'll manage the deference nicely. You'll create a court-and a half! No worry about to your account. What'll happen is that our misdeeds will be credited to your account. We do it; our Kotwal pays for it [...] (385).

Having got the powerful post Ghasiram starts misusing his power on the inhabitants of Poona indiscriminately. Desperately, he brings a hell in the city as he had pledged after being badly thrashed by the police and Brahmins:

> I will come back. I'll come back to Poona. I'll show my strength. It will cost you! Your good days are gone! I am a Kanuaj Brahman, but I've become a *Shudra,* a criminal, a useless *animal*. [...] I'll come back like a boar and I'll stay as a devil. I'll make pigs of all of you. I'll make this Poona a kingdom of pigs. [...] (emphasis added-77).

And eventually he terrifies all the citizens to their core. Quite naturally by the order of same Nana he is brutally killed by the people.

If we see the journey of rise and fall of Ghasi, it starts from the ill-treatment and forced profession of dancing so to speak and which caused him to nourish a grievance that he lost his caste, i.e., Brahmanism, by the occupation of dance and singing. Wittingly he succumbed to 'ill-design of power' by bartering Gauri Lalita to Nana, the chief minister of Peshwa. Here power is defined horizontally in terms of individuals against individuals—from Ghasi's humiliation, his assertion to revenge to his eventual execution—played out against a backdrop of political and moral decadence and degeneracy with sexuality impinging on power politics and ideology. The hymns and sacred ceremony create the ironic screen, which penetrated through and through by the most perverse debauchery and violent exercise of power as we see in personality of Nana popularly dubbed as the Indian Machiavelli.

Ghasi's wounded ego that he was no longer a Brahmin but a thief and scoundrel let him to go in the black business of power. In other words the sense of high caste, i.e., Brahmanism was threatened which he was supposed to maintain at any cost. Having been involved in the profession of dancing and singing he lost his own identity, Brahmanism, while the Poona Brahmin were enjoying the high respect and position, no matter visiting the prostitute at the late night and which is beautifully rendered by the *sutradhar* and choral song. Ghasiram was treated as a low caste man by the Poona people and state-power or authority. When the playwright was interviewed regarding the exposition of Brahmanism and its moral corruption he stated:

> It is rather difficult to go back to the point when I thought of writing this play and recollect everything that happened to me on the conscious and subconscious levels. Broadly speaking, I had in mind the emergence, the growth and the inevitable end of the Ghasiram; also those who create, and help Ghasiras to grow; and the irony of stoning to death a person pretending that it the end of

> Ghasirams...The decadence of the class in power (the Brahmans, incidentally, during the period which I had to depict) also was incidental, though not accidental.[4]

This notion of caste has been used more as a literary trope to discuss the profession of acting and singing which was supposed to be derogatory in the early eighteenth century in Indian society. It idea gets revealed when we encounter the *sutradhar*'s dialogue and his deplorable condition amid the so-called Chitpawan Brahmin. There is a perceptible allusion and interconnection of caste system and dramatic activity. Since caste system in Indian society is inbuilt and dance and drama have been associated with lower caste. This notion gets concertized from the analogy of drama/*natya* genesis. As the popular belief ensues dance and pretension area low caste's profession.

From the poststructuralist point of view sexual orientation of a person determines the nature of sexuality: whether s/he is hetero or homosexual or more specifically gay or lesbian. Gender is not only the social and cultural phenomenon but also the very much premise of 'subject' construction. Genderinzation has become a trope to categorize the nature of subjectivity—is the subject famine or masculine. The perspective also gains significance by the fact that Nana's behaviour and relations with man and society are highlighted instead of his stately activity so as to feel the cultural, political and social mores of a historical context. Hence the dominance of Nana and his lust for sex overrides the manliness of subservient man like Ghasiram also. In the course of the action of the play he is perceived to be feminine male. Thus to study sexuality in the article is concerned with the sexual activity of Nana—the historical figure who was a lewd womanizer. And which simultaneously without failing also signifies at large level the India of seventies and its immorality, political corruption and social degeneration at local level in Maharashtra as well. Here the author has used the historical incident as the vantage point or base narrative to make the audience sense that "the past cannot simply be considered to be 'out there', as a thing which is somehow' available', but most be read as an effect of the very narratives that would seek to describe it" (Kaye *Postmodernism and Performance*, 20).

Here history is dramatized for the contemporary social and political causes as Herbert Lindenberger pertinently views, " to the degree that a segment of the past is intended to the link up with the present–day reality of the audience"(Dharwadker, *Theatre of Independence,* 221)

The notion of gender here has been implicated to study the subjugation, exploitation of woman (Gauri) as a girl and later as a forced wife with Nana, who by no means was monogamous without bothering about her desires and likings. The complete denied privilege of Gauri and woman's freedom only as an entertainer for man and not as a social being as we encounter in the sketch of Gulabi legitimizes the interspersed issue of gender and sexuality. Throughout the play, Ghasiram's desire for 'power' and Nana's 'sexuality' are appropriated theatricality. Here Foucault's notion of power is functioning in the text, because his sexuality becomes the locus of state authority and since power can be realized only in relations and hierarchies of the society. The relation between Nana and Ghasi is the relation of power and resistance. As an individual father he could not disobey the order of the state (Nana) and further as an agent of organization or system. Hence power is the decisive factor in the narrative of sexual implication.

Nana's marriage is the structures of non-monogamous relationship with several women including Gauri. This is how his relationship with women or his sexuality explicates the mechanism of power-state by which an individual's life might be affected and transformed. So the fall of Ghasiram in the end as Bandhopadhyay observes, "is often regarded by the people as a political relief; and it is the powers-that-be that take advantage of that delusion to tighten the stranglehold of their power" (Bandhopadhyay, *Collecetd Plays* 591). By this means the sexuality has been in the centre of resistance and vengeance—both. Bartering a daughter for power is the example of vengeance and after being drunk the power victimizing the people is resisting the authority.

After the observation we reach two conclusions which are an integral part of a woman's life: the role of, father the hence patriarchy, and the role of cultural systemcaste system. Since, women as dancers in the public sphere stand against the idealized model of Indian women, they are considered by the Brahminas and Nana as loose women and the objects of sexual entertainment gratification. Father (Ghasiram)'s preoccupation of power at the cost of relations (daughter) explores conflicting archetypal desires of male hegemony and sexuality as the only bond of relation between man and woman, father and daughter. This also reminds us of the bond between Prospero and Miranda but the bond between Ghasi and Gauri is the inversion of the former. In both the instances we have a different sort of hegemony and sexuality in varying degrees. Gauri is unable to resist the coercive norms of her father. The domination of his daughter is the corresponding unrecognized presence or projection of Ghasiram–his own anima if we view it from the psychoanalytical perspective. Power of hegemonic institutions like Nana intends to affect even his most personal experience and social decorum to a daughter. This consciousness towards women in the play is the nodal point for gender reflection in the theatrical space. The issues are gender and caste if we reflect over function at the two theatrical levels: Nana as a stage-manager and Ghasiram as an actor and observer. Ghasiram is functioning as dramatic persona/impersonation of Nana when he wages oppression of common people, especially Brahmins who were also a threat to Nana. Nana takes a back seat to the whole happenings of the play enjoy sexual life with Gauri. This act of defence mechanism towards the wrath of dominant Brahmans has been instrumental in his downfall.

Tendulkar has tried to portray the nature of violence, be it caste-based, gender-based or economic-based because as he says, "As a writer I feel fascinated by the violent exploited-exploiter relationship and obsessively delve deep into it instead of taking a position against it. That takes me to a point while I feel that this relationship is eternal, a fact of life however, cruel, and will never end. Not that I relish this thought while it grips me but I cannot shake it off" (cited by Samik

Bandhopadhyay, Introduction to *Collected Plays in Translations*, xiii-xiv).

Thus the play underpins the plethora of issues like caste, gender, sexuality and their outgoing/overriding trajectory. By not providing any final solution to such issues responsibilities of resolution are handed over to the spectators or readers. He juxtaposes the tender love of father (Ghasi) with crudity and violence of powerful state (Nana), innocence of a daughter (female) with harsh patriarchy of father (male).

Nana's mischievous seductive nature and sex orgies have been inflated with his power and higher caste system of society. His lewdness has been projected in the play a recurrent motif of the play. His sex orgy has been objectified in his behaviour, gestures and speech he uses to capture the prey, Gauri. He is mesmerized with her first appearance:

> NANA: Oh, can we? Can we find her? How beautifully formed! What a lovely figure! Did you see? *Erect! Young*! *Tender!* Ah! Ho ho! We've seen so many handled so many, but none who *she* is (emphasis added, 379).

His lewd sexual urge is objectified in his utterance and also the Machiavellian framework in which the historical figures like Nana works. The very tempo of the deviant time can be sensed when he asserts: "if she is not found, no one will keep his head! 'Our grandeur's gone if she is not had'", to which *Samik* Bandhopadhya rightly remarks, "the brilliant innuendo" (Bandhopadhyay, Note on G.K. 587, *Collected Plays in Translation*-Appendix II). His reckless surrender to sexuality has been intensified by the playwright dramatically and symbolically by letting her off the stage. However, Nine Court Nana is made to encounter Gauri's father Ghasiram Salaldar not by chance or co-incidence but with a far reaching dramatic plan where he "in blind lust grabs the servant (Ghasiram) as the door". This 'dramatic irony' serves the double purpose and proves the turning point not only in the life of Nana and Ghsiram but also in the development of the plot since the entire plot revolves about the contract of Ghasiram with Nana when the latter barters his daughter for the post of the chief of police of Poona and finally his execution by the order of Nana as a reward of action. Nana needs Ghasiram to get Gauri and the latter needs the former equally for sexual fulfilments. Their dependency equation or reciprocity, if we minutely observe, is also the power—game between the two opportunists, permeating the whole play. No matter whosoever is the exploiter or the exploited (as the *sutradhar* reveals to Nana in the play itself, "may be your are, may be you not. In this place it matters not a jot" (387). This equation has been highlighted into dichotomies: state-power (Nana) vs. individual (Ghasiram). The dialogue between Nana and Ghasi bear the impression of a skilled artist of language and connoisseur of word meaning, *bhava*.

> NANA: Bastard!. You have got me in a narrow pass.
>
> GHASIRAM: Yes, the narrow pass of my only daughter (384).

Samik has perceptively stated about the method of delineation of 'macrocosm' into 'macrocosm' of Tendulkar, "Tendulkar has shown religiosity and sexuality combined into the strategies of power. The sexuality and the strategy of deputation have been shown working hand in hand" (*Collected Plays in Translation*—Appendix II, 588).

Tendulkar has jerked the conscience of the whole society by letting power pervade in its crudest form the play. *Ghasiram Kotwal* is a social documentary, a piece of dance-drama meant more for performance than a play text to be read. This is through and through a lyrical drama extending into 'Two Acts'. The play is extensively drawn on the *Tamasha* form of Maharashtra where the *sutradhar* is supposed to have influential and varied roles: as a stage manager, actor, singer, chorus, and commentator over the incidents. Tendulkar has used two forms of song: *lavani* that is love ballad and *abhanga* as religious. He has brilliantly juxtaposed both the songs to highlight the hypocrisy of high caste Brahmins, politicians, and at large, of society. The dialogue of Brahmins and the *sutradhar* is of cenrtral concerns to understand the social deformity like casteism and the drama profession as associated with the low caste or untouchable.

Through the skilled use of song form Tendulkar has tried to explore not only the psyche or Nana's state of mind but also the degeneration of whole religiosity that society was under grip. As we see in the prayer of Ganpati Haridas singing devotional songs Nana is lost in *lavani* and ogles at Gulabi. Therefore, Nana is portrayed with subtle humour and irony as the young Krishna playing flute in the dance of Gulabi as Krishna would play it among the *gopis* (cowherd). This mixture of songs and dance makes the sense of theatrical reality very obvious. This is how he has created a theatre space which automatically encourages spontaneous interaction between audience members and actors. To break any kind of realistic boundary at the theatrical levels as such the author successfully employed the improvisation technique in the method of acting. When the seven men including the *sutradhar* come in the form of actors and later on characters and in between as a human curtain before the eyes of the audience the notion of theatre as community and public space gets authenticated.

The play opens with twelve dancing men coming on stage and later on they are joined by Ganapati, Saraswati and Lakshmi. This celebratory beginning ends with the chanting of God's mantra. Six people from various professions come before the *sutradhar* and the remaining from a pilgrimage from Shringeri, Tangore, Rameshwarm, Kumbakonam, Banaras and Poona respectively. Thus the story begins from the dialogue between the *sutradhar* and a Brahmin where, by the exquisite repartee of the *sutradhar,* we come to know about the prostitution of the state:

> SUTRADHAR: The Brahmins go to Bavannakhani. And the Brahmins wives stay at home. They stay at home. They wait. They cannot sleep. Do you know what's happening in Bavannakhani in the house of Gulabi, Gulabi the courtesan? (367).

This aphoristic use of language as we see in the preceding dialogue by Tendulkar is also part of his broader aim of 'decolonization of canon' initiative along with his contemporary counterparts. Such experimentative use of language with coinages and aphorism has been the benchmark of not only Tendulkar but also of all other post-independence modern, theatre vanguards like Rakesh or Girish Karnad among others to evolve an Indian theatre idiom. This type of use of language sometime poetic and metaphorical, and sometimes prosaic, is the modern innovation and source of richness of the text. A similar use of language pregnant with meanings, for instance, can be seen in Karnad's *Hayavadana* when both Devadatta and Kapila have got their heads exchanged by the mishap of Padmini. They expressed their gratitude, as thus:

> KAPILA: We are now blood relation! Body relations! (Laughing.) What a gift!
>
> DEVDATTA: Forfive you? We must thank you...
>
> KAPILA: *We'll never be able to thank you-enough...*" (*Hayavadana,* 144 emphasis added).

Coming back again to the play, similar kind of verbal experimentation we get in the choruc's salutation of Nana. "There is only one Nana, the rest is na-na-na-na" (380). In Hindi language if Nana is dissected, it would be na+ na= nothing. 'Na' stands for 'No', in English. Thus no one, only Nana, can exist.

Tendulkar as an astute artist portrays the most debauchery and sexuality of Nana with an underlining current of devotional songs which becomes more dramatic and gives an extra edge to the notion of sexuality. This love-making undercuts the sincerity of divine play of Krishna with the cowherds. In the significant presentation where he is presented playing the flute deconstructs his personality as a sincere statesmanship. The personality of Nana is highlighted as the decline point of moral deformity of the society. The role of Gauri as a victim of her father who barters her for his personal gains is another significant gesture to understand the gender subjugation under the patriarchal system. How dance and drama are associated with the caste system and how it is accredited as a lower caste activity get concretized in the play itself. This implication of 'theatre as the low caste activity' can also be found in Girish Karnad's most ambitious mythical play *The Fire and the Rain* where a Brahmin man Arvasu loses his caste when he decides to take the profession of dance and drama. Thus *Ghasiram Kotwal* is a brilliant musing over the issues of caste, gender and sexuality in the most gripping manner.

References

1. The time of Manu, a Brahmin author who wrote *Manusmriti* stipulating that *shudra* or low caste men are not qualified for holy texts and scripture.
2. The stand points of the both ideologues are in the sharp opposite line. Gandhi was in the favour of *Varna Ashram* while Ambedker was a hard core critic of the system. For details see "Ambedker vs. Ghandhi II—Religious Break", *The Dalit Movement in India: Local Practices, Global Connection.* 66-69. By Eva-Maria Hardtmann. Oxford University Press, 2009.
3. Again who was an enlightened Brahmin, in fact a Brahmin sage—priest-writer-actor generally held to be the initiator of drama or *natya* by the divine inspiration in India? But unlike the former, Bharata preferred the profession of acting and dance, and hence he migrated from northern part of India to south to flourish the tradition of drama. In another instance it is pointed out that instead of lord Brahma he himself created 'Natyashastra' (*NS)* and accredited it as the fifth Veda, and it is he who implicates *NS* with divine origin though it is untenable.
4. See pp. 58-87 'Appendix II: Note on Ghasiram', Samik Bandhopandhyay, *Collected Plays in Translations*, 2003.

Works Cited

Babu, Munchi Sarat. *Indian Drama Today: A Study in the theme of Cultural Deformity.* New Delhi: Prestige, 1997.

Dharwadker, Aparna Bhargava. *Theatres of Independence: Drama, Theory, and Urban Performances in India since 1947*. New Delhi: OUP, 2006. India Paperback.

Jagger, Gill. Judith Butler: *Sexual Politics, Social Change and the Power of the Performance*. London & NY: Routledge, 2008.

Tendulkar, Vijay. *Ghasiram Kotwal: Collecetd Plays in Translations*.Ed, Samik Bandhopadhyay New Delhi: OUP, 2004.

Grainger, Roger. *Theatre and the Relationships in Shakespeare's Later Plays*. Bern: Petre Lang, 2008.

Richardson, Diane. "Patterned Fluidities: (Re) Imagining the Relationship between Gender and sexuality". *Sociology,* 41.3(2007): 457-474 *SAGE. Web.* 22 Sep, 2010. <http://soc.sagepub.com/content/41/3/457>

14

Tendulkar's *The Vultures*: Body and Soul

—Shailaja B. Wadikar

Spiritual Deformity

Human civilization has witnessed all through its history a kind of schism between body and soul, leading to spiritual malady and disease. The quest for power and position renders people blind and cripples their souls. This leads to spiritual deformity, which manifests itself in human violence and destructiveness. Most of Tendulkar's plays deal with the themes related to love, sex, and violence. They have become rather noticeable in some glaring light ever since the presentation of *The Vultures*. The play projects violence in human nature through the depiction of an upper middle-class family. Hari Pitale, the father of the two sons Ramakant and Umakant and a daughter Manik, prospers in his business by cheating his brother. The two sons and the daughter inherit his treacherous ways. Ultimately, "they form a family of vultures." [1]

Not satisfied with the magnitude of their father's property, Ramakant and Umakant decide to blackmail the Raja of Hondur, their sister's lover. However, they cannot carry out their plan due to the Raja's death. In anger and frustration, they cause abortion of their sister's baby.

Constant drinking of liquor affects Ramakant's health adversely and he grows impotent. So, his wife Rama turns to Rajaninath, the illegitimate son of Hari, Pitale for emotional support. The relationship results in her wilful conception or pregnancy. Anyhow, she gets her urge for motherhood fulfilled. However, Manik seeks her revenge on her brothers by manoeuvring Rama's abortion.

Feeling insecure, Hari Pitale turns to Rajaninath for protection. The father tells the illegitimate son that he has a mind to change his will, but Rajaninath has no attraction for any worldly possessions. It is these material considerations that turn the Pitales into loveless vultures. Without showing compassion, he asks his father to leave his garage.

The play is realistic not only in the portrayal of characters and their actions but in the language and setting also. The playwright, here, depicts educated, modern generation. But the language used by them is full of abusive terms such as bastard, swine, lecher, etc. All the actions take place in a dim light quite away from the outer world of cultured, refined people. Due to the presence of this dim light, the play appears to present a detective story. The picture of a huge tree having curved, crooked, bare branches, and a big hollow, in the background symbolizes the living place of the characters is not a home but a hollow of wild vultures as "home is built by hearts." The dark green shade cast on Rama's *tulsi vrindavan* indicates how the virtuous suffer in the company of vulture-like people. A fierce wind, and a shrill screeching of vultures incline the audience to perceive the play as being full of violence and sensation. Even the name of the family, viz., "Pitale", suggests that the family members are rather brazen, shameless, and insolent.

However, Tendulkar projects something more than wickedness and sensuality. If the world of Ramakant, Umakant, Manik, and Papa represents evil aspects inherent in human nature, the world of Rama and Rajaninath represents its tender aspects. Although Rama's relationship with Rajaninath is illicit one, one should not ignore the fact that it is the only human and genuine one. The poems of Rajaninath help one realize the past history and the present state of the Pitales. Similarly, they indirectly express the playwright's compassion for the victims of viciousness.

Tendulkar succeeds here in depicting the tragedy of Rama and Rajaninath in naturalistic terms. Similarly, by pitting these two worlds of tenderness and violence against each other, he sets a new trend of avant-garde movement—the "Theatre of Cruelty" in Marathi. Manchi Sarat Babu rightly observes:

> The spiritual deformity facilitates ruthless exploitation and oppression and destroys human relations even within the family.[2]

Metaphor of Violence

The play *The Vultures,* published in 1971, stands apart from the other plays of Tendulkar in that it is a play, which displays the unmitigated violence arising from selfishness, greed and sinfulness. On its first production on the stage, there was a great storm in the society around. The conservative Maharashtrian people were stunned to observe the vulgar reality of their lives presented through the sexual relations and the scenes of violence in the play. It is for this reason that Girish Karnad says: "The staging of *Gidhade* could be compared with the blasting of bomb."[3] The play was bitterly criticized by the theatre-going public. The censor-board, too, felt that it was obscene and suspended its public performance for the time being.

The Theme of Love, Sex and Violence

The play is a ruthless dissection of human nature as it depicts violence, avarice, selfishness, sensuality, and sheer wickedness inherent in man's life. The title of the play *The Vultures* itself indicates the unpleasant subject-matter of the play. The characters belong to the middle-class family. Ramakant's and Umakant's greed and viciousness, their father's degenerate nature, and their sister Manik's sensuality throw a glare of light on the baser aspects of human nature. In Arundhati Banerjee's view:

> The beating up of the father by his own sons, the two brother's forcible abortion of their sister's child, the mutual hatred among the members of family underline the fundamental evil inherent in human nature.[4]

The play deals with contrasting situations. The playwright, here, explores two worlds: (i) a stormy, sentimental world that is characterized by greed, wickedness, sensuality, and (ii) a fragile, sensitive world that is characterized by love, tenderness, and generosity. Ramakant, Umakant, Manik, and their father represent wickedness, whereas Rama and Rajaninath represent love and tenderness. Through the character of Rama, the playwright creates a naturally kind, tender-hearted and good-natured individual. Helpless and submissive, she is a birdie among the vultures. Ramakant, who is an extreme addict to liquor, fails in his duty as a husband. Therefore, Rama, his wife, turns to Rajaninath and conceives a babe by him. However, Manik, her sister-in-law, successfully tries to abort it as a part of her revenge on her brothers. Rama, once again, remains as calm and patient as a stone "Empty of pain / And empty of desires." (206)

Rama's illicit relationship with her half-brother-in-law Rajaninath raises the question of morality as she is portrayed as an embodiment of an ideal Indian woman who is religious, virtuous, hardworking and impressive. However, of all the relationships in the play, this seems to be the only one which, though illicit, is, perhaps the most human. The sexual aspect is so used as to throw light on their love-relationship, which according to Arundhati Banerjee, "is the only redeeming feature in the morbid and claustrophobic atmosphere of the family."[5]

Rajaninath, the illegitimate son of the family, is a poet. His role is reminiscent of the role of the *sutradhara* or the Greek chorus. His poems throw light on the past history and present situation of Pitale family. He recites three poems in the course of action, the one at the beginning of the play, the other at the end of the first act, and the third at the end of the play. The compassion of the playwright for the victims of viciousness is manifest in these poems.

The play is extremely morbid not only in the portrayal of its characters and their actions but in the setting and language also. The scenes of violence, the open exhibition of sexual relations, and the abusive language shock the sensibility of the conventional audience. Never has such violence been depicted nor experienced before in the Indian theatre. It has stunned the audience and made them introspective.

The language, the setting, and the stage directions make the violence vivid and the play alive. In the background, there are a huge tree having curved, crooked branches and a big hollow, a drawing room consisting of old, unpolished, worn-out furniture, a small country-yard having a *tulsi-vrindavan* and an old garage. When the play opens, there is a constant sound like wind howling over a plain and a shrill screaming of vultures for some time. When the curtain is raised, the lights on the garage and the *tulsi-vrindavan* are green and those on the bedroom and drawing room are dirty gray, almost black.

The language used is coarse and roughshod. There ensued a long war with the censor-board that asked to omit one hundred and fifty words. All the characters except Rama and Rajaninath are foul-mouthed. However, as pointed out by Dr. Shriram Lagu, "It is the language of the vultures, not of civilized, cultured people. They have to speak only in such abusive language."[6] He further says:

> While reading the play, the abusive terms such as "bastard", "swine", "ruffian", "wolves", "bullies", "lecher", "bugger", etc., appear foul and filthy but, in the course of dialogue, they fit in like punctuation marks! The omission of these roughshod terms will turn the play of vultures into the play of sparrows.[7]

The movements and mannerisms are in harmony with the subject-matter. The characters' way of speaking, their modes of behaviour, their habits of scratching bodies, of thoughtless spitting, of eating food rapidly, and their peculiar dresses indicate their selfish, sensual, and bar baric ways. The lighting technique also helps to make the characters appear violent and blood-thirsty from the play's beginning to its end.

V.A. Dahake, an eminent critic, examines the play *The Vultures* on this assumption: "The characters therein belong to the middle-class society, but their actions are suitable for the upper or higher class people."[8] However, in this play, Tendulkar exposes the vulture-like tendencies that are common not only among the lower or middle-class people but among the upper-class people also. Actually, the world projected here is not one of white-collar people but of high-class, affluent industrialists.

According to Dr. Lagu, the director-actor of the play, "The characters in the play are not wicked by birth. They are victims of cultural degradation of the so-called civilized society."[9] By depicting the tragedy of Rama and Rajaninath, Tendulkar, like Artaud, succeeds in presenting the Theatre of Cruelty. In Artaud's opinion, "The Theatre of Cruelty has been created in order to restore to the theatre a passionate and convulsive conception of life and it is in this sense of violent rigour and extreme condensation of scenic elements that the cruelty on which it is based must be understood."[10] Therefore, this pitting of the two worlds of violence and tenderness against each other is the essence of the play. The tragedy also indicates, likewise the rule of naturalism stated by Darwin in his *Origin of the Species*, that the weaklings are ruthlessly crushed by the strong and the mighty in the contemporary society. Physical, moral, and spiritual powers are needed for the preservation of good and for the extermination of evil. Otherwise, the world would be the most suitable abode for vultures only to live in.

In an interview, referred to by Arundhati Banerjee, Tendulkar says:

> *Gidhade* was born out of personal crisis in his life. He wrote it just in four days. He himself was shocked that he could give expression to so much violence. It was a kind of cathartic process. Soon after writing *Gidhade,* he commented that he did not think that he could write such a play, wrought (sic. fraught) with sex and violence, again. But he did. Just sixteen months later, he wrote *Sakharam Binder.* It evoked more resistance from the censor board than *Gidhade* had.[11]

References

1. Manchi Sarat Babu, *Indian Drama Today*, Prestige Books, New Delhi, 1997, p.139.
2. Ibid., p.150.
3. Arundhati Banerjee, Introduction, *Five Plays of Vijay Tendulkar*, OUP, Bombay, 1992, p.xii.
4. Ibid.
5. Ibid., p.xiii.

6. Dr. Shriram Lagu, "*Gidhade*, Censorship ani Mee", in Narendra Dabholkar (ed.), *Sadhana: Diwali Special,* Pune, 2001, p.55. The extract is translated into English by the research worker herself.
7. Ibid., pp.55,57.
8. Vasat Dahake, "Krauryanatya ani *Gidhade*", *Satyakatha*, Sept.,1995, p.12-13. The extract is translated into English by the research worker herself.
9. Dr. Shriram Lagu "*Gidhade*, Censorship ani Mee", in Narendra Dabholkar (ed.), *Sadhana : Diwali Special,* Pune, 2001, p.58. The extract is a translation in English by the research worker herself.
10. Eric Beautely, (ed.), "The Theory of the Modern Stage", Penguin, London, 1983, p. 66. Quoted in Asha S. Kanwar, *Ghashiram Kotwal : A Study Guide,* IGNOU, New Delhi, 1993, p.50.
11. Arundhati Banerjee, op. cit., p.xv.

15

Gender in Question: Vijay Tendulkar's *Silence! The Court is in Session*

—Vishwanath Bite

Vijay Tendulkar is one of the outstanding Indian playwrights. He has mastered different genres of literature like Essays, Short Stories, Criticism, Screenplay Writing and Drama. He is known for his plays, *Shantata! Court Chaule Ahe* (1967), *Ghâshirâm Kotwâl* (1972), and *Sakhârâm Binder* (1972). He has received awards including the Padma Bhushan, Sangeet Natak Akademi Award, Filmfare Award, Saraswati Samman, Kalidas Samman and Maharashtra Gaurav Puraskar. He is ranked with great playwrights like Badal Sarcar, Girish Karnad and Mohan Rakesh. In the preface to his collection of *Six One Act Plays Raatra (night)*, he has mentioned:

> Recently, my name has been repeatedly counted amongst the followers of the new drama sect. I have felt no great urge thus, far to determine which sect I belong to, nor do I expect to feel the need to do so in the future. I have written on any theme that has occupied my mind over time, stubbornly insisting that I write on in which ever form I thought best...It is wrong to support that everything different from the establishment is bad, childish and irrelevant. It is equally wrong to think that only which is different is good, true or valuable. Personally, despite being counted amongst the new dramatist, I love to lose myself in the best of Deval, Gadkari, Khadikar and Warerkar...
>
> (Tendulkar 197)

Vijay Tendulkar has powerfully articulated the socio-political situations in his plays. He has expressed it by saying:

"As an Individual or rather as a social being, I feel deeply involved in the existing state of my society (because I am affected by it though not immediately in some cases or not as much as some others are) and in my way brood over it. Once in a way I even do something to relieve myself of the tension and anxiety and agitation produced by this brooding. I participated in a protest meeting or dharma or a fast or morcha or a satyagragh I align myself with some civil liberty organization...

"As a writer, I find myself persistently inquisitive, non conformist, ruthless, cold and brutal as compared to the other committed and human .....

"As a social being, I am against all exploitation and I passionately feel that all exploitation must end...

"As a writer, I feel fascinated by the violent exploiter and exploited relationship and obsessively delve deep into it instead of taking a position against it. That takes me to a point where I feel that the relationship is external fact of life however cruel, will never end. Not that, I relish this thought while it grips me but I cannot shake it off". (Tendulkar 92)

In *Silence! The Court is in Session*, Tendulkar has depicted the difficulty of a young woman, who is a victim of the male dominated society. He has criticized the follies prevailing in the society. The original name of the drama in Marathi is *Shatata! Court Chaule Ahe* (1967). It was translated in English by Priya Adulkar. The play carries all the vitalities of contemporary life. It focuses on the human mind and detects the ugliness in it. All the plays of Tendulkar are the result of his surveillance of the life, society and different incidents of his own life. He has noted in an interview that:

> I personally don't bother about people who haven't seen life. They close their eyes at the sight of suffering as if it doesn't exist. The fact is that life is dark and cruel, its just that you don't care for the truth. You don't want to see it because it might make you uncomfortable. If escapism is

> your way of living then you will fail to see the truth. I have not written about hypothetical pain or created an imaginary world of sorrow. I am from a middle class family and I have seen the brutal ways of life by keeping my eyes open. My work has come from within ... an outcome of my observation of the world in which I live. If they want to entertain and make merry, fine go ahead, but I can't do it, I have to speak the truth.

Miss Leela Benare is presented as an extraordinary and crucial character in the play. She is a young middle class woman of 34 years who is working as a teacher to earn her livelihood. She was loved and appreciated by her students in the school. She was punctual in coming to the school every morning, carrying out her assignments and her courses. She says to Samant:

> I never had been behind with my lesson! Exercises corrected on time too, not a bit of room for disapproval, I don't give an inch of it to anyone!
>
> (*Silence*... 4)

She admits to Samant, a local villager who escorts the amateur dramatic troupe members to the village hall, that little children are much better than the adults. She says:

> They don't have the blind pride of thinking they know everything. There is no nonsense stuffed in their heads. They don't scratch you till you bleed, then run away like cowards.
>
> (*Silence*...4)

She is a member of an Amateur Theater group. They arrive in a village to perform an awareness raising play on the social and current issues. She is preparing to present a play titled 'Mock Trial of Lyndon B. Johnson' at Suburban Village. She is accompanied by Samant and was enjoying his company. She admits to him that: "I felt even more wonderful coming here with you. I am so glad the others fell behind" (*Silence*... 1). She introduces all her co—stars to Samant in their absence. She sarcastically calls Mr. Kashikar as 'Mr. Prime Objective' and

Mrs. Kashikar as 'Mrs. Hands that Rocks the cradle' She further says that the "Hands that Rocks the cradle has no cradle to rock" (Silence...2). Mr. and Mrs. Kashikar are childless and have adopted Balu. According to Benare, they have made him a slave:

> Mr. Kashikar and the hands that Rocks the cradle, in order that nothing should happen to either of them in their bare house and that they shouldn't die of boredom, gave shelter to a young boy. They educated him—made a slave out of him
>
> (*Silence*... 6)

She sarcastically introduce Sukhatme, one of her co-stars as:

> An expert on the law. He's such an authority on the subject; even a desperate client won't go any where near him! He just sits alone in the barristers' room at a court, swatting flies with legal precedents!
>
> (*Silence* ...6)

According to Ms. Benare, Ponkshe is 'Hmmm.... Scientist, Inter failed' (*Silence*... 6). She calls Prof. Damle as:

> And we have an intellectual too. That means someone who prides himself on his books learning. But when there is a real life problem, away he runs, hides his head. He's not here today. Won't be coming either. He won't dare.
>
> (*Silence*...6-7)

Benare want to live a free life, free from the patriarchal dominance and the conservative norms of the society. She displays self-determination, self-assertiveness and cynicism but is also receptive to the conventional norms of integrity. Tendulkar has tried to initiate the new form by commenting on the mendacity of the social and ethical standards existing in the society. This conversation between Benare and Samant throws light on the character of Benare.

> *Benare*: I am the soul of seriousness: But I don't see why one should go around all the time with the long face... we

> should laugh, we should play, we should sing! If we can and if they will let us, we should dance too! Should not have any false modesty or dignity or care for anyone! I mean it. When your life is over, do you think anyone will give a bit of theirs? What do you say, Samant? Do you think they will?
>
> *Samant*: You are quite right. The great sage Tukaram said... at least I think it was him...
>
> *Benare*: Forget about the sage Tukaram. I say it—I, Leela Benare, a living woman, I say it from my own experience. Life is not meant for anyone else. It's your own life. It must be. It is a very very important thing. Every moment, every bit of it is precious...
>
> (*Silence*...8)

The actual play is scheduled to be staged in the night. Characters want to rehearse the drama, a mock trial and also find opportunity to dig up Leela's past life. Balu Rokde, Ponkshe, Karik and Samant appear as witnesses for the trial against Benare. Samant is forced to accept and act as the fourth witness in the play on behalf of Prof. Damle. Sukhatme suggests the theater artists make Ms. Benare as the accused in the mock trial. She has to perform the role of a woman who is indicted for infanticide. Mr. Kashikar plays the role of the judge. Leela is accused by the Judge of the 'Mock Law Court' as:

> Prisoner Miss Benare under section No. 302 of the Indian Penal Code, you are accused of the crime of Infanticide (foeticide). Are you guilty or not guilty of a fore mentioned crime...?
>
> (*Silence*...25)

Benare replies:

> I don't like your word at all! Infanticide...Infanticide! Why don't you accuse me instead of snatching public property...? I plead not guilty. I could not kill even a cockroach. I am scared to do it. How could I kill a new born child...?
>
> (*Silence*...29-30)

Mr. Kashikar quotes a Sanskrit proverb: "Mother and the Motherland both are even higher than heaven"(*Silence*...30). Sukhatme is playing the role of the Counsel of Defence and the Counsel for the Crown. He adds:

> Considering this what would we respectable citizen say if any woman were to take the life of the delicate bundle of joy she has borne, we would say, there could be no baser or more devilish thing on the earth. I intend to establish by means of evidence that the prisoner has done this same vile deed.
>
> (*Silence*...31)

Benare is smart, educated and good looking but is unmarried. About this, Mrs. Kashikar states:

> Anyone who really wants to can get married in a flash... when you get everything without marrying....they just want comfort. They could not care about responsibilities. In my time even if a girl was snub nosed, sallow hunchbacked or anything whatever, she could still get married. It's the sly new fashion of women earning that makes everything go wrong. That's how promiscuity has spread through our society... look how loudly she laughs, how she sings, dances, cracks jokes...and wandering alone with how many men, day in and day out.
>
> (*Silence*... 54)

Mrs. Kashikar further adds with firm assurance that all the unmarried girls are, "a sinful canker on the body of society, that's my honest opinion of these grown up married girls" (*Silence*...54). The play is a satire on the hypocrisy of the middle class society. The playwright exposes:

> ...their characters, dialogues, gestures and even mannerisms reflect their petty circumscribed existence fraught with frustration and repressed desire that find expression in their malicious and spiteful attitude towards their fellow being. (Preface VIII)

Kashikar, Sukhatme and others form a group to torture Leela at the mock trail. She is charged as a licentious woman who is always ready to sell her body. She is even charged with having an illicit relationship with her maternal uncle and later with Prof. Damle. Ms. Benare was in love with her maternal uncle at the age of fourteen but it was a failure due to the cultural bounding and limitations. Benare explaines the way in which she was abused by her own maternal uncle at the age of just fourteen. She says:

> Why, I was hardly fourteen! I didn't even know what sin was, I didn't! I insisted on marriage. So I could live my beautiful lovely dreams openly... But all of them-my mother too—were against it, and my brave man turned trail and ran. (Silence 74) She failed in the love affair with her maternal uncle. He exploited her at such a tender age to satisfy his hunger for bodily pleasure. She uttered while remembering him that: "Life is a poisonous snake that bites itself. Life is a betrayal, life is a fraud. Life is a drug. Life is drudgery... Life is a dreadful thing...
>
> (*Silence*...75-75)

The character of Ms. Benare reminds us of Ammu, the protagonist in *The God of Small Things* by Arundhati Roy. She is also identical to various female characters presented by Shashi Deshpande and Anita Desai in their books. They have also exposed the naked realities of women suffering at the hands of the male-dominated society. Ms. Benare studies and establishes herself as a teacher. She falls in love with Prof. Damle as a young woman in spite of her previous failure in a love with her maternal uncle. Prof. Damle is a married man who also wants to satisfy his bodily thirst. She is pregnant without marriage and this is the reason that she is discharged from her school. The chairman of the education society, Mr. Nana Saheb Shinde, also fails to drop an inquiry against her. According to Ms. Benare:

> Again I fell in love. As a grown woman. I throw all my heart into it. I thought, this will be different. This love is intelligent. It is love for an unusual intellect. It is not love at all-its worship! But it was the same mistake. I offered up my body on the altar of my worship. And my intellectual god took the offering and went his way He

> didn't want my mind, or my devotion—he didn't care about them! He was not a god. He was a man for him everything was the body, for the body? That is all.
>
> (*Silence* 73-74)

She pleads with Rokde and Ponkshe to marry her but her proposal is rejected by them. Vijay Tendulkar has created a satire on the unjust male-dominated society and on the working of the court. Mr. Kashikar, the judge, should be free from prejudice but he is just the opposite. He quotes the proverb: "Janani Janama bhumischcha Svargadapi Gariyasi" (*Silence*...30). This is a mockery on the judge who is talking about motherhood and innocence, and who himself does not follow what he says. The court allows Prof. Damle to enjoy his married life and does not accuse him of exploiting and abusing the life of a woman. The irony of the mock trial is that Benare is accused in the court without the presence of Prof. Damle. This depicts the condemnation on the Indian society and the prejudices it carries against women. According to Veena Dass, in her *Women Characters in the Plays of Tendulkar*:

> It is important here to note that theses charges became verbalized only in the absence of Prof. Damle. If he were present, the typical backbiting attitude of the self righteous Indian male would not have helped reveal the truth. Miss Benare was thrown into the dock and there she remained trying to joke herself out of it, but trapped too murderously by the male vultures around her. Witness after witness, charges upon charges we heaped upon her. The defense lawyer was so frightened that he only asked for a little mercy on her behalf. Miss Benare who is on the offensive at the beginning found herself trapped at the close of the play.
>
> (*Dass* 10)

All the characters drawn by Tendulkar except Ms. Benare represents the male-dominated Indian society. According to C.Coelho: "In his portrayal of human relations and tensions, Tendulkar depicts the violent tendency of egoistical man and equally self-centered society" (Coelho 34). Ms. Benare has been loyal to her profession. She declares in the final act that she has always kept her professional life away from her personal life. She has justified her role of being a teacher. She stated:

> I just put my whole life into working with the children... I loved it, I taught them well... Emotion is something people talk about with sentiment. It was obvious to me. I was living through it. It was burning through me. But do you know? I did not teach any of this to those tender; young souls. I swallowed the poison, but did not let the drop of it touch them. I taught them beauty. I taught them purity. I cried inside and made them laugh. I was cracking up with despair and I taught them hope.
>
> (*Silence*...75-76)

The Judge, Mr. Kashikar, orders Ms. Benare to abort her child. According to him, to have the child without marriage is against the tradition of Indian culture. The judgment passed to her seems to be absurd. Mr. Kashikar says:

> The crimes you have committed are the most terrible. The mortality which you have shown forgiveness for them...through your conduct was the mortality you were planning to impart to the youth of tomorrow. It must be said that the school officials have done a work of merit in deciding to remove you from the job...There is no forgiveness... No memento of your sin should remain for the future generation. Therefore the court hereby sentences that you shall live. But the child in your womb shall be destroyed...
>
> (*Silence*... 67-68)

She screams to this: "No! No! No! I won't let you do it. I won't let it happen, I won't let it happen" (*Silence*... 76). The character of Ms. Benare also reminds us of Ibsen's heroine Nora in *The Doll House*. Nora abandons her children and her husband due to the annoyance and dominance created by her husband. She questions the male-dominated society and finds her escape. According to Arundhati Banerjee: "Benares's monologue is reminiscent of Nora's declaration of Independence" (Banerjee 40). Mrs. Kashikar does not help the helpless Ms. Benare in the court in spite of being a woman. She is against Ms. Benare because she is a conventional Indian housewife who has accepted all the norms framed by the society. She accepts the role of a woman as a beautiful flower to be decorated in a flowerpot with no existence of her own. Benare, on the other hand, is a progressive contemporary woman. She is psychologically tortured but is still striving to search for her existence. According to P. Obula Reddy and P. Pramila Devi:

> Benare, the principal character in the play is as sprightly, rebellious and assertive as the heroine of Shakespeare romantic comedies... Of course, Benare is a lovely spark from the thunder bolt of Tendulkar. She is a new woman pleading for freedom from the social norms...
>
> (*Reddy and Devi* 36)

Ms. Benare is a victim of male chauvinism, used simply to gratify quench bodily thirst and deserted at the end to her own destiny. Man has all the rights to be sinful in society. He can be harsh, notorious and innocent too. All the rights are reserved specially for him. On the other hand, a woman must be deserted, abandoned, ignored, thrown away and should be tainted for her sins. There is no escape for her in our society. She must be brutally destroyed for her actions both physically and mentally. The character of Mr. and Mrs. Kashikar, Ponkshe, Rokde, Sukhatme represents hypocrisy and inferiority complex. One can clearly notice a conflict raised by Tendulkar between the real self and the performed self in the play. Tendulkar digs the inner self of all the characters in the plays, how they present themselves and what they actually are. He has identified the role of society in shaping and determining their identities. In an interview, Tendulkar divulged: "This play is a caustic satire on the social as well as legal justice." (Tendulkar 40)

Benare represents all the women in India who are suppressed, oppressed and are marginalized. She breaks down during the mock trail because the story of the character in the play she is performing at the mock trail is identical to her own. The last speech of Ms. Benare is skilfully constructed by Tendulkar. It echoes the irony, sorrow and lampoon present in Indian society. She says:

> But I was ignorant Instead; I threw myself off a parapet of our house-to embrace death. But I didn't die. My body didn't die. I felt as if feelings were dead-but they had not died either then....
>
> (*Silence*... 74)

Tendulkar has left the play open without suggesting any solution to the problem of Ms. Benare. He has highlighted critical problems like the squalor of Indian Judiciary system, male dominance in the society and the ostentatious institutional social organizations. The play is derision on the middle class probity, where people have all the rights to pass judgments and silence is the only alternative left for the victim. The words of Candy Elizabeth quoted in *The Introduction of Feminism in Our Times* can be the best to conclude. According to her: "Thus far women have been mere echoes of men. Our laws and constitution, our creeds and codes and customs of social life are all of masculine origin. The true woman is yet a dream for future..." (Candy XIV-V)

Works Cited

Candy, Elizabeth. (1994) Quoted in Introduction of *Feminism in our Times*, Vintage Books: New York, pp. XIV-V

Dass, Veena Noble. (1994) 'Women Characters in the plays of Tendulkar', *New Directions in Indian Drama*, ed. Sudhakar Pandey and Freya Barya. Prestige Books: New Delhi, pp. 10.

R.K.Dhawan Ed., *Indian Literature Today*. (1994) Vol. I, New Delhi: Prestige Books, pp. 34-42

http://passionforcinema.com/a-conversation-with-sir-vijay-tendulkar/

Tendulkar, Vijay. (1992) *Silence! The Court is in Session*, Oxford University Press: New Delhi.

____ . (1974) *Silence! The Court is in Session* translated by Priya Adarkar, *Five Plays*, Oxford University Press: New Delhi, p. VII

____ . (1994) Preface to *Raatra Ani Itar Ekankika*. 2nd. Ed. Continental Publication: Pune. p 197.

____ . *A Testament' in Indian Literature*. No. 147, Jan-Feb, p.92

16

Representation of Women Characters in Post-Independence Indian English Drama

—Vikas Raval

The image and the role of the woman have been observed through the centuries and studied in various ways, and the acquired knowledge has been recorded in literature, works of art, religious texts, mythology and codes of social behaviour. As Junaita William rightly says in *Psychology of Women: Behavior in a Social Context:* "Mostly understandings of women have taken the form of strongly held beliefs which served to validate and to order experience, or have emanated from such authoritative sources, that few would questions them" (1). Man has always felt the need to explain woman, and to accommodate her within his rational system. Woman has been worshipped as a goddess, as Mother Nature as well as condemned as a witch and a seductress. She has rarely been perceived simply as a human being.

The present paper is an attempt to analyze the delineation of the Indian women characters in the selected plays of major dramatists of the post-independence period of Indian English drama. Identified with respect to the evolution of the position of women in India, Parth N. Mukherji points this out:

> In the sphere of structural elaboration, sex differentiation gradually but inevitably evolved in a manner such that societal roles which were linked with production, governance and ecclesiastics, became more or less, the exclusive domains of the male sex. Concurrently, the

> biological capacity of the female to reproduce the human species and ensure its survival, led to her being assigned roles which progressively tied her down to the home and withdrew her from the wider economic, political and religious arenas of social participation. Paralleling these two processes, these took place the progressive elaboration of an ideology which rationalized this shift from differentiation to discrimination and institutionalized it by means of customs, rituals and religious or social prescriptions (40)

Thus, there was a dichotomization that propelled man into the outside world, and confined woman inside the home, and positioned them on either side of an ever-widening gulf. Prominent factors which aided this dichotomization were socialization, the influence of religion and mythology, and representation of women in literature. Women appear in the stories of men, but only in roles defined by men. It is men who create polar image like virgin and whore, saint and witch, good mother and wicked stepmother. These binary concepts fit conveniently into the schema of a phallocratic society.

Change began to appear in Indian society in the mid-twentieth century. The changes in the life and position of women and in the attitude towards them were due to many factors. Some of them are the reformist movements of the time in India, the spread of education, participation in the freedom struggle, the influence of women's movements abroad and the movements for the liberation of women in India.

The freedom struggle gave Indian women a golden opportunity to come out of the four walls of the home and become participants in bigger issues. Hundreds of women took part in the picketing of liquor shops, in demonstrations and marches. They courted arrest and faced lathi charges and bullets. A series of peasant and tribal rebellions spread through India then. Women were involved in these. Many of Mahasweta Devi's stories, novels and plays deal with these movements. In several villages, when the men were arrested or had to go underground, women moved into positions of leadership and continued the fight. In the peasant movements of Telangana nad Tebhaga, women were involved in large numbers and as key figures. The participation of women in the Congress-led freedom movement was remarkable. They picked shops selling foreign goods and burned foreign cloth in bonfires.

After independence, the position of women has greatly improved. The Constitution of India states that no citizen shall, on the ground of sex, be ineligible for any employment or office under the state. One of the most striking contrasts in modern Indian history is the one between the position of the upper caste Indian women in the mid-nineteenth century—subservient, uneducated, secluded—and their position in the mid-nineteenth century-articulate, educated and active in professions and public life. (Everett 1)

Although this observation is only partially true, some changes can be seen in the lives of the middle class women of Indian society. This change is reflected in the Indian drama of the fifties and sixties. Many plays depict women who are trying to deconstruct the myth of male sovereignity; who are trying to come out of the margins and to occupy subject positions. A more realistic picture of the Indian woman began to emerge from the Indian drama in English too. An exegesis of the culled plays of selected dramatists of the post-independence period reveals the changes in the portrayal of the Indian woman. With women dramatists also making a mark in the field, the change has become more marked.

In this survey seven major dramatists have been selected as representative dramatists of the post-Independence period in Indian English Drama. These dramatists have written in English. Girish Karnad wrote in Kannada, but translated his plays into English himself. Women characters have precedence in the plays of the chosen dramatists. An analysis of the women characters in their selected plays will show the shift in perspective of the post-Independence Indian English dramatists towards the Indian woman. The dramatists in the chronological order are Bharati Sarabhai, Nissim Ezekiel, Asif Currimbhoy, dina Mehta, Girish Karnad, Manjula Padmanabhan, Mahesh Dattani.

Among the few women playwrights to make a mark in the Indian English drama of the fifties was Bharati Sarabhai

(b. 1912). The foremost among these women playwrights is Bharati Sarabhai who has, to her credit, two plays: *The Well of the People* (1943) and *Two Women* (1952). In both the plays the author tries to give a new meaning to age-old beliefs and customs. Bharati Sarabhai has a poetic and sensitive mind and this is reflected in both her plays. *The Well of the People* and *Two Women* present different aspects of the then prevalent notions of Indian womanhood. While traditional womanhood and the Gandhian social doctrine are dealt with in the pre-Independence play, the complex nature of the incipient educated woman with aspirations of her own, as exemplified in Anuradha and Urvashi, forms the theme of the post-Independence play.

In his article, "The English plays of Bharati Sarabhai: With a Note on English stage", Gowda observes that the play's message is: "God is not found in the hermitage in the Himalayas, but should be sought in Samsara, the wheel of life and death" (56-57)."...Bharati Sarabhai's style and her writing are like flies in amber today" (Varma 38). But they provide a starting point for the study of Indian women in the post-Independence Indian English drama. Traditional Hindu culture encourages a wife to see husband as her lord. In Bharati Sarabhai's *Two Women*, Anuradha, Kanak Ray's wife, speaks of her worship of her husband: "You were Sri Rama to me...what her husband was to Sita. I wanted also to worship you" (19). She needs his permission even to have a chat with Urvashi, her childhood friend. She tries to make her husband happy by becoming the woman he wants her to be. It is this attempt to fit into a fixed role model, that blurs the contours of identity of the woman as an individual.

Nissim Ezekiel (14 December 1924-9 January 2004) was an Indian Jewish poet, playwright, editor and art critic. He was a foundational figure in postcolonial India's literary history, specifically for Indian writing in English. As he admits in an interview with P. Bayapa Reddy, "I have never wholly identified myself with the Indian sensibility." But his plays reveal his insight of the Indian family. He is the author of *Three Plays (TP)* published in 1969 which contains "Nalini: A Comedy",

"Marriage Poem: A Tragi Comedy" and "The Sleepwalkers: A One-Act Farce" (henceforth to be referred to as "Nalini", "Marriage Poem" and "The Sleepwalkers"). He also published a short one-act play, "Song of Deprivation" in July 1969 in *Enact*, the theatre magazine. A two-act play *Don't Call It Suicide: A Tragedy (1993)* (in further references *Don't Call It Suicide)*, was first staged by the British Council in Mumbai in 1989. Women characters play a prominent role in these plays. In the interview with Reddy, he says that his women characters "are certainly as important as the men characters" (16).

Through his plays, Ezekiel makes one scrutinize established institutions of society like art and marriage. He takes a look at the world of art and the reaction to a woman artist in "Nalini". Raja Rao observes in *Nissim Ezekiel: The Authroized Biography* that, "...one of the themes of the play is the dispelling of stereotypes by presenting the real Nalini as a woman of greater intelligence and substance that Raj or Bharat" (188). Marriage, and the compromises within marriage form the theme of "Marriage Poem" and *Don't Call It Suicide.* Ezekiel draws a contrast between illusion and reality in married life in "Marriage Poem" through the marital problems of Naresh and Mala. "Ezekiel probes a subject already tackled in many of his poems. It is a cynic's observation of the failure of a brutal truth" (Rodrigues 125)

Wry humour is often used by Ezekiel to sweeten the bitter taste of reality. This characteristic feature is prominently displayed in "The Sleepwalkers" which is a satire on Indians and their fascinations with everything American. The play provides insights into the attitudes of Indian men and women, especially husbands and wives. The satirical note is also to be seen in "song of Deprivation" which presents two frustrated lovers-"She" and "He"—who cannot meet and consummate their love. "She" represents the urban, young women of the post independence period. He presents a cross section of middle class society in "Marriage Poem". Mala in the play is the best example of the wife who apparently enjoys playing a submissive role. The play "represents the dull and drab life of a couple, Naresh and Mala, who quarrel and compromise, love and hate and finally strike a helpless reconciliation with life itself". (Rahman 57). Many Indian women submerge their identities in those of their husbands. Mrs. Shah in Exekiel's "The Sleepwalkers", is a caricature of such wives.

Asif Currimbhoy (1928-1994) deals with the ennui of the modern youth in "the Doldrummers", schizophrenia in "The Drum Dancer", the Indian take-over of Goa in "Goa", the evolution of an artist in *Throns on a Canvas* and the alienation of an Indian Jewish family in *This Alien...Native Land.* Although there is no play of Currimbhoy's which deals exclusively with the image of the Indian woman and her position in society, his female characters provide us with different facets of the Indian woman. Liza and/Rita in "The Doldrummers", Prema and Shakuntala in "The Dumb Dancer", Malini in *Thorns on a Canvas*, Mirinda and Rose in "Goa", and Rachael, Sarah and Tara in *This Alien...Native Land* present the Indian woman in her variety and complexity. "His women characters, major or minor, are frequently more memorable than is male charactes....In Currimbhoy's best plays, his woman characters are central to the provocative and sensitive issues that stimulate his creativity" (Meserve 423). Senhora Miranda in "Goa", sees Alphonso as her potential savior. She is always uncertain of his affections and is alert to the slightest change in his mood. She seeks constant assurance from him that he will never leave her and go away. She wishes to keep him drunk for, she finds him more amenable then. As a result of this insecurity, Miranda becomes hard and cynical. These are the consequences of the dependency syndrome which adversely affect the actualization of a woman's potential. Too much dependence on a husband or a man leads to a further decline in the self-image of woman.

Dina Mehta (b. 1928) focuses on the precarious position of the Indian woman in her plays. The insecurity of a single woman past her prime, as exemplified in Pramila, forms the theme of "The Myth-Makers". *Brides Are Not for Burning* deals with the scourge of dowry. The characters of Laxmi and Malini stand at two ends of the spectrum of Indian womanhood. While Laxmi is the conventional, submissive daughter-in-law, who is tortured and humiliated for bringing insufficient dowry, her sister Malini is a fighter who will not take things lying down. The play is dedicated to "All the angry young women who can be whatever they choose to be" (5). The vulnerable girl child, the trauma of child sexual abuse, childlessness and infidelity are the issues dealt with in "Getting Away with Murder". The struggles of the modern Indian woman to overcome these "body blows" are seen in Malika, Sonali and Raziya. Dina Mehta's "The Myth-Makers" encapsulates the vulnerable position of a single woman in an androcentric society, and her vacillating mind. Pramila, the aging actress in the play, invites the sympathy of the readers.

Girish Raghunath Karnad (born 19 May 1938) is a contemporary writer, playwright, actor and movie director in Kannada language. He is the latest of seven recipients of Jnanpith Award for Kannada, the highest literary honour conferred in India. For four decades Karnad has been composing plays, often using history and mythology to tackle contemporary issues. He bases most of his plays on folklore and myth. He finds contemporary values in these lores and myths, and combs the past for myths to analyze the present. "A legend, a myth, a page of medieval history: but the ambience is strictly contemporaneous" says Prema Nandkumar in her review of *Three Plays: Naga-Mandala; Hayavadana; Tughlaq* (435).

All the three selected plays problematize female sexuality, and the woman's freedom to make choices. *Hayvadana* is based on the "Story of the Transposed Heads" in the Sanskrit *Vetala Panchavimsati* (twenty five stories about King Vikrama and Vetala), which forms part of Kshemendra's *Brihat Katha Manjari* and Soma Deva's *Kathasaritsagar* (both belonging to the eleventh century AD). A modern source of the plot of *Hayavadana* is Thomas Mann's story *The Transposed Heads* (1941). This story is imbricated with the Hayavadana story, which describes a horse's search for completeness. The characters in Karnad's play are called Devadatta, Kapila and Padmini. Padmini is the pivot of the play, for her action causes the story to come about. Through her Karnad presents the existential angst.

> ....the central figure is a woman, Padmini, that embodiment of the life force. \Selfishness and sexuality find expression in her desire for both brain and brawn symbolized by Devdatta and Kapila respectively. Married to the former, Padmini craves for the 'muscles' and 'body' of Kapila.
>
> (*Chakravartee* 36)

Karnad subverts the conventional concept of marriage in *Naga-Mandala* which tells the story of Rani and Appanna. Rani "is perhaps Karnad's emblem for the New Woman, unshackled from the repressions of a terrible past", remarks Prema Nandakumar in her review of *Three Plays: Naga-Mandala; Hayavadana; Tughlaq* (434). The evolution of Rani is the highlight of the play. As Goel says "Karnad traces the movement of Rani (or the Indian women in general) from enslavement to empowerment. Into this metamorphosis are woven the themes of patriarchal tyranny, female and male sexuality, adultery and chastity..."(111)

Karnad takes a philosophical look at the idea of non-violence, as exemplified in the Queen, in "Bali: The Sacrifice", taken from the thirteenth century Kannada epic, *Yashodhara Charite* by Janna. The conflict between the Queen who believe in Jainism and in non-violence, and the Queen Mother who follows the Vedic practice of blood sacrifices represents the universal conflict between violence and non-violence. The Queen's decision at the culmination of the play proclaims her volition, and her refusal to live under patriarchal endorsement.

The recipient of the first ever Alexander Onassis Cultural Award for Theatrical Plays 1977 for her full-length play *Harvest*, Manjula Padmanabhan (b. 1953) tackles many genres at the same time. She is a playwright, a short story writer, a cartoonist, an illustrator and a painter. As she states in 'The story of Harvest" (105-108), an appendix to her play, it was written for the Alexander S. Onassis Public Benefit Foundation International Competition which asked for a new, original, unproduced, unpublished play which "deals with the problems facing Man on the threshold of the 21st century" (105). She presents "from a futuristic angle a dark, bitter, cannibalistic future that awaits the poor, helpless, innocent, gullible folks of the third world nations like India" (Gnanamony 21). The play, set in 2010, has two groups of characters-The Donors and The Receivers-the former, from the Third World (probably Mumbai) and the latter, North America. The Third World has become the supplier of body organs to the First World. In the course of the play, Jaya grows from a submissive wife and daughter-in-law to an assertive woman who spurns the tutelage of phallocentric society. The social evil of rape, and the contradictory reactions of men and women to this crime are vividly portrayed in "Lights Out". Vijaya Ramaswamy says in her newspaper article, "Psychological Disrobing". The play brings out the insensitivity of a patriarchal society to such incidents, and demonstrates the way women become complicitous agents and acolytes of patriarchal injunctions. The wife's lack of initiative and her readiness to believe anything her husband tells her can be seen in Manjula Padmanabhan's "Light's Out". The two women, Leela and Naian, depend on their husbands to do something about the rape taking place in full view of the colony. Leela is the typical over-sensitive, hysterical wife who needs constant consolation from her husband, Bhaskar. Naina is quickly subdued into silence by her overbearing husband.

Padmanabhan raises a whole range of issues: Is a prostitute not a woman? Can she not seek justice against sexual violation? The men in the play clearly believe that "only decent women can be raped", " a whore is not decent, so a whore can't be raped". Naina responds, "If not decent women can be raped, what is the point in being decent?" (xi)

Mahesh Dattani (b. 1958) is the first playwright in English to be awarded the Sahitya Akademi award. At the heart of every Mahesh Dattani play is the family "fount of love and hate, of smouldering discontents and resentments, of bitter strife between the generations" (Kagal 38). In his plays "Dattani portrays a gallery of women characters who in their own way try to subvert the patriarch" (Brahma 59). Uma in "Seven Steps Around the Fire", Lata in "Do the Needful", Smitha in "Final Solutions", Dolly, Alka and Lalitha in "Bravely Fought the

Queen", Tara in "Tara", Ratna in "Dance like a Man", Kiran and Preeti in "Where There's a Will" and Mala in *30 Days in September* are all women who adopt direct and indirect methods of survival in a patriarchal society. Mahesh Danttani's plays abound in complex men and women. He makes a bonsai plant the symbol of the suppressed wife in "Bravely Fought the Queen". In the play Lalitha's bonsai becomes an apt symbol of the suppressed dependent woman who tries to fit into the straitjacket created for her by a patriarchal society.

In most Indian English Drama, "the emphasis is on women's behavior in relationship to men: wife/husband; mother/son; daughter/father, sister/brother". The stereotyped woman has little in common with the real woman. In most cultures, women are categorized as two distinctive, yet paired types: the wife and the mistress, the lover and the vamp, the good and the bad stepmother. This hides the fact that women's roles and functions are diverse.

A change take began to be perceived in the post-Independence phase of Indian literature. This was reflected in Indian English literature too. The plays of Bharati Sarabhai, Nissim Ezekiel, Asif Currimbhoy, dina Mehta, Girish Karnad, Manjula Padmanabhan, Mahesh Dattani reveal a truer image of the real Indian woman who is in conflict with the conventional fictional image. Women have to struggle against prejudices of society. Western education, participation in freedom struggle and women's movement have encouraged women to assert themselves. Such women can be seen in the plays of the above dramatists. There is thus a drastic change in the earlier idealized image of women that was mainly visible in the pre-Independence Indian English drama.

Works Cited

Brahma, Tamabay. *Mahesh Dattani: A study of the father figure in his plays*, Kolkata: Kreativemind, 2004.

Chakravartee, Mautushi, "Myth and Symbol as Metaphor: A reconsideration of red oleanders and Hayavedana". *Literary Criterion* 26.4, 1991.

Goel, Savita. "Girish Karnad's Nagamandala The Metaphor of Transformation" *Contemporary Indian English literature: Position and Expositions* Ed. Santosh Gupta, Jaipur: Rawat pub, 2000.

Gnanamony, S. Robert. "Manjula Padmanabhan's Harvest and Paradigms of subversive construction". *New Quest* 153, 2003.

Gowda, Anniah H. "Nissim Ezekiel's Plays", *Literary Half Yearly* 14.1.

Junita William, Psychology of women, New York; W.W. Norton, 1983.

Jacobson and Wadley, *Women in India: Two Perspectives*, New Delhi: Manohar, 1977.

Kagal Carmen " A Bright, particular star" Rev of *Tara*: A play in two acts by Mahesh Dattani, *Indian Review of Books* 6.8, 1997.

Kumar, Nand. *Indian English Drama: A Study of Myths*, New Delhi: Sarup and Sons, 2003.

Mukherji, Partha N. "Sex and Social Structure", *Charana*.

Meserve, Walter J. "Shakuntala's Daughter's: women in contemporary Indian Drama." New Delhi: World literature Today, 1989.

Mehta, Dina. *Bridges are not for burning: A play in two acts.* Calcutta: Rupa, 1993.

Rodrigues, Santan. "Two Plays", Rev. of three plays by Nissim Ezekiel. *Journal of Indian Writing in English*, 14.2, 1986.

Rao Raja, *The Authorized Biography*. New Delhi: Viking, 2000.

Rahaman, Ansur. "Technique and Motif in Nissim Ezekiel's Three Plays", *Indian Writing in English. Ed.* Krishna Nandan Sinha, New Delhi: Heritage Publishers, 1979.

Sarabhai Bharati, *Two Women*, Bomaby: Hind Kitabs, 1952.

Varma, Monika, "Bharati Sarabhai". *Facing Four*. Varma, Calcutta: Writers Workshop, 1973.

17

Interrogating the Savage and Bitter Indictment in Manjula Padmanabhan's *Harvest*

—M. Ibrahim Khalilulla

There is a paucity of drama in Indian Writing in English. Compared to other literary genres its output has been scanty. Indian English Drama saw the first light of day when Krishna Mohan Banerji wrote *The Persecuted* in 1831. It is, however, pertinent to note that the real journey of Indian English drama begins with Michael Mudhusudan Dutt's *Is this Called Civilization?* which appeared on the literary horizon in 1871.

In the Post-Independence era Indian English drama does not make a noteworthy presence unlike poetry and fiction. A prime factor for this is that "drama—essentially a composite art involving the playwright, the actors and the audience in a shared experience on the stage—has its own problems of which the other literary forms are free."[1] However, the post-Independence Indian English drama was benefited by the increasing interest of the foreign countries in Indian English literature in general and Indian English drama in particular.

The form and facet of post-modern drama have crystallized and have become galavanised because of the overwhelming impact of G.B. Shaw, Tchekhov, Ibsen, Eliot, Yeats, Pirandello and Bertolt Brecht. In comparison to other literary genres Indian English drama has achieved a little during post-modern era, the changing perspective realm is full of fruit-bearing possibilities. In this connection it will not be an exaggeration to quote Dr. R.K. Dhawan who observes: "Very recently Indian

English drama shot into prominence. Younger writers like Mahesh Dattani and Manjula Padmanabhan have infused new life into this branch of writing".[2] Manjula Padmanabhan is the great voice in the recent Indian English drama. She has won the first Onassis International Cultural Competitions Award for Theatrical Plays in 1997 for her play *Harvest*, and no other Indian writer has been able to effect as strong an impact as her. Her pioneering play *Harvest* bagged the Onassis Award and got tremendous popularity throughout the world. She portrays a mean and moribund world where mothers sell their children for 'the price of rice.' Her play *Harvest* deals with a miserable family dwelling in a single room in a chawl of Mumbai. Population explosion is responsible for the increasing pauperization and dehumanization of the city people. Om Prakash, a young man of twenty, driven by hunger and unemployment, decides to become an organ donor and ultimately mortgages his body to a Whit First World buyer.

Harvest centres on Om, who signs up to be an organ donor for an American woman named Ginni because there are no other jobs available. Ginni pays him to lead a 'clean' and 'healthy' life (terms she defines) so she can harvest healthy organs whenever she needs them. Ginni begins to control every aspect of his life, from when and what he eats to whom he sees and how he uses the bathroom. In fact, she begins to control the entire family. *Harvest* is a personalization of the politics of organ donation in a global economy, and a play about how the First World cannibalizes the Third World to satisfy its own desires. In this case, the Third World is located in Delhi, but it could be anywhere. The play has a science fiction feel, although the science fiction elements are merely exaggerated versions of familiar things: Ginni communicates with Om through a globe that hangs centre-stage, referencing video-conferencing technology. The pseudeo sci-fi set pieces are designed to heighten the surreal nature of Om's gutted lifestyle. They are reminders that *Harvest* is written not from Ginni's perspective but from Om's. *Harvest* focuses both on questions of an individual's moral choice and on the social structures that make those choices seem necessary. Through Om's wife Jeya, who in the end refuses to participate in an economy of greed and degradation, the play ultimately offers the possibility of a world in which there are no winners or losers, only partners.

Manjula Padmanabhan, in her intensely gripping play, *Harvest*, presents from a futuristic angle a dark, bitter, cannibalistic future that awaits the poor, helpless, innocent, gullible folks of Third World nations like India. The play won the coveted international prize of US$ 250,000 announced in 1997 by the Alexander S. Onassis Public Benefit Foundation in Athens. Critics have hailed the play as theatre-worthy of international production.

The play is set in Bombay in AD 2010, when the sale of vital organs between the rich and the poor nations become a routine affair like any other commodity transaction. The poor people of the Third World unsuspectingly come forward to sell their vital organs. The donors are mostly hapless slum dwellers living in single rooms in the high-rise tenements of the crowded Indian cities like Bombay living without any basic amenities of life. They sell their organs to rich customers in North America through sophisticated, foolproof, internationally registered and approved agents like Inter Planta, so that they may taste a bit of luxury in the form of electronic gadgets, before they die an anonymous death. In other words, they exchange their organs in return for escaping from their matter-of-fact, humdrum real life that is mere hand-to-mouth survival.

The playwright, through creating paradigms of subversive strategies, presents a multiplicity of perspectives such as the males and females of the twenty-first century who lack a will of their own, the city dwellers' totally addicted to watching television, the pointlessness of their life, and their absolute dependence on modern gadgets. Some of the issues they face in their prison-like existence are inhospitality, unemployment, the closure of factories, moral decline and a weakened morale, the lack of privacy, the partiality of parents towards bread-winners among their children, the pathetic condition of women, organ donation, human body donation, cloning, artificial insemination, and the comprehensive spread of cyberspace. Though the playwright is working in the realm of fantasy, the spectator gets from the very outset of the play, a realistic picture of modern times. To an average reader Manjula Padmanabhan's presentation of human relations will look subverted.

In the play, the mother, Ma(Indumati) is presented not as a very docile, passive typical Indian mother. Here Manjula Padmanabhan subverts the mother character in the play. She is sitting all the time in front of the TV. Shortly she will be a slave to the *Video Paradiso* of the future *Super Deluxe Video Couch Model XL 5000* specially ordered by herself, in exchange of her son's vital organs, in fact, her son himself. Always finding fault with her daughter-in-law Jeya, her preference is for her first son, Om, the husband of Jeya. Her second son Jeetu is a loafer and a male prostitute "a pimping rascal" (Harvest 8) in his mother's words. Jeya, instead of loving her husband Om, loves her brother-in-law Jeetu. Om is presented as Ma's darling, her "Soul", her "Hearbeat" (9): but in reality, he is a weak-willed, docile and an impotent man who makes his wife his sister. Unlike the quite familiar modern feminist discourse, where the father figure is presented as a butcher, a knife-wielder and a male-chauvinist pig, the father is conspicuously taken out of the play. It's a female-dominated world where Ma rules and Ma's words are law. Ma is physically more powerful than her daughter-in-law, Jeya. When Jeya snatches the remote control from Ma's hand, Ma pushes Jeya off balance and snatches it. A minute earlier, Ma had threatened her with the harsh expression: "Pig-faced buffalo! Give it back or I'll...I'll shit in the water-supply.... I'll microwave your entrails!"(84).

The play presents us with photographic realism that though the twenty-first century is spectacularly rich in everything else. Though four people live in a small room, two of them think, "the other two don't exist" (*Harvest* 8). Everyone is selfish, selfish to the core. The mother, Ma, never even cares, when her younger son, Jeetu is taken away for the transplantation. She is unperturbed when her daughter-in-law informs her of what has happened. With total indifference, she answers, "Why should I care what happens to Jeetu? I'm through caring about anybody" (83). Human predicament in the third millennium is very disquieting and unsettling, precisely because in this era civilization ruthlessly invades man's inner privacy. In order to eke out a living, he is even prepared to ignore his wife. Om does so when he mindlessly signs off his name for organ transplantation. In classics like the *Mahabharata* and the *Ramayana*, the wives of the heroes stood with them through thick and thin without the slightest murmur of complaint. Every Indian knows that when Yudhishthira lost everything in a game of dice, and when the Pandavas were sent out of their city, their devout wife, Draupadi did not lose heart, but "*went with them, no longer in rich garments, but a bare footed beggar-maid*" (*Harvest* 18). Similarly, in *Ramayana*, when Lord Rama was banished for a period of fourteen years into a jungle, his dutiful wife Sita happily threw her lot with her husband. In 2010 in metropolises of India, Padmanabhan cannot visualize any ideal womanhood of this kind. She has only a sad spectacle to offer. Even blood-brothers are presented as utterly selfish. The legendary brotherly affection that Rama, Lakshmana and Bharata mutually shared fails to inspire the brothers Om and Jeetu in *Harvest*. Manjula Padmanabhan subverts ideal brotherhood and makes the brothers go for each other's throat. Right in front of her mother-in-law, Jeya makes love to her brother-in-law, Jeetu. Though feeling a little guilty, she offers herself wholly to him. Jeetu cracks a crude joke with her when he does not find any privacy in their beehive-like apartment, "If we can shit in public, we can just as well screw in public too...especially since you're now officially my wife!"(31). The teenage boy Jeetu has clearly lost all his moral moorings when he says that he will service all "*cows, pigs, horses….for a price*"(32). Jeya "by offering herself to Jeetu proves that there is a false marriage.... Uhh!.... False'...'false'…. False…life"(34). The spectator/reader is remained of the bitter words of the Ecclesiastes in the Holy Bible, "Vanity of vanities; all is vanity"(640).

One thing that surprises the spectator most is the way the youth of the play are ready to accept authority and most anxious to have it 'laid on the line'. They behave as if they knew the direction. They are not in revolt against anything. They are too nice to be rebellable against. Nothing provokes them into hostility. Knowing that his wife carries an illicit relationship with his younger brother, Om is not at all provoked. He lies like a dog at the door fawning on its master. He lies down "like a corpse" (*Harvest* 69). Jeetu, the 17-year-old youth looks like "Death's first cousin" (46). With the enormous amount of freedom he gets in the new millennium, he thinks that he enjoys life, but in reality, it costs a handful of years off his life. There is nobody to check him. Not even his mother because her eyes are stuck to the TV screen "from staring at it twenty four hours of the day!" (38). Not just the couple of Doordharsan channels, but 750 video channels from all over the world. Jeetu is ready to offer any organ of his body to a beautiful phantom seen in a contact module. He doesn't know whether that person is young or old, whether it is male or female. Jeya tries to make him see reason:

Jeya: (bitterly): But she wasn't real!

Jeetu: She exists. That's enough for me She's a goddess and she exists. I would do anything for her-anything! (81)

Sheepishly he follows the gay guards for the transplantation. Like him, even Om comfortably compromises: "Nothing matters. Whatever happens it's fate" (69). The play focuses on a mingled admiration and horror of the suburban lifestyle, and the suburbanites' increasingly compulsive craze for electronic gadgets. They have, in front of them, a bewildering multiplicity of gadgets to choose from. Soon after the negotiated barter and the nefarious agreement with the recipient, through which they sacrifice their self-respect and dignity, the family of Om start obtaining what they have longed for. They can now have direct contact with the recipient thousands of miles away through a contact module fitted in their house. It is quite natural that they wish to change their pathetic existence from "living day in day out, like monkeys in a hot-case" (23), lulled to sleep by their neighbour's "rhythmic fasting! And starving" (23).

At the time of Om's signing the contract there is no toilet in his house. There is only one toilet in the whole apartment. And forty families share that. To Ginni, the American Receiver,

"It's wrong! It's disgusting! It is unsanitary!" (28). She installs a sanitary system in Om's house. "It's a wonder", she says, "You're all not dead of the plague years ago!" (28).

Fuel Preparation Equipment will supply the family with enough fuel. Ginni sends everything for the family like jewellery, perfume, flowers and even chocolates to humour Om's people. In two months, time, Om's single room apartment is transformed into a sleek residence, with chrome steel and glass, convertible type bed-cum-sofa, TV set, computer terminal, mini-gym, an air-conditioner, cumbicles containing bathroom and toilet. A low-Japanese style dining table is also there.

Women look over-dressed. Their faces look heavily made up. They deck themselves with jewellery on their ears, wrists, ankles and throats. The foreign receiver (from Viriginia) is a heartless crook with a cynical design that gets gradually unfolded before the spectator. In the beginning, the spectator as well as the donor and his family see the face of a young lovely girl. Even the stoical Ma falls for her and describes her as "an angel" (27). Ma is in a fix to understand why the foreigner loves her son so much. Only a little she understands that her beloved son has "sold the rights to his organs! His skin! His eyes. His arse"(23). In a mellifluous voice, Om falls in love with her voice and the phantom of her profile and tell her: "Madam! It's our pleasure! Our duty, I mean! Anything we can do the help..." (Harvest 25).

The irony of the situation is that the Indians are not able to decolonize themselves even after some 50 years of the colonizers' exit from India. Independence for the Indian is like a pompous brass plaque that covers their squalor, wretchedness and ignorance. Om's unconditional surrender to the white rich American shows the unmistakable slavish attitude or the 'dependence complex' of the Indians.

Ginni by offering electronic comforts tries to keep everyone 'happy' in Om's house. She speaks through the electronic device: "The most important thing is to keep 'Auwm' smiling. Coz if Auwm's smiling, it means his body's smiling and if his body's smiling, it means his body's smiling, it means his organs are smiling. And that's the kind of organs that'll survive a transplant best, smiling organs" (41). Though there is an ironical humour here the audience knows that she is not at all sincere. The sympathy she expresses for Om's family members is just skin-deep. The luxury that she promises to the donor family will in fact be a trap that offers neither comfort nor peace, but it only increases their disillusionment. And their little apartment shortly becomes a veritable tower.

No one can fool or cheat Ginni. She knows everything. She notices even a cold or sneeze or a whisper. All the visitors, including the neighbours for toileting purposes, are watched. When Jeya tries to hold back something, Ginni's voice booms "....Zhayat! I can see it in your lying scheming little face! You think you're such a cutie-pie, Zhaya, but you don't fool me! Not for one instant!" (42).

Surprisingly, all through, Ginni has been angling not for Om but for Jeetu, "a health hazard" (45), "a walking, talking health Catastrophe" (45), and a really very sick person. But that doesn't matter to her. He will be cured and used by the receiver. Jeetu is administered a hypo and is carried away in a stretcher very much against the protest of Jeya: "Don't hurt him, don't hurt him—Please! Oh! Oh! They'll make mincemeat out of him" (62). Much to the shock of Jeya and Jeetu, the latter's eyes are taken out, and in place them, they have fitted a pair of imitation eyes. He keeps on asking: "This...is my reward?" (73).

Deplorably, Jeetu weeps, that the rich woman who has plucked his eyes is a she-demon. Jeetu's ecstatic love cry in a day or two earlier is turned into a pathetic cry of despair. He has become a somnambulist like Lady Macbeth. He pays for his sins by being sightless and all through his life has become like Lady Macbeth, haunted by terrible visions:

> ...I am in a place worse than death...
> bleached and pitted place. Scars and
> slashes no stillness, no dimensions. No
> here, no there—I see in molten bars and
> blinding shapes, I see symmetries and con-
> fused fragments—sparks, shadows, water
> on mad glass, heat dreams, trains flying
> on fever tracks....
>
> *(Harvest* 75).

Jeetu is rocked in his sleep violently. He has lost his sleep and mental peace. Seeing his plight, the spectator is reminded of Lady Macbeth and her in strutting and fretting about in her chamber with her eyes wide open and with a lighted taper in her hand, speaking to her doctor absent-mindedly: "To bed, to bed; there is knocking at the gate: come, come, come, come, give me your hand; what's done cannot be undone: to bed, to bed, to bed (*Macbeth* V i n.l.n). Lady Macbeth's tortures of her mind and her restless ecstasy soon come to an end with her untimely tragic death. But Jeetu's problems are perennial. He is condemned to endure a never-ending nightmare. He is taken away for the "Next Phase" (78), with transfer of not just one particular organ, but the entire body, not for the 'angel' Ginni, but for the "Vampire" (29). In Virgil's words, "In exchange for the life supports we offer poorer sections of the world, we gain fresh bodies for ourselves" (96). And Virgil will live forever. And Ginni is only a fish for the fish, or a bait to hook the fish. With Jeetu's body, the phantom even offers to make Jeya pregnant by prolonging his life by artificial insemination. Virgil says: "the guards will make the child possible, Zhaya. It's just a formality. A device...an implant....Something I sent for you, which they're ready to deliver" (98). But Jeya emphatically says, "No more madness" (98).

In act II, scene ii, when Om's wife and the others are afraid to observe the knocking on the door, Om thinks that the gray guards of the Inter Planta Services have come to take him away for taking out the organs. Sometime ago the gray guards were his "dearest friends" (53). But now his legs refuse to move. Nobody opens the door. Jeya taunts him, "Such a hero, my man" (52). Her words have no effect on him, as she is not Lady Macbeth. Om pleads:

> Another month—another week, another,
> day, even....The smallest pimple on my
> chin is more precious to me at this mom-
> ent than a diamond mine in someone else's
> first! Oh—how could I have done this to
> myself? What sort of fool am I?...No!
> No! I beg of you-Please! Please! Leave

> that cursed door alone! Seal it with cement
> and fire! I cannot bear to see its gape, admitting
> those vile, those cruel, those vicious guards! ('Groans')
> Ahhhh.....(53).

Om, with a barely audible cry, agonises:

> "Where'll I hide? In the fridge. That is where I'll just crawl
> along here, all the way to the fridge and I'll sit
> there—Yes"
>
> (*Harvest* 54).

The play is not only futuristic, but also contemporary. There are many allusions to organ transplantation, organ selling, artificial insemination, cloning, browsing websites, information super highway, and innumerable video channels.

Harvest explores the spiritual poverty of a "citified age" in the third millennium. In fact, there is no place for God or religion in that age. Thus in a godless world, to the rich Westerners, the hapless Indians are like "human goldfish bowls" (43) and the goldfish inside "don't have a choice" (45). Indians are "a game to play with" (95). Their life is "one long joke" (31). They realize only at a later stage that "a peaceful shit is more precious than money in the bank" (46). The organ-receivers like Ginni, though pose "such a divine being" (49) are really crooks. Ginni cares, as Jeya says, "just as much as she cares about the chicken she eats for dinner" (50) and the donors are just "another kind of dinner" (50). Sleep or waking has no significance to the twenty-first century suburbanites. Om does not know, soon after signing off his organs-whether he is living or dead. He asks Jeya: "Why? What's the point?" (66). Human beings are reduced to the level of insignificant beings. The enigmatic receiver would even use Jeetu "for research" (67); the donor will become "a trophy for some industrialist's daughter" (68). There is no hope, there is no courage, and there is no struggle (leave alone heroic struggle). Concern, care, wanting have lost all their significance. The conversation between Om and Jeya reveals this disillusionment:

Om: You betrayed me. Seduced my brother. I feel
Nothing but contempt.

Jeya: You never cared for me. You never wanted me.

Om: Wanting-no wanting-what meaning
do these words have in our world? (68).

Organ donors seldom look like human beings. Jettu appears "like a first time visitor from Mars" (73) and he is "moving like a madman" (80). Their existence is prison-like; they have absolutely no freedom; their will is conditioned; they are always under surveillance. The Inter Planta grey guards once even lock them in. Om can only moan: "Ah ...you've locked us in, you bastards! You've locked us in"(83). A poignant silence is always ominously present in the fancy-prison house of Om. Some of the features of post-colonialism like doubleness, centre-shift, boundary-blur, intertextuality and irony are found in the play. Though Indians got their freedom some 55 years ago, still they are not able to cut off their umbilical cord with the whites, be it the British or the Americans. They sheepishly emulate the coloniser's culture, their life-style and their language. As a result, a sense of duality marks their existence. Such a contradictory doubleness reveals itself through the narrative strategies employed by Manjula Padmanabhan, in the use of irony, reinforced through polarized imagery and intertextuality.

As all great literatures of the world are related. *Harvest* too is linked not only to the present-day literatures of the world but also to the literatures of the by gone era. Consciously or unconsciously, Manjula Padmanabhan redefines the ancient myths and legends, and juxtaposes them with facts and facets of future life. In this way she brings out the similarities and contrast between the past, and future. In the ancient myth, it is categorically narrated that the sin involved in the violation of sex codes in all ages and in all countries led to decay and degeneration, and the necessity of purifying the sinner's soul through suffering as the sole way of salvation. Jeetu, in this sense is like Oedipus who unwittingly kills his father Laius and marries his own mother Jocasta, and then on, knowing the sin, calls down upon his head the curse of the gods. Jeetu doesn't commit any murder but breaks the sex taboos of the society by committing adultery with his elder brother's wife Jeya, who in the Indian context is given the elevated place of a mother. This is an instance of ironic intertextuality signifies a continuity of tradition.

In *Harvest*, Jeetu has seen his sister-in-law's nakedness and not only that, he calls her "my darling wife" (45), and for this sin he goes blind, and just as Tiresias is granted with the gifts of immortality and prophecy, Jeetu is also granted both the gifts. He can now see the real meaning of life: "Life is a strange thing. When your pockets are full with it, you throw it away like rich whores buying silk bed sheets" (58). He sees his mother for the first time as "a bundle of red desires" (75); Jeya is "an epileptic kitten" (75) and his brother Om is a man "with a blaze of friend nerves and straining bones, his eyes like ping-pong balls jottering in their orbits" (75). Like Tiresias, he cannot turn his head away; he cannot end this poison vision; he cannot sleep, he cannot dream, and he cannot even cry. He is "reduced to a cabbage" (57). The cabbage imagery is an instance of polarized imagery found in the play.

The sense of futility which pervades in *Harvest* is actually based on the chilling response of the characters' sudden consciousness of their empty, meaningless life. Each of them is imprisoned in his/her own; consciousness. In the modern jargon, Jeya with increasing despair tells her brother-in-law, Jetu, "It's not really a life any more. We're just spare, parts in someone else's garage" (*Harvest* 34).

Harvest resonates a dark fantasy about a high-tech racket in body organs. The play presents a sense of the interconnectedness of the world in which we live—this world of impoverished donor's and wealthy receivers—and some of the moral dilemmas that arise from this contact. In the play, in which an unemployed Indian man sells the rights to his body parts to a buyer in the United States, pointedly critiques the commoditization of the healthy Third World body, which, thanks to significant advances in transplant medicine, has now become a bank of spare parts for ailing bodies in the First World i.e. phenomenon of 'neo-cannibalism'. Wealthy but ailing patients in the First World are increasingly turning to healthy if poverty-stricken populations of the Third World in order to procure 'spare' body parts. It is tempting, at first glance, to read this illicit global economy as yet another example of the exploitation of Third World bodies that global capitalism gives rise to the trade in human organs, best understood in the context of global capitalism.

Harvest launches a scathing critique of the organs market and of the global, predatory capitalism resulting in the commoditization of the Third World body. Indian writer Manjula Padmanabhan's 1997 play confronts us with a futuristic Bombay in the year 2010, a time when legal, moral and bioethical debates about organ sales and transplants have been overcome. The trade in human organs is now fully institutionalized and smoothly operated by the entity embodying all the rapacious forces of global capitalism: a transnational corporation named Inter Planta Services.

In the play *Harvest* Padmanabhan explores the Third World dilemmas. She deliberately opens the play with the act of the protagonist Om Prakash's attempt in searching for a job. His unemployment makes him helpless and he makes an agreement with an American Company Inter Planta to sell his body organs to get money. This act of selling the body parts to Inter Planta suggests the dependence of Third World countries on First World countries. Here, Inter Planta is the Ideological creation of Padmanabhan, which symbolizes the domination of First World countries on Third World countries.

Padmanabhan employs a dystopian satire full of a psycho-economic aberration and challenges the social conscience of the Western predator and the indifferent Indian bureaucrat who has as yet shown no interest in intervening. In a technically advanced Bombay of 2010, a world of the immoral, criminally and diabolically insane, the author invokes sympathy in us for a poverty-stricken family in their slum. The eldest son Om is accepted as a donor in return for all amenities necessary for a healthy, civic life. They are the representatives of the Third World who are exploited by the racketeers in human organs and blood trading through the hedonistic, materialistic streak that is bound to destroy consciousness.

Harvest presents the paradigm of the totalitarian neo-imperial state as an enormous workshop for the transformation of human nature, the creation of a species whose personality has collapsed and the ego eliminated. We also meet Ginni, the receiver, an "epitome of an American-style youth goddess" who stands for the Inner Party depending for its dictatorial power on an unending process of victimization to assure her own immortality and vitality. *Brave New World* or *Nineteen Eighty-Four* are parallel texts that show the working of such terrors of science and the mechanism of the totalitarian super-state. The whining and insignificant mother of Om, the totally mindless brother Jeetu, a gigolo who secretly is a lover of his sister-in-law Jeya, are all mediocrities overpowered by an absurd world of human exploitation.

Manjula Padmanabhan's *Harvest* deals with the darker, oblique side of realism that would, perhaps, interrogate a bleak, gullible future that dominates the futuristic dimension of the Third World living. The "mistaken notion of wealth for happiness" (Pande 24) involves transaction that alters the basic conventions of the contemporary spectators. The presence of multiplicity of perspectives such as the will-less males and females of the twenty-first century, addicted to a visual spectacle that stimulates their immediate present, subverting their living concerns to pointlessness is the quality that Manjula Padmanabhan's *Harvest* underscores as an elementary 'lack' suggestive of the artificial insemination compelling people to savagely imbibe cyberspace. The playwright seems to go beyond the realm of theatrical fantasy; recalling the subversion of human relationship that the spectator is easily able to identify and the inevitable violation of the cultural forms from within. The onlooker is able to perceive subversion replacing coherence with perversity, dislocations and crudities. The play constructs human predicament invading the vital privacy of human beings where the escape route for the individual seems almost a bleak tragedy. The 'authoritative' patterning of the characters 'on the line' subverts the act of resistance in dealing with the traumatic situation as a prominent motif covering the inner life of the characters. *Harvest* relates contemporary concerns; as reading a Third World text, also means interpreting the ancient and age-old chilling ironic continuity of a tradition that stands more unique to the Third World experience. The imprisonment of the characters into their conciousness evidently revitalizes the powerful dilemma of Third World experience.

Works Cited

Padmanabhan, Manjula. *Harvest*. New Delhi: Kali for Women, 1998.

Pande, Ira. "Thirty Pieces of Silver". Rev. of *Harvest. Biblio: A Review of Books*. 3. 3-4 (1998): 24.

Shakespeare, William. *Macbeth. The Complete Works of Shakespeare*. London: Spring Books. n.y.p.

The Holy Bible. London: Cambridge University Press, Trinitarian Bible Society, 1995.

18

Girish Karnad's *Tale-Danda*: A Drama of Social Retribution

—Prafull D. Kulkarni

Revenge as a feeling always has its source in psychic injury. It takes birth, consciously or unconsciously, in an individual's imagination out of his disgruntled state of mind, out of his personal loss of pride, incessant insults or out of his unfulfilled ambitions. Such an individual can go to any extent to calm down the fire of retribution raging in his mind, and, in the process, may hurt his enemy seriously or even get hurt his own self quite badly. The present paper deals with such a situation in the Indian context as dramatized by Girish Karnad, in his celebrated play—*Tale-Danda*.

The critically acclaimed play is all about the revolt of the suppressed lower castes, their revengeful retaliation and eventual bloody civil war which took place in the twelfth century India. It is also an adoration of the religious and the legendary Saint Basavanna, his lofty idealism, his zeal for social reformation, but his eventual failure in establishing the egalitarian society due to the revengeful tendencies of his followers. Despite the wholehearted efforts and sacrifices of such great social reformers and revered personalities as Lord Budha, Mahatma Basaweshwara, Mahatma Gandhi, Phule, Shahu, Dayanand Saraswati, Dr. Ambedkar, etc., over the years, the Indian society and its mentality is still caste-ridden in every sphere of life. The impact of advanced science education and the advent of casteless computronics could not eradicate this age-old Indian malady even in the postmodern age. The country's politics, too, is based heavily on the caste calculations. Now and then, the media flashes incidents of upper caste atrocities upon the struggling lower caste masses and the resultant retaliatory reactions by the victims. In such a scenario, the strong message generated by the play is quite significant for the caste mongering people of post modern India. The playwright's aim here hence seems not so much to give a historical account of the events actually happened in the past but to show their relevance to the contemporary India and to ponder over this cancer of the society which is growing day by day, year by year, since its initiation millennia before leading to social retribution and resultant chaos. By recreating the socio-religious character of Mahatma Basweshwara in this play as Basavanna, Girish Karnad emphasizes the intellectual urge of the modern Indians for social reformation towards an egalitarian society free of any caste inhibitions. Accordingly, the author comments in his "Preface" to *Tale-Danda*:

> I wrote *Tale-Danda* in 1989 when the 'Mandir' and the 'Mandal' movements were beginning to show again how relevant the questions posed by these thinkers were for our age. The horror of subsequent events and the religious fanaticism that has gripped our national life today have only proved how dangerous it is to ignore the solutions they offered. (Karnad, 1994, Preface)

In such a light the historical message of Basavanna becomes quite important. The play is hence an eye-opener for the Indian masses to bring the ideals of such great men as Basveshwara in practice and avoid bloodshed resulting out of revengeful tendencies. Karnad succeeds to deliver this message through *Tale-Danda* by employing social myth of religious revenge as a tool in the caste conflict of the past.

Basavanna and King Bijjala are the key figures in *Tale-Danda*. The play takes into account some of the events from the history of Lord Basweshwara of twelfth century Karnataka, India. The Lord believed that man becomes great, not by his birth, but by his worth to the society. Hence, every kind of manual labour associated with lower castes and looked down by the higher castes, was now looked upon with love and reverence because of Basava's revolutionary ideals. He propounded such a cult which believed in the equality of humans, and made his followers eliminate the barriers of caste, respect the menial work, remove untouchability and consider women-folk equal with men. All, including the Brahmins who enjoyed the most favoured status those days, were welcome in this social structure. Thus, a new foundation was laid down in the social history of the country with the advent of Basavanna's cult. They were called as 'Sharanas', who later came to be known as Veerasaivas or Lingayats. This 'Sharana Movement' thus brought all the classes of people, including even a few courageous Brahmins, under its fold. Soon the cult's popularity prejudiced the minds of some disgruntled orthodox individuals and their followers. They started making a big hue and cry for Basava's defying of the ancient religion. He was so accused of misappropriating the state funds for his cause. On verification, however, the king found nothing wrong in these allegations. Soon an incident of intercaste marriage in the region arranged by these sharanas turned the social world of the city of Kalyan upside down. The supportive king was assassinated and the blame was thrown on the sharanas. His dictatorial son Sovideva usurped the throne. The new tyrannical king crushed the sharana movement. Once again the casteless Indian society was forced to follow the age-old casteists Vedic ideology of the past. Basavanna then moved to Kudal Sangama along with remaining followers and preached for the cause of one of the greatest social ideals in the history of the country until his samadhi. Ironically, however, centuries after, his sharanas moulded themselves into yet another caste of the Hindu society. Girish Karnad himself says in this connection:

> You can perceive deep irony because, after all the martyrdom of the sharanas, when they re-emerged after three centuries of underground survival as Lingayats, they were totally caste-ridden. (Karnad Preface).

This is the failure of Basava's grand ideology. It could have been due to the inherent tendency for revenge existing in the individuals due to the conflict between the oppressive upper castes and suppressed lower castes. Karnad seems to have drawn his *Tale-Danda* on this theory. Basava's social and religious movement, though was unsuccessful at the time, brought to light the social evil of Indian casteism for the first time in thousand years after Budha and became a source of inspiration for such great social engineers as Mahatma Phule, Chatrapati Shahu, Mahatma Gandhi, Dr. B.R. Ambedkar, etc. in later times.

The "Literal translation of 'Tale' is 'head' and 'Danda' means 'punishment' (beheading). You think with your head, worse still, you dare to feel with head. And that's why it must be chopped." In our day-to-day life also, such a thing happens due to the pent-up feelings of hatred of an individual or a group of individuals for the oppressive individual or vice versa. Over the years, the troubled party feels that some injustice has been forced upon them. That leads them to retaliate. Sometimes they take revenge to satiate their troubled psyche. In turn, the other party thinks likewise. They do find themselves questioned or challenged and they throw everything to overcome the other's attack. To preserve their dignity and social standing, they feel it necessary to crush the thinking abilities of the opponent. Eventually, the conflict leads to bloody end. In the process, a few miscreants from either side jump in the fray to fulfil their individual ambition and utilize every opportunity of revenge for their own selfish ends. This very feeling of individual or collective revenge in the society is framed by Karnad in *Tale-Danda* using history as a social myth to highlight the contemporary evil of casteism. The result is an enthralling play with a gripping plot framed in three acts of fifteen scenes. It so tells a story of collective social uprising of the casteless masses initiated by the adored character of Basvanna against the Brahminical tendencies of casteism, class distinctions and gender bias.

Unfortunately, India is the land of numerous castes, since time immemorial. They are supposed to have been formed out of a dastardly mythical concept of Chaturvarnya (Division of Society in 4 Classes) found in the age-old religious treatise—

Rigveda, and an ancient book of social laws—*Manusmriti* or *The Laws of Manu*. Those controversial verses found in these books, and also referred by Dr. B.R. Ambedkar in his world famous scholarly article "The Riddle of Shudras", are scripted below:

> 12. The Brahman was his mouth, of both his arms was the Râjanya made.
>
> His thighs became the Vaiúya, from his feet the Úûdra was produced. (Griffith)
>
> 31. But for the sake of the prosperity of the worlds he caused the Brahmana, the Kshatriya, the Vaisya, and the Sudra to proceed from his mouth, his arms, his thighs, and his feet. (Buhler).

These four heirchical verna distinctions, namely, the Brahmins (priests), Kshatriyas (warriors), Vaishyas (traders) and Shudras (menials), as interpreted by Dr. Ambedkar, were essentially an open 'Class System' which later on encapsulated as closed 'Caste System' due to the practice of endogamy observed by the priestly classes. Girish Karnad seems to know fully well his idea that "as long as caste in India does exist, Hindus will hardly intermarry or have any social intercourse with outsiders." (Ambedkar 17). The dramatist so presents in *Tale-Danda* the age-old issue of the caste problem in the light of the 'intercaste marriage incident' which took place during Basava's time and which resulted in the crushing of his humanitarian movement. The dramatist also seems well aware of Dr. Ambedkar's study of Manu and the behaviour of Brahmins. Dr. Ambedkar in his thoroughly researched seminar paper entitled "Castes in India" comments:

> One thing I want to impress upon you is that Manu did not give the Law of Caste and that he could not do so. Caste existed long before Manu. [......] The spread and growth of the Caste system is too gigantic a task to be achieved by the power or cunning of an individual or of a class. Similar in argument is the theory that the Brahmins created the Caste. After what I have said regarding, I need hardly say anything more, except to point out that it is

> incorrect in thought and malicious in intent. The Brahmins may have been guilty of many things, and I dare say they were, but the imposing of the caste system on the non-Brahmin population was beyond their mettle. (Ibid.).

However, in later days and as generally believed, the Brahmins held the distinguished upper hand in every field of Indian society. The Shudras or menial workers were the last in the social ladder and became the untouchables. They were denied even the most basic human needs by the upper class people and forced innumerable atrocities upon them. Their miserable life was nothing short of a living hell. Since antiquity, it is the most troubled social class in India. Naturally, they would seek an opportunity to avenge this social injustice whenever the opportunity came their way. According to Sigmund Freud, "the exploited persons in society foster feelings of hatred and animosity towards the exploited classes in their unconscious minds." (Sharma, 1997, 459). After Buddha, there was no one to guide these neglected people until Basava emerged in twelfth century. His emergence with the humane ideals of the casteless society was a sort of boon for these oppressed masses. And they grabbed the idea with both hands, became sharanas and looked upon him as their leader in the protest. In the process, their pent up feelings of hatred and centuries old emotion of revenge burst to life leading to bloody upheaval. Karnad's *Tale-Danda* deals with this mass uprising of the oppressed social classes against the upper castes, especially the Brahmins, in this high-tension drama of social revolution.

The play revolves around two major incidents in the life of Basava, i.e., the treasury miracle and the intercaste marriage. Basavanna is the Finance Minister to King Bijjala. Sovideva, the disgruntled Yuvaraj of the King, doesn't see an eye to eye with Basavanna. In the King's absence, he invades the treasury of the King to check the accounts suspected to be swindled and utilized by Basavanna for the propagation of his cult and to malign his image among his followers. The sharanas get an air of the intentions of Sovideva and immediately they surround the treasury in thousands to prevent any mischief by the Prince. Sovideva doesn't find anything wrong with the treasury.

That is supposed to have been happened due to some divinely perpetrated miracle by the Basavanna himself. Sovideva so is jeered by the assembled sharanas and hence feels humiliated by these followers of Basavanna. After his return to the capital, however, the king unleashes his full fury upon Sovideva and physically kicks his son for attempting to dishonor Basavanna. That makes him an enemy of Basavanna and also of the king. His angry remarks against the sharanas in his mother's presence before the treasury event foretell his intentions when he screams: "I shall bury them alive! Hack them to pieces and feed them to my hounds!" (Karnad, 1993: 8). He doesn't like the King to be soft against the sharanas. "It's he who's encouraged those sons of slaves" (ibid.), Sovideva thinks. The king, however, is a Basava sympathizer since he himself is a barber by caste and looked down by the Brahmins even though he was their king. In the play, he says to the Queen:

> His Majesty King Bijjala is a barber by caste. For ten generations my forefathers ravaged the land as robber barons. For another five they ruled as the trusted feudatories of the Emperor himself. They married into every royal family in sight. Bribed generations of Brahmins with millions of cows. All this so they could have the caste of Kshatriyas branded on their foreheads. And yet you ask the most innocent child in my Empire: What is Bijjala, son of Kalachurya Permadi, by caste? And the instant reply will be: a barber! (Karnad 14).

This anguished cry of the king itself tells the whole story of the tortured predicament of the lower caste people in the Indian society. That's why, though an atheist and secular king, he reveres Basavanna and his people who have brought hope of better social stature to him and to all such lower caste people along with abundant finances to his treasury through their honest, hard working enterprises. He further comments:

> In all my sixty-two years, the only people who have looked me in the eye without a reference to my lowly birth lurking deep in their eyes are the sharanas: Basavanna and his men. They treat me as—as what?—(Almost with a sense of wonder.) as a human being. (ibid.)

All such pent-up feelings of constant humiliation of the lower castes eventually resulted in a retribution that shook the very foundation of the age-old caste system in the twelfth century Karnataka. The socially oppressed masses found vent in the form of social revolt on the occasion of an arranged intercaste marriage of a Brahmin girl, Kalavati, and an untouchable cobbler's son, Sheelavanta, as dramatized later in the play by Girish Karnad. This unworldly alliance becomes a sort of myth for the sharanas to exploit at an opportune time. The social psychologists, Rajendra K. Sharma and Rachana Sharma rightly point out:

> When the exploitation and disorganization in the society increases, the progressive individuals resist it and object to it. Then some myths are formed in society on the basis of the thoughts and ideas of the progressive individuals. These myths help to circulate this mode of thinking in the public and the people become acquainted with it.
>
> (Sharma, 1997: 452).

The lower caste people turned sharanas here find a wonderful opportunity to avenge the age-old and oppressive Brahminism, challenge their social and religious superiority and annihilate the Brahmin might. For them it is:

> Another way of combating the continuing increase in casteism is the encouragement of intercaste marriages. Intercaste marriage provides an opportunity for two families belonging to different castes to come together not only for two individuals, one male and the other female, to do so. In this way, the seed of casteism shall be unable to strike root and even if it does the resulting sapling will be so weak that it will subsequently be wiped out. (382).

Dr. Ambedkar is also of the opinion that the four social classes turned into the castes due to the continual practice of "endogamy" or the "marriages arranged within one's classes by the priestly class" (Ambedkar 1-22). The system was later imitated and followed by other classes. That further led to the encapsulation of the classes and then led to the formation of the castes. Hence, this endogamy is the actual basis of the rigid Varnashrama Dharma. Girish Karnad and so his sharanas in *Tale-Danda* are quite aware of it and also of the fact that it is the root-cause of their trouble. Hence, they grab the opportunity by both hands and almost force the proposed intercaste marriage to take place despite the reluctance of Basavanna. The following Sharana dialogues of the play over the news of this unworldly alliance clearly point out to this feeling of hatred and revenge against the Brahmins:

Sharana One: The whole city is abuzz with your news.

Sharana Two: Every sharana's home is wearing a festive air already. You've done it!

Sharana Three: The Brahmins are in a state of uproar. All credit to you!

Sharana Four: Excellent! Excellent! (Karnad, 1994: 43).

The earlier treasury incident actually prepares the ground for this revolt in the intercaste marriage. The orthodox Brahmins, represented by Damodar Bhatta and Manchanna Kramita, play a key role in the happenings from this point onwards. They provide the brain to the insensible and impetuous Sovideva's muscle force. These two characters have been drawn by Karnad as prototypes of that Brahmin community which is supposed to be selfish, opportunist, and hypocritical in their behaviour. Anything unorthodox becomes a challenge for their religious superiority and their social might. Hence, they would not tolerate Basavanna's cult based on social equality. For them "He cannot grasp the elementary fact that a hierarchy which accommodates difference is more humane than an equality which enforces conformity" (57). However, in Karnad's *Tale-Danda* though the Brahmin prototypes are drawn in the characters of Damodar Bhatta and Manchanna Kramita, it is the individual selfishness that gains significance. The cunning and selfish Damodar Bhatta hence actually is belated when the sharanas arrange the accursed wedding. For the followers of Vedic traditions, the incident was a blow to their beliefs. But for him, "The whole city is like tinder—ready to ignite into flames. … It was impossible which way the wind will blow" (56). That has given him a lifetime opportunity to exert his influence upon the disgruntled Prince and gain a position of political strength with his help. Hence, he forces the wind to blow his way. He himself prepares Sovideva for the coup against his own father King even risking his social morality at the concubine Indrani's den and treacherously arranges for his kingship.

Thus the intercaste marriage upon which Karnad's *Tale-Danda* thrives becomes a tool of revenge for both—the upper caste Brahmins and the lower castes turned sharanas. Basavanna knows the situation by heart. He is fighting for the cause of equality with the wonderful tool of non-violence and non-cooperative movements. He has been leading the battle of inequality. But he knows that the sharana movement is still in its infancy. It is not yet ripe for the social revolution of the magnitude of such an incident of the intercaste marriage. Any haste at such an inopportune time may lead the movement to failure. He says: "We are not ready for the kind of revolution this wedding is. We haven't worked long enough or hard enough!" (44). He also knows that it would be far too dangerous for the newly wed couple. His concern for the well-being of his followers finds expression in these words:

> It's a question of life and death for these children. From tomorrow the wrath of the bigoted will pursue them like a swarm of snakes, to strike as they pause to put up a roof or light an oven. Who will protect them then? (38).

Similar concerns are also voiced by a Brahmin turned sharana woman Lalita whose daughter was to get married to Sheelavanta. She herself retells the prophecy of Sheelavanta's grandmother that "Rivers of blood will flow if the marriage takes place" (41). Hence, Basavanna is reluctant to bless the occasion. However, the sharanas are too vengeful to bother for the safety of a poor couple against the opportunity of avenging the Brahmins through this marriage. The intercaste marriage between a Brahmin girl and a cobbler's son thus becomes a sort of myth for these sharanas and a tool of revenge against the tyrannical priestly class. In this agitation, they are so incensed that they would not even grasp the logical considerations of Basavanna. Their arguments and incessant pressure force Basavanna to bless the occasion. Finally, he persuades King Bijjala to give his consent. Bijjala at first is reluctant to incur the wrath of his orthodox subjects; but he bows under pressure of the dominant Basavanna's larger than life image and provides security to the marriage ceremony. Here he risks his own authority in the complicated matter of society for the cause of the sharana movement. The wedding finally takes place without any untoward incident but later results in the treacherous move by Damodar Bhatta to make the king captive. The revenge of the sharanas is complete. They now have nothing to do with the supportive King. The sharanas are simply happy that they have forced vengeance on the orthodoxy through this intercaste alliance. Now they become totally indifferent to the troubles of King Bijjala and desert their own saviour. Even after Basavanna's humanitarian plea to save Bijjala from Sovideva's captivity, they keep themselves away and attempt to save their own skin in the matter. The words of the sharana father of the bride, Madhuvarasa, spoken to Basavanna clearly point out to this feeling:

> The world is awe-struck at the wedding of Sheela and Kalavati. We sharanas have at last shown our mettle, our indomitable spirit. And after all that, you want to lay the credit at the King's feet? (67).

On the other hand, Jagadeva (or Jaganna as he has been referred to in the play), the disgruntled follower of Basavanna, forces his own and personal revenge against Basavanna, by assassinating King Bijjala to show his worth for the sharana movement. He later commits suicide. The excited Damodar Bhatta now comments: "The sharanas lie inert, lost, adrift in a void of their own creation. Excellent! Now we must act" (78). Here, by offering his advice, he wants to be a political advisor to the new King. But another Brahmin aspirant to that position, Manchanna, is smarter than Damodar Bhatta. His timely judging of the situation compels Sovideva to turn to him for advice. The cunning Brahmin here kills two birds with a single stone. He removes the obstacle of Damodar to satisfy his own political ambition of becoming the advisor of the king and also incites the revenge motive of Sovideva for the insults from sharana at the treasury. The revengeful Sovideva immediately orders for the tale-danda, i.e, the beheading, of the sharanas involved in the intercaste marriage. Damodar Bhatta is killed in the confusion. Mayhem follows, people are killed, the followers of Basavanna are beheaded and the sharana movement is crushed by this decree of the new atrocious king:

> From this moment all sharanas, foreigners, and free thinkers are expelled from this land on pain of death. Women and the lower orders shall live within the norms prescribed by our ancient tradition, or else they'll suffer like dogs. Each citizen shall consider himself a soldier ready to lay down his life for the King. For the King is God incarnate! (90).

Thus, a myth of social revenge is formed from the history of Basaveshwara in Girish Karnad's *Tale-Danda*. This revenge motive runs all through the action of the play in a gripping plot. The great humanitarian movement of the past was a failure in Basava's time. But the message it delivered through this play is applicable even to the present. Unmistakably, it refers to the two key events of the contemporary times that put an indelible mark in the country's present make up. The Mandir and the Mandal movements erupted and corrupted the already prejudiced minds of the countrymen in the nineties. The treasury incident of the past dramatized in *Tale-Danda* corresponds to the Mandir agitation of the present time. This dramatic action exposes the meanness of Sovideva as the Mandir agitation exposes the meanness of the power hungry politicians involved in it. The holy place of worship of the millions in India becomes the miraculous treasury in Karnad's *Tale-Danda*. This treasury incident led to the intercaste marriage and ultimately to the bloody vengeance and a civil war. Similarly, the Mandir agitation resulted in the Mandal movement. To counter the political gain of the Mandir party the ruling one threw in the weapon of the Mandal Commision's report supposedly to benefit the Other Backward Castes and to form the social equality. However, that further enlarged the gulf between the upper and the lower castes and produced massive pro and anti Mandal agitations and caste-based riots. Similarly, the Mandir agitation made the tolerant Indians blood thirsty. It divided the secular India on communal lines and resulted in unparalleled communal riots. For the purpose, Mahatma Gandhi of India and his non-violent ideals were thrown into the museums for a structure of brick and mortar. Basavanna of *Tale-Danda* would denounce such a thing in no uncertain words as: "Violence is wrong, whatever the provocation. To resort to it because someone else started it first is even worse, And to do so in the name of a structure of brick and mortar is a monument of stupidity" (29). In these words of Basavanna, we find a pained and humanitarian Karnad who denounces the violence that gripped the whole country in the religious fanaticism and revenge for cutting each other's throat in the name of possessing a structure. The treasury miracle in the play, too, produced discontention, jealousy and division among sharanas just like it did among the masses of Indian society after the Mandal agitation. The following dialogue of Jagadeva points out to these feelings implicitly:

> I was at the Treasury! [...]To make sure that Basavanna's honour remained untarnished. To establish his glory in perpetuity. [...] I told myself, I shall be the hero of the sharanas. [...] (but) I was told—Basavanna has performed a miracle. Basavanna! No mention of me. In front of my own house, only hosannas to Basavanna! (43).

These pained words of a Brahmin-turned sharana youth makes him intolerant and eventually leads him to destroy the nonviolent image of Basavanna and his egalitarian movement by assassinating King Bijjala. He, thus, represents the common man who is torn between the secularism and religious fanaticism, the right and the wrong and also between his own jealousy and integrity. In this way, the play represents the contemporary world of socially disturbed India in which the personal gains, ambitions, enmity and revenge gains significance.

On the way, the dramatist has deftly made use of two myths—of Lord Shiva and of an ancient sage Maharshi Markandeya—to deliver his message of selflessness, love, non-violence and social equality for the betterment of common masses. Madhuvarasa, one of the Brahmins-turned sharana, says: "... Like Lord Shiva himself, we shall drink that venom and hold it blocked in our throats." (38). It is the Shiva myth from *Shiva Purana* (the Mythology of Lord Shiva) which points out to the benevolence and sacrificing attitude of Lord Shiva towards all other Gods and mortals when he supposed to have drunk a pitcher full of venom found during the 'Sagar Manthana' (the Ocean Churning) episode for the retrieval of Amrit (the Sacred Nectar). Here the sharana pressurizes Basavanna for the intercaste marriage between his daughter and the untouchable Sheelavanta. For the purpose, he wouldn't even mind to incur the wrath of the orthodox Brahmins. He is the devotee of Lord Shiva, a true sharana, hence he wants to sacrifice his caste of birth for the propagation of Basava's cult. The venom referred to here represents the intercaste marriage and the wrath of the orthodox. Ironically, it becomes a reality when by Sovideva's orders he meets a horrifying death. Lord Shiva drank the venom judiciously and saves the world from the dangers of the deadly poison. But Madhuvarasa, or for that matter all the sharanas, do it injudiciously at an unripe time for their revolution only to destroy it. Here, Karnad's message is quite clear—to avoid impetuosity and maintain restraint for the betterment of such a cause. He further refers to the Markandeya myth in one of the final utterance of King Bijjala before he was killed by Jagadeva. The atheist King, before his impending end, takes the help of the religious idea prescribed by Basavanna earlier to cling to the Linga of Lord Shiva at the time of crisis. Jagadeva and the sharanas cannot kill him clinging to their Lord Benefactor. Here the tired and defeated Bijjala says to the waiting assassins:

> I have a message for Basavanna. Will you deliver it to him? If you promise, I'll step out. On my own. If not, I'll stick to this linga: I'll be Markandeya and you play the messengers of Death—(86).

The mythical sage Markandeya sought the blessings of Lord Shiva to save himself from being carried away by the assistants of Yama, the God of Death. Here, Karnad points out to the mythical meaning of such a gesture for the people under threat from the opponents of a good social cause. He so desires to continue the humanitarian movement propounded by Basavanna, unafraid, and by trusting the Lord Shiva of the sharanas—the common people of the country. And expects the people of the country to follow the doctrine of egalitarianism as envisaged even in the Vedas:

> *Na viseso'sti varnanam sarvam brahmam idam jagat*
> *Brahmana purvasrstam hi karmabhir varnatam gatam* | |
>
> [Trans.: There is no distinction of castes. This world, which, as created by Brahma, was at first entirely Brahmanic, and has become divided into classes in consequence of men's deeds.]
>
> (Singh, 1997: 19)

Works Cited

Ambedkar, B.R. 1990. "The Riddle of the Shudras", *Dr. Babasaheb Ambedkar: Writing & Speeches*, 7. Bombay. Education Dept., Govt. of Maharashtra.

Buhler, G. (Trans.) *The Laws of Manu,* Chapter I. Access Dt. 26 January 2008. < halsall@murray.fordham.edu.>

Griffith, Ralph T.H. (Trans.). 1896. *Rig Veda*, Book X, HYMN XC. Puruca. Access Dt. 26 January 2008. www.sacred xts.com\hin\rigveda\rv100-72.html .

Joshipura, Pranav. 2000. "*Tale-Danda*: A Problem Play". *Indian English Drama Critical Perspectives*. eds. Jaydipsinh K. Dodiya, K.V. Surendran. New Delhi: Sarup & Sons.

Karnad, Girish. 1994. *Tale-Danda*, New Delhi: Ravi Dayal Publisher.

Sharma, Rajendra. Rachana Sharma. 1997. "The Psychology of Revolution". *Social Psychology.* New Delhi: Atlantic Publishers.

Singh, Nagendra, Kr. 1997. *Indian Legends,* New Delhi: APH Publishing Corporation.

19

Girish Karnad's *Tughlaq*: "Absolute Power Corrupts Absolutely"

—Sophia Jaychandran

Tughlaq by Girish Karnad is a historical play. There is a remarkable mixture of fact and fiction in the play. Its plot is based on history. The central character Muhammad Tughlaq is a well-known historical figure. Besides, a number of characters who surround him are historical. But characters like Aziz and Aazam are the dramatist's own invention. The action covers over five years. It begins in Delhi, then shifts to the road to Daulatabad. The comic sub-plot dealing with the story of Aziz and Aazam parodies the story of *Tughlaq*.

Girish Karnad's *Tughlaq* depicts the state of a man in extreme debilitation and despair, a man who sees the crumbling down of his ideals right in front of his own eyes, a man who symbolises corruption, misappropriation and dishonesty. George Orwell's quote "Absolute Power Corrupts Absolutely" is justified when we study the character of Mohammad Tughlaq in the light of this statement. Bernard Shaw's statement, "Power does not corrupt man, but fools, when they enter into a position of power, corrupt power", also echoes this predicament. The entire administration is in ruins. The play brings to light the contradictions in Tughlag's ideals. He is not able to strike a chord between idealism and realism. The play projects a succession of events that ultimately lays bare his crimes and sins. Though he is in control of the Sultanate, he is not able to ensure peace and normalcy for his people. Karnad's apt portrayal of Tughlaq is quite in apt in the present day situation. He has rightfully signified that ideals devoid of substance are bound to incapacitation and failure. His ideal thoughts are reflected when he tells his stepmother:

> "But then how can I spread my branches in the stars
> while the roots have yet to find their hold in the earth?
> (*Tughlaq,* 10)

In spite of promising "greater justice, equality, progress, and peace—not just peace but a more purposeful life" (3), all that the people experience is riots and bloodshed, poverty and starvation and chaos. Eventually, his meaning of "purposeful life" is disillusioned and rendered barren. His hasty and shortsighted decision of shifting his capital from Delhi to Daulatabad proves catastrophic. He deliberates this pseudo-ideal to his people.

Owing to Tughlaq's ambitions and greed many of his close aides and acquaintances turn hostile. One of them is Ain-ul-Mulk, his childhood companion, who marches to Delhi with his army with a view to usurp Tughlaq's sultanate. With the administration in shambles and the subjects in a state of despair, Tughlaq has made his state a model of utter collapse. In seven years' time the state has been ruined in every respect. His stepmother accuses him of the same.

> It's only seven years that you came to the throne. How glorious you were then, how idealistic, how full of hopes. Look at your kingdom now. It's become a kitchen of death.
> (*Tughlaq,* 65)

Tughlaq is a futuristic Muslim ruler of the fourteenth century India. He has an excellent craving to achieve esteemed ideals like goodwill, material comfort, justice, egalitarianism and harmony in his state. As a consequence of these beliefs, he decides to implement specific policies. There are five radical decisions, viz. (1) prayers five times a day and punishment if one fails to do so, (2) the provision to protese against His Majesty, (3) the shifting of the capital from Delhi to Daulatabad, (4) circulation of copper coins alongwith the silver dinars, and (5) executing all those hindering his plans.

Tughlaq is a distinguished scholar whose vision is magnified and fashioned by Sukrat (Socrates), Aflatoon (Plato), Zarathushtra or Buddha and Greek literature. So he isolates religion from politics and does not allow himself to rely on God, religion or prayer merely, though the word of God was his breath of life. The superlative ideals like peace, truth, justice, equality, affluence and regeneration of people are very much important than religion and religious people for him. Naturally he does not allow the religious leaders like Sheikh-Imam-Ud-din to interfere into politics and to spread illegitimate and deceptive doctrines of religion in society. When they try to do so, Tughlaq either imprisons or exiles or kills them strategically. However, he knows the spirit of religion which aims at the transformation of human heart, self-realization and social regeneration. Thus he tries to teach wisdom and truth, to mend the minds, to enlighten people's souls and to free their minds from the shackles of false religion. While doing so, he crosses the principles of religion but not defies nor sacrileges the religion. He knows that there is a divine power in prayer that controls human mind and provides enormous strength in desperate situation. So he makes Namaz compulsory and allows people to read the *Quran* in the streets. Severe punishment and torture is meted out in case a person fails to do so.

The play has a remarkable story, a spontaneous plot, scope for exhibition and use of dramatic practices like the comic pair, Aziz and Aazam. Besides it, the play reflects the complex political mood of disillusionment which followed the Nehru era of idealism in the country. In *Tughlaq*, the game of chess has its own symbolic value. For example, in Scene II, we find that Muhammad is bent over a chessboard. He is excited and his face is shining with a mysterious smile. Just then his stepmother appears and Muhammad welcomes her saying that he has got success in solving a difficult problem in chess. In fact he is not talking about a problem related to chess but the revolt of Ain-ul-Mulk who is marching on to attack Delhi. In childhood, he was the Sultan's companion. At present, problems for the Sultan have multiplied as he was short of force. With only six thousand soldiers, he plays cunning and invites Sheikh Imam-ud-Din to address a public meeting in Delhi though he knows well that the Sheikh has been inciting people to defy the Sultan. In appearance, the Sheikh looks like the Sultan. When he holds a meeting nobody goes to hear him. Now Tughlaq requests the Sheikh to go to Ain-ul-Mulk as a royal representative to ask him not to rebel. If a battle takes place, thousands of innocent Muslims will die unnecessarily. The plea appeals Sheikh who puts on a royal robe to represent the Sultan. When Ain-ul-Mulk sees Sheikh, he takes him for the Sultan. Just then the Sheikh is killed. Ain-ul-Mulk has to surrender and seek pardon. It is thus, every political problem is a chess problem to him and he solves accordingly. Thus, the Sheikh is murdered in a cold-blooded manner.

Tughlaq has made the optimum use of his power but he has diverted it to suit his plans and schemes. It is in a negative and an evil manner that he has used his power. Under the garb of beneficial plans, he devises his improper intentions as well. Hence, when he seeks eternity in history, he finds himself peering down the abyss of nothing:

> Tell me, Barani, will my reign be nothing more than a tortured scream which will stab the night and melt away in the silence?
>
> (*Tughlaq,* 185)

His zeal to construct a secular heaven in his kingdom is an effort to revive a lost spiritual vision and to force that vision to its zenith by way of translating it into reality. The vision had broken over him like a sudden wash of rain when he was young. The assembling lunacy of years, perched on the periphery of another breakthrough, recalls that vision in a night of pitch-black despondency. He is silently envisaging retracing the steps to Delhi, drawing the decimated people along once again when the memory strikes:

> Nineteen. Nice age! An age when you think you can clasp the whole world in your palm like a rare diamond. I was twenty-one when I came to Daulatabad first, and built this fort. I supervised the placing of every brick in it and I said to myself, one day I shall build my own history like this, brick by brick.

> One night I was standing on the ramparts of the old fort here. There was a torch near me flapping its wild wings and scattering golden feathers on everything in sight. There was a half-built gate nearby trying to contain the sky within its cleft. Suddenly something happened—as though someone had cast a spell. The torch, the gate, the fort and the sky—all melted and merged and flowed in my blood-stream with the darkness of the night. The moment shed its symbols, its questions and answers, and stood naked and calm where the stars throbbed in my veins. I was the earth, was the grass, was the smoke, was the sky. Suddenly a sentry called from far: 'Attention1 Attention!' And to that challenge the half-burnt torch and the half-built gate fell apart.
>
> No, young man, I don't envy you your youth. All that you have to face and suffer is still ahead of you. Look at me. I have searched for that moment since then and here I am still searching for it. But in the last four years, I have seen only the woods clinging to the earth, heard only the howl of the wild wolves and the answering bay of street dogs.
>
> (*Tughlaq,* 194)

The half-burnt torch and the half-built gate remain uncompleted. Mundaneness interferes to wrap the vision in its dull shimmer once the vision has been disrupted. The guard's interruptive "'Attention! Attention!'" breaks the reverie and returns the youthful Tughlaq to the passing instant, to the process of history. Paradoxically, he would seek to penetrate into history and overdetermine it ahead of its happening. He tells Barani:

> Sweep your logic away into a corner, Barani, all I need now is myself and my madness—madness to prance in a field eaten bare by the scarecrow violence.
>
> (*Tughlaq,* 219-20)

Girish Karad has also used irony in order to achieve the desired effect on the stage. Irony in all the forms of expression—of situation, of dialogues and of characters etc.—has been used effectively. The element of irony regularly enhances the theatrical appeal of the play; it also contributes to a dramatized manifestation of Tughlaq's own tortured divided self. Both Tughlaq and his foes at first carry the illusion of being idealists. Yet in the actual pursuit of the ideal they strike its opposites giving the rare impression that the 'way to hell is paved with best of intention'. The whole play is structured on these 'opposites' the ideal and the real. Tughlaq is what he is his self-cognition and deep desire for divine mercy not withstanding. In the end, Mohammad Tughlaq and his kingdom become indisputably identified with each other vis-à-vis the pandemonium that clenches them equally. The modus operandi of swinging the scenes work on the mind of the spectators, who though enjoy others things as well, focus on the tragedy of Tughlaq. Girish Karnad has dexterously of symbolism and motifs to divulge the inner landscape of the character.

The characters of Aziz and Azam have been presented as symbols. They stand for opportunistic and dishonest people who take undue advantage of the liberal ideals and welfare schemes of the democratic government and fill their own pockets. Karnad has presented chess as symbol. In the play it symbolizes that the whole kingdom is as complicated and full of problems as the game of chess.

Karnad has presented the python as symbol. The python is a symbol of increased brutality and blood thirstiness of the Sultan. It symbolizes the complete disintegration of his persona. Tughlaq's asking Barani not to cover the dead body of Shihab's dead body, the presence of the witty Aziz pitied against the gentler Aazam all stand out as striking examples of situational irony. Lying alongside the situational irony are the example of verbal irony represented through Barani(the historian) who is interested in "playing chess with the shadows of the dead". In a despondent state he utters:

> Tell me, Barani, will my reign be nothing more than a tortured scream which will stab the night and melt away in the silence?
>
> (*Tughlaq*, 185)

Historically speaking, Tughlaq has been a miserable failure in the history of all the emperors that India has ever witnessed.

In fact, the glorious Mughal deteriorated when he became the self-crowned monarch. In the play, we find the portrayal of the emperor who has failed in striking a balance between idealism and realism. He has used power in a dubious manner. Not only that, he has also alienated himself from his subjects. Priya Srivastav observes:

> Karnad's Tughlaq has been compared by critics to Camus' Caligula and Eisenstein's Ivan the terrible, where in the play he is seen as a deracinated monarch whose absolute individualism alienated from his people, from society and from himself. He emphasizes on the personal reality of individual existence and so as a man he is doomed to suffer the corrosive impact of alienation.
>
> (*Srivastav,* 75)

As an emperor Tughlaq has proved to be disastrous, and his policies futile and ineffective. He has not been able to optimize his vision. With a vast kingdom and huge territories under his control, he has strayed from his path, thereby snatching away peace, security and prosperity from his people.

Works Cited

Karnad, Girish. *Tughlaq* Oxford: Oxford University Press, 1972.

Srivastav, Priya. 'Social Alienation in Karnad's *Tughlaq', Perspectives and Challenges in Indian English Drama*, Ed. Tandon, Neetu. New Delhi: Atlantic Publishers & Distributors (P) Ltd., 2006

20

Social Transformation and Hidden Contemporary Realities in the Works of Mahasweta Devi

—Sri Latha Golakoti

Mahasweta Devi was born in 1926 at Dhaka, Bangladesh in a family of literatteurs and social workers. A prolific and best-selling author of novels and short stories in Bengali, she is equally well known for her pioneering work among the most downtrodden in the Indian society—the dispossessed tribals and the marginalized segments such as landless laborers of eastern India. Her writings are often based upon meticulous research, conducted sometimes via unconventional means (such as oral history), into the history of the peoples she writes about. She has received many awards, including Sahitya Akademi (1979), Jnanpith (1996), Ramon Magsaysay (1996), and for her work among the tribals, the Padmashree in 1986.

Mahasweta Devi believed in documenting her own time and history which she thought was a professional concern of a writer. This paper examines her works. *Aajir* is a story of a bonded tribal as a potential work reflecting contemporary realities. Five plays are used to indicate the spirit of the times that marginalized them. Her deeper social awareness and Marxist consciousness helps her to portray the condition of exploited tribals. Truly, she has created a "novelist theatre."

Mahasweta Devi desired for a transformation of the present social system without believing in "narrow politics". The five plays containing *Mother of 1084, Aajir, Bayen, Urvashi and*

Johny and *Water* deal with hunger, landlessness, indebtedness of villagers and bonded labour of advasis or tribals. Most of the characters are set in anger, burnings and speak in passionate utterances. She likes to protest against the social system that has "failed to liberate from the horrible constraints of independent India."

Mother of 1084 or *Hajar Churashir Ma* (1973, Bengali) first appeared in *Prasad*. She elaborated the same and published in 1974 with the theme of "the awakening of a political mother." The crying voice of the second scene shouts:

> Bring him back to me
> Let me hold him close to
> My breast for once, and
> I will no more, My sonu. (IAD)

The above lines have to be attributed to the political mother, which concept for the first time might mean the natural mother. In other words, Mahasweta is assigning the children of lesser Gods to her. The mother is desperate and crying for her sons who are encountered by the oppressive police in rural Indra. This is a recurrent and running image in all her works. She doesn't mind or create any sentiment because her ideology and legacy do not permit the same. Her works and themes only campaign for the oppressed millions who are fighting for their constitutional rights. This awakening is the voice of girijans and adivasis of Bengal.

Condemnation of the police is also part of her narratorial voice:

> Sujata shuts her eyes. Inscriptions
> In shadows pass across the screen at
> The back of the stage: saroj Pal,
> Bloody cur of the police, no forgiveness
> For you! Quick promotion for Saroj Pal,
> In recognition of his heroic role in
> The suppression of the Naxalite revolt.
>
> (*Mother of 1084*)

This is related to immature ideological and her activist temperament. Sensitive women writers like Arundhati Roy,

Sudha Narayana Murthy, have emphasized this point in portraying society, disintegrated and shattered lives of tribals across India. Disopossed tribals communities have occupied the central stage in the narratorial dramas of women writers. Political activists like Brinda Karat and Medha Patkar have adopted similar ideologies in the movements they are sphereheading.

Middle class women like Saroj, Tuli do not consider police encounters as important. Tuli "does not feel anything of this "and feels that "it's only natural to try to hush it up when something like this happens." Their conversations are dry and disconnected because they are aware of brutal killing of the persons and criminalization of politics.

The bitter fight against the establishment helps Mahasweta to rotate her plot around the lives of advasis. Anti-establishment ideology is rampant among them and the police officer says "you won't get the body." Sujatha's face "like a whiplash" makes him feel and she kneels with her face upwards, shocked. The lights are off and the curtain comes down. There are several such suggestions in her plays.

The pathetic agony of a mother is clearly shown and Mahasweta uses this as an archetype or main repetitive image of her works. The entire scenes of *Mother of 1084, Aajir* are devoted to mourning because she documents the annihilation of urban naxalites during 1971. These images are distinctly communist and she acknowledged this fact. Even the mothers portrayed exhibit activist features. Nandini's voice is "metallic, indecipherable," Tuli the youngest demands "fuming importance." Boni's attachment to prayer is 'a sham,' and laughs at other people's beliefs. Saroj Pal, a character, calls these as cancer worms growing on the body of democracy. Sujata as a wailing mother is possessive and wonders at the lack of affection of other members. In this urban drama family situations are depicted indicating lack of human relationships. Mechanical lives without any enjoyment and purpose are sarcastically portrayed in Kolkata.

The alienation of urban people from rural countryside has made their lives purposeless. Sujata says, "with Brati, they have cast me too in the opposite camp. If Brati had been like Jyoti or drunkard like Neepa's husband, Ansh or a hardened fraud like Tony, or had run after the typists like his father, held have belonged to the camp." The dialogues of the characters of Mahasweta indict the middle class lives and particularly those of government employees. These people are those government employees who are "homeless" and the mothers mourns their sons are Sonu, Bijir, Parsha, Brati and Laltu. Mahasweta sympathizes with the mothers whose sons were killed by the police suspecting and branding them as terrorists. This idea appears to be controversial as an communists glorify the dead as martyrs and their killings as fake encounters. This ideology behind the writer affects these political activists as social reformers.

A social reformer like Brati knew that his mother bore everything of her father's humiliations and insults. She was all pomp and was full of concern for his affairs. Her friends troubled Sonu's mother. She says to Sujata:

> It hurts sister. But we cannot
> annoy them and stay here.
> Sonu's sister never got a job
> in a school. She's always in a
> temper. She rages at me, all
> this for that one son of yours!
> They won't let me work to earn
> food for my stomach. (p.27)

Caste and regional disparities and discriminations arising from feudal society are condemned by Mahasweta. The above passage is a hidden reality. Contemporary reality in AP has changed because of reservations and reimbursement of fees for education. But the like of that situation cannot be found in India.

Mahasweta's punch line emanates from comparison and contrasts of a rich, influential mother and a poor, struggling mother. The role of urban gangsters is highlighted in humiliating poor women. She tells that these mafia men are paid by the rich people. Nandi Mitra, Brati's college mate, is the mouthpiece of the writer. She talks about "failing's mistakes, deviations and betrayal since 1947." She voices the anguish of her generation:

> Betrayal was rampant, but
> we hadn't been taught to be
> suspicious. When began to
> suspect, and could analyze
> our past experiences, only then
> could we become more
> confident of ourselves. (p.20)

Nandini's angry youthfulness is typical of Bengali youth who think 'they were bringing in a new era." But she has become a witness to arrests, torture, murders in the name of encounters by the police.

Mother of 1084 is a dramatic conflict of mothers mourning their young sons killed in fake encounters. Saroj Pal lights a cigar and presses it to Nandini's cheek to extort information about the gang members. The police questioning and the pattern of behavior interlines in the scene. She talks about thousands of young men ruffians in "without trial." They are denied the status of political and "you would say it's all settled down again?" Torture of these people is done in secrecy using Third Degree methods. The punch line of Mahasweta is "what do you need to get it who your heads that nothing's quiet" (p.26). It appears that she created a "novelist's theatre" to create awareness and protests and the minds of viewers about fake encounters and detention without trial.

To put it in brief, the hidden realities of rural India as consequences of liberalization, privatization and globalization are reflected by Mahasweta. The division between rich and poor seems widening and as desired by some activists the extinction of middle class bourgeois has set in. Middle class represents and cultivates certain traditional values which communists hate. Although she grew in a cultural milieu of Bengal she preferred to work among tribals and the underdogs. She was harassed and retrenched from government jobs as she was a communist having the works of Marx, Engels and Levin in her possession.

Struggle and odd jobs in her life deepened her social awareness and she was against the tradition-bound middle class society. Hence, she preferred to live with people she writes about.

Works Cited

Mahasweta Devi, Five Plays, Calcutta, Seagull Books. Pvt. Ltd. 1999.

___ . *Bitter Soil*, Calcutta, Seagull Books. Pvt. Ltd. 2002.

___ . *Mother Of 1084,* Calcutta, Seagull Books. Pvt. Ltd. 1997.

Amin Mulouf, " on identity," London: The Harvilli Press, 2000.

Interview to a journalist in April 1983.

21

Women in Vijay Tendulkar's Plays: A Socialistic Study

—T.K. Kanthale

Vijay Dhodopant Tendulkar (1928-2008), born in Kolhapur, India, is absolutely a writer of independent thoughts. So far as his characterization is concerned, he is matchless in the subcontinent. He has dealt with all social issues that are commonly seen in Indian social life. He deftly portrays his characters and fits them into situations that are easily visualized by his spectators in the theatre. In fact, the adversities around Tendulkar helped him to produce plays containing social issues in Marathi. His women characters are strong and focus on social issues.

Silence! The Court Is In session! is a play of plight and predicament of a woman who is violated several times. It is the story of Miss Leela Benare, a dutiful and punctual school teacher, who becomes the victim of the carnal lust of some men who seldom take care of her modesty, and her ardent wish to live a peaceful and domestic life of the husband and wife. In technique, the play is artistically structured and contains almost all the features of socialistic modern problem play. The images and symbols are highly suggestive. They speak volumes of things in a nutshell. Miss Benare unknowingly falls in love with her maternal uncle. He betrays her. At a mature age, again she comes in contact with Prof. Damle, who is deliberately absent in the court. This shows that from hell to heaven man's sexual urges and instincts are more or less the same thinking about woman and her privileged body parts. In the rehearsal, Sukhatme, Ponkshe, Mr. and Mrs. Kashikar, Samant—everyone criticizes and humiliates her. This piteous predicament of Leela obviously reminds us of Ammu, the protagonist in the famous novel *The God of Small Things*. Leela Benare says in her soliloquy:

> Again I fell in love. As a grown woman, I throw all my heart into it. I thought, this will be different. This love is intelligent. It is love for an unusual intellect. It is not love at all-its worship ! But it was the same mistake. I offered up my body on the altar of my worship. And my intellectual god took the offering and went his way. He didn't mind or, my devotion, he didn't care about them ! He was not a god. He was a man. For him, everything was the body, for the body ! That is all.

The play *Sakharam Binder* also reveals critical condition of women and explores the complications of human nature, two necessary components of which are sex and violence. A comment on *Sakharam Binder* soon after its production by a critic is worth quoting here:

> For many decades no play has created such a sensation in the theatre world of Maharashtra as Vijay Tendulkar's Marathi play *Sakharam Binder*.

This play may be termed as Tendulkar's most intensely naturalistic play. The play as Tendulkar has stated in an interview, expands around the central character Sakharam, a book-binder, who though a Brahmin, is the antithesis of the general idealized conception of member of that caste. Vijay Tendulkar explores the manifestation of physical lust and violence in a human being. Sakharam offers and gives shelter to the helpless Laxmi and Champa, who have been abandoned by their husbands. Both the females are his keep. Sakharam's straightforwardness in dealing with helpless women such as Laxmi demand a certain admiration . Laxmi, on the other hand, is the embodiment of the ideal Indian woman who has been the puppet in the hands of Sakharam as well as Destiny, so to speak. Champa, the other character, becomes a victim of lust and violence. Sakharam does not believe in the institution of marriage and arranges contractual cohabitation based on the convenience with such women who have been deserted by their husbands or who have separated themselves. Champa has to satisfy Daud Miyan also. Sakharam can't bear it any longer and throttles Champa brutally.

'Kamala' in *Kamala,* another play by Vijay Tendulkar, is a girl from a rural flesh market. She is presented at a press conference. Tendulkar raises certain cardinal questions regarding the value system of a modern success-oriented generation which is ready to sacrifice human values even in the midst of humanity itself. Kamala, an advasi woman, is an object for Jaising Jadhao, a journalist, and can be the cause for his promotion in his job and a reputation in his professional life. Sarita, his wife, is an object like Kamala who provides physical enjoyment, social companionship and domestic comfort. Kamala's entry into the household reveals to Sarita the selfish hypocrisy of her husband and the insignificance of her own existence. Sarita rightly sums up her husband's character.

> .... a man who is in the year 1982 still keeps a slave, right here in Delhi.
>
> *Jaising Jadhao.* I am going to say: this man is a great advocate of freedom. And he brings home a slave and exploits her. One can use and throw away. They (Women) must only slave away. Dance to their master's whim. Laugh, when he says, laugh. Cry, when he says, cry!!

The situation of women has not undergone a social change in the current scenario also. This is what the modern saint Rashtrasant Tukdoji Maharaj expectes in his *Gramgeeta* in the Mahilonnati canto:

> *Koni Bhogvastu samjoni Bhali I*
> *Sajvoni theviti nusati bahuli II*
> *Tyane gharoghari shirala kali I*
> *Abala banali Maibhoomi II*

Gidhade (Vultures) is a story of selfish brothers who become mad for money and kill their father and sister. After the first production of this play, Girish Karnad wrote,' "The staging of *Gidhade* could be compared to the blasting of bomb in an otherwise complacent marketplace. It was with the production and publication of *Gidhade* that Tendulkar's name became associated with sensetionalism, sex and violence". Tendulkar is able to create a sensitive, naturally kind, good hearted individual. Rama, Ramakant's wife, is like a helpless, submissive, tender little bird among the vultures. Her illicit relationship with her half brother-in-law, Rajaninath, who is a bastard and an outcaste from the family, may raise a few conservative eyebrows and evoke questions of morality. Thus, *Gidhade* is a play of family dispute in which Tendulkar has dramatized the proverb, "As you sow, so shall you reap".

Kanyadan is a play based on intercaste marriage of Jyoti, the daughter of Nath Devalikar with Arun Athawale, a Dalit Youth. Jyoti falls in love with Arun who is a drunkard and uses rude language. Her decision to marry him leads to a crisis which worsens after marriage. She is forced to come to terms with her fate and as Arun's wife, as she realizes that it is not possible to improve people and change society. Tendulkar has focused on a social problem that there is a want of a useful social bridge between the various sections of society, and that the attempt to overcome a taboo often leads to greater pitfalls than one can handle. The problem of difficulty in living a happy and peaceful life by couples indulging in inter-caste marriages has not yet found a concrete solution even in the twenty-first century. We may even question the success of literature like *Kanyandan* regarding social issues in our country.

Ghashiram Kotwal is a play of power, politics and sex exploitation. Ghashiram gets Kotwalship at the cost of his loving daughter, Gauri. He surrenders Gauri to Nana Phadnavis to get power and to take revenge. Many a time, Gauri is seduced as Nana is obsessed by her physical beauty and signals his desire to have sex with her. When Gauri is pregnant, she is murdered by Nana. The report of Gauri's sudden death makes Ghashiram mad and ferocious. He rues his action, but has gone too far to return. So, he, too, thinks, like Macbeth, " Returning is as tedious as go over'". Thus, Vijay Tendulkar explores the sorry state of affairs as far as in Indian society is concerned. The idea projected is that women have to subsist or survive at the whims and caprices of their male counterparts. The situation of women characters in Vijay Tendulkar's plays seems not far different even in present times.

Vijaya, in *Encounter in Umbugland,* is another powerful female character who is in sharp contrast with other female characters in Tendulkar's plays. Her encounter with her ministers and her victory in it throw light on women's inherent power. Hostile circumstances play little, negligible role in shaping the good fortunes of such dominant people. The play is depiction of Vijaya's triumph over her rivals signals the inauguration of Women's Empowerment Decade. The play *Encounter in Umbugland* differs from other plays in that the problematic aspects presented her are related to the dangerous game played in power politics. Treacherous ways are devised and adopted to gain the position of authority as to help Princess Vijaya triumph over her ministers by suppressing her humanity. Through her character, Tendulkar seems to state the idea that the people who believe in the truth of the axiomatic statement, "My mind is my master and my thoughts are my powers", always remain victorious.

To sum up, the total portraits of Vijay Tendulkar are captivating of this traditional and exploited society. Today, if we analyze the several modes of exploitation of various strata of this society, it seems that there is a long chain. The serial of women's exploitation is a part of that chain. This part has been justifiably portrayed by Vijay Tendulkar by his diversified and multifarious genius.

One can find a great surprise on the world level if we ponder over the women's exploitation. Comparatively, Vijay Tendulkar has outlined this issue in a limited form; even though he has presented some unexpected issues before the world. The great respect is expected in *Gramgeeta* by Tukdoji Maharaj when he say :

Samaji jo purushasi adar I
Taisachi mahilanshi asava vyawahar I
Kimbahuna adhik tyancha vichar I
Jhala pahije samaji I

It is a progressing movement in the women's life to think over the women's exploitation on the world's dais having socialistic view. Tendulkar's images make us to think over these topics. In the view of the researcher, this is the very success of Vijay Tendulkar's writing prowess. There are many types right from the pre-historical period to the contemporary period regarding the exploitation of women and also studying them. Today also, the modern woman is standing as a slave before the world. The images of Tendulkar like Kamala, Leela Benare, Laxmi, Champa, Vijaya and Rama are the burning and exploiting examples of the society. It is the need of the time to think on the progressing dais positively. Thus, Tendulkar has delineated several central points of exploitation and brought them into limelight. He has rendered great service to his literature as well as society.

I read an article by Sudha Murty which was published in the *Hitwad* where she says about the present condition of women:

"When women in India won the right to vote, it was seen as a sign of equality and freedom. But in reality, their social status is not good.

"I attended a seminar on women's issues. During the talks, something very interesting was read out. It was a list of countries where women enjoy freedom in all respects economically, socially and politically. The countries where women were more emancipated featured at the top of the list. While countries which lagged behind in empowering women came lower in the list. I assumed that India would feature somewhere in the middle of the list. In fact, it was second-last country to be named.

"I was curious to know about the listed three countries. The top three countries were all Scandinavian, Sweden, Norway and Denmark. Women are usually identified in relation to men—as a daughter, a wife or a mother. Often, Indian women do not have a say even in personal matters, There services are not rewarded nor is their efficiency appreciated. They have to live in a male-dominated society. It is ridiculous that often those of their own gender are their worst enemies. It is a different matter, a matter of pride, that the Indian women have learnt to live and excel in such an environment.

"In contrast, women are respected in the three Scandinavian countries. We just talk, but they practise. The saying, 'Where women are happy the goddess dwells,' holds true only in such places."

Works Cited

Unpublished Dissertation for M.Phil. By Kantale, T.K. YCMOU, Nashik, 2008.

Prasad, Amar Nath / Satish Barbuddhe, *The Plays of Vijay Tendulkar, Critical explorationss,* Sarup and Sons New Delhi, 2008.

___ *British and Indian English Literature, A Critical Study*, Sarup and Sons, New Delhi, 2007.

The Hitwad Article by Sudha Murty, "My Inspiration".

Wadikar Shailaja B., *Vijay Tendulkar, A Pioneer Palywright,* Atlantic Publication, 2007.

22

Do Until You Die: Usha Ganguli's *Rudali*

—Durgesh Ravande

> As subject for history woman always occurs simultaneously in several places.
>
> —*Helen Cixous*

Usha Ganguli (b.1945) is among the well-known theatre personalities in India today. Her name is taken with dignity in *theatrum mundi*. She can be responsible for, as Laxmi Subramanyam observes: "Increasingly theatre has been seen as a useful means of foregrounding issues that are largely suppressed or considered as nonexistent by mainstream theatre" (30).

Usha has been directing a number of plays for her Kolkata-based theatre company Rangkarmee, formed basically to create "a meaningful theatre for masses" (Deshpande, intro: 9). She took the challenge of doing Hindi theatre in Bengal with a considerable measure of success.

The play *Rudali* (1992) is a metamorphosis of Mahasweta Devi's Bengali short story. Usha Ganguly has a deeply-rooted inclination for lifelike issues. As Brecht innately urges for creating new realism of objectivity and social relevance through his Epic Theatre, Usha Ganguly with similar fervency takes the social issues for dramatic presentation. *Rudali* is all the way a woman's text because it matches closely with author's inner experience of being a woman with protagonist's personal experience. Anjum Katyal explicits in her criticism on this play:

"*Rudali* is a powerful woman's text which communicates a feminist message" (67). Noted film director Kalpana Lazami's film *Rudali* too focuses on the same issue with a comprehensive concern. Usha Ganguly's intention behind adaptation of short story for performance is very clear. She asserts: "There are two subjects that I have wanted to work with. One is how the political parties are exploiting our religion....The other is the women's problem" (35).

Being a competent post modern text, the play provides enough details of an individual's suffering and constant combat for survival. The play is based on an age-old convention of rudali, countered on the pages of history. As a part of custom, the act of rudali was rooted well in most of the parts of Brazil, Greek, Africa and Middle East. In India, it is observed as a culture in certain areas of Rajasthan. The word 'rudali' (roo-daa-lee) is defined as a female weeper. The professional weeper (rudali) would wail and tear her cloths to encourage others for weeping. The low caste women are generally hired to mourn on the death of a high caste person.

The present research paper proposes to focus on a woman's constant contend for survival through commodifying her grief and mourning. The playwright denies docketing her play as 'a feminist text' though it provides a profound heed in relation to the issues of women in our society. The social conscience of Usha Ganguli meets here with an everyday struggle of a woman for survival on different frontiers. This realistic fervour to the play fuses with playwright's conviction: "Theatre should show what truth is, how it is" (10). Therefore Sanichari, the protagonist of the play, though forfeitures almost everything, shows the spirit of the 'show must go on.' Sanichari represents the millions of women in our society who receive minimum care and consideration within family and outside. Neglecting their over-age, they are forced to face physical and mental torment for everyday persistence. Sanichari, like Brectian Mother Courage, endeavours the struggle of life with a dominant spirit. She earns *roti* for her family of five members by grinding grains for others.

The play attributes largely an interpersonal tension. Sanichari is a victim of humiliation and lack of prudence. She has been considered as an unrosy woman for her birth on Saturday. She strives constantly for family but receives disregard, discomfort in return. The women in her family are more responsible for her desolation. Her daughter-in-law Parbatia has a manifold defaming personality whereas her mother-in-law has a whiplash tongue. Though the playwright expounds a gender issue in the play, she never denies the fact of a woman becoming worst rival of another woman in family.

The play also establishes a social association by handling the issue of prostitutes and cavalier *malik-mahajans*. The zamindars are largely responsible for ruining the life of a great number of low caste women who used to work on their farms. Their footing as prostitutes is nothing but a worthwhile gift awarded in the form of a curse of becoming whores. These zamindars are now interested in hiring these women as mourners to mourn for death of their nearest. Since these *malik-mahajans* believe in the more rudalies you have, the more rich and famous you are formula, they are ready to pay heavily for the rudalies. This flamboyance of opulence is observed almost all the time in our community.

The play comprises twelve short scenes. Sanichari appears in all the scenes. The play opens with a quarrel between Somri and Sanichari. Somri complains to her for not giving her *roti* since the morning. It is difficult for Sanichari to stop her mother-in-law from yelling. Sanichari is unable to feed any of her family members until she completes her work of grinding the grains for others. She may get her payment in kind only after completing her work. Unable to have patience Somri calls out: "You bitch, just watch out Jackles will eat your dead body" (*Rudali:* 117). It seems as there is no end to humiliation, despair and gloom in Sanichari's life. Her son, Budhua, is a TB patient, knocking the door of death. Parbatia, her daughter-in-law, tries her level best to stand away from the family responsibilities. She sells the vegetables in a nearby market. Budhua has grown them in the backyard of the house. Their son Haroa receives from them nothing but the curse of poverty, complete negligence and doomed future. Sanichari has to grapple for survival on a number of fronts. She is unable to provide medical treatment to her son. Further it is beyond her capacity to provide proper meal to her family. She can't even expect anybody's support in her battle for existence. Parbatia strives no way for family. Instead of extending her help to Sanichari, she blames: "... you can't even provide a few *roties* for your family! And you think you can push me around, you bitch?" (118). It's shocking to listen from her: "I'm only staying here as long as he's alive. The moment he dies, I'm leaving—or I'm not my father's daughter" (120). Therefore Budhua's death causes no harm to her. She remains normal as she was earlier. Sanichari's predicament is nobody's concern. Instead of understanding her properly, she was blamed for almost everything.

Time passes and the difficulties for Sanichari almost increase. In course of time she has to confront Somri's death, the death of her son and to the worst, Parbatia's elopement—leaving behind her son Haroa by forgetting her accountability as a mother. The plight of Sanichari can be equated well with Maurya's plight in J.M. Synge's *Riders to the Sea*. Like her Sanichari never shades a single tear even though she confronts utmost distress in personal life. Afterwards she weeps more on death of others as a professional mourner but fails to mourn for her personal sorrow.

Usha Ganguli further strikes at a conventional hypocrisy observed at the time of Budhua's death,in following way:

> *BIJUA*: Arre, there's lots to be done. Do you think a kriya ceremony comes cheep?
>
> Mohanlal Pandit's fee, chivda, dahi, gur—and won't you need to sacrifice goat?
>
> *A VILLAGER:* All this....?
>
> *BIJUA:* What else? On the forth day one has to feed five Brahmins on dahi and gur. I tell you living is tough for us poor people but dying is even worse (125).

Sanichari is compelled to sell her *chakki*—the sole earning source to get money for last rituals. *Chakki*, as Anjum Katyal points out, "is an aural-cum-visual metaphor signifies Sanichari's act of grinding poverty, labour, and food for existence" (39). Budhua might have hardly received proper meal throughout his life. But now on his death the Brahamins are fed with a tasty meal. The playwright directs us towards this real social deception.

The next phase of gloom and despair occurs in Sanichari's life with Haroa's absconding. Like her mother he too blames Sanichari: "Can't provide a square meal, and orders me around!" (132). A half-hearted Sanichari interrogates:

> *SANICHARI*: What did you say? I don't feed you well? my whole life has gone in feeding and raising you, and now you turn around and say I don't give you enough to eat? !
>
> *HAROA*: No, You don't. You never gave anyone enough to it. You starved my grandmother, you drove out my mother, and you killed off my father (132).

Sanichari's life, as one witnesses, is full of turns and twists. Knowingly or unknowingly she is kept away from the pleasures of life. The members of her family expect a lot from her but fail to accept their personal responsibilities. Her son dies without performing his duties as a son and now Haroa, her grandson, leaves home. In this way he leaves her in misery and dispair. Sanichari as a child might have cursed herself for her birth on Saturday. She is immensely tortured as a daughter-in-law; denied pleasures as a mother; Haroa, the only descendant of her family, runs away by shuddering his accountability. Usha Ganguli contemplates on the present different stages in life of a woman. The pain she receives and the plight in which she is found are less because she is of a low caste but more because of being a woman. But as the writer herself professes "... her stance shouldn't be taken as feminist but as humanistic" (Katyal, 64).

The most crucial move in Sanichari's life occurs with her old mate Bikhni's converge meet. Like Sanichari, Bikhni is also terribly troubled in life. They share the sorrow and ignominy that they have received in their respective lives and add, "... this is what happens when a woman doesn't have a man in her life" (137). For the first time Sanichari expresses her feelings before Bikhni. She asserts: "My life has been nothing but the stove, the chakki, and outside jobs" (138). Sanichari and Bikhni decide to initiate life on completely different terms and for the first time they determine to live for each other.

The sixth scene in the play is all about Sanichari's expression of sorrow in her personal life. The family members of Sanichari passed away one after another but as she says, "... I didn't shed a single tear. They call me *daain*—say it's as if I was born just to devour others" (139). The sorrow of Sanichari fuses with Bikhni's sorrow. They develop a mature relationship with each other. Usha Ganguli hits here at a social tangibility. The millions of women like Sanichari and Bikhni have denied love, sympathy and care. They are forced to experience the utmost pains of life. It is only after Bikhni's arrival that, Sanichari starts feeling better. When Bikhni gives her a gift, she remarks: "This is the first time in my whole life that anyone has given me a gift..." (139). Sanichari's frank details of two *Kriya* ceremonies of her husband unearth the selfish motives of Brahmins. These selfish and narrow-minded people are ready to prey on these poor people without taking notice of their scrape.

Dulan brings an offer of becoming rudalis or professional mourners. This offer is for both Sanichari and Bikhni. He comes to know about the murder of Madho Singh's father. Madho Singh is all the way prepared to have a grand *Kriya* ceremony of his father. Actually Madho Singh has murdered his father but now pretends to be a good and loyal son. Initially Sanichari denies the offer of becoming a rudali: "I haven't been able to shed a single tear ever. When Budhua's father died, I thought at least then I would really cry hard.... I'll cry now, I'll cry—then it became evening and I hadn't shed a single tear" (145). But at last she accepts the job of becoming a rudali to satisfy her hunger. She and Bikhni reach Madho Singh's *haveli* to mourn upon his death. The women from the red light area are also hired for this cause. Being indebted to the original story, the writer doesn't give up any chance of criticizing the social tendency. The zamindars in the rural part of the country pretend their superiority on such occasions. Madho Singh orders a great number of rudalis to mourn on his father's death. But after finding only three rudalis to mourn, he shouts: "What's this, only three rudalis? (Loudly). Arre Madho Singh's father dies, and you arrange just three rudalis? Why didn't you get the whole whores quarter here?" (150). Sanichari and Bikhni wail loudly before the corpse to create a different atmosphere. The public performance of women like Sanichari and Bikhni is considered as subaltern since they represent the poor class of society. The satire in this part of the play is quite poignant. The people are ready to do anything possible to maintain the status of superiority. There is a noticeable change in the lifestyle of Sanichari and Bikhni. Initially it was arduous for them to acquire sufficient food and now they are offered *puris and laddus*. The death of any rich person is a guarantee of getting tasty and sufficient food for them. Misri speaks out sharply: "And this one—her father died, her husband died, but the woman, never much as shed a tear! Why should she, after all, there was no *halwa-puri* to be had, was there?" (155).

The momentous scene in the play is Thakurain's visit to Sanichari's hut. Her visit can be considered as a lowering down of high class people for their personal requierments. Thakur Nathuni Singh's middle wife approaches Sanichari and Bikhni to hire them as mourners to mourn for her father's expected death. As Anjum Katyal observes: "This (the visit) signifies cross-class culture gender bonding which is, in fact illusory" (56). The zamindars took the matter of rudali as matter of reputation.

Bikhni's sudden death develops a sense of loneliness in Sanichari, but to continue with life she has to continue her job as a rudali. Sanichari visits whore quarters to offer the job of a rudali to mourn on Gambhir Singh's death. He was a womanizer. Lavishness brought an early death for him. To her surprise, Sanichari meets Parbatia there. She finds no change in her attitude. She has a similar aversion for Sanichari. Initially the whores reject the offer by saying: "People don't die everyday, do they?"

"No, I don't go. This rudali work is too uncertain. There may be a job today but what happens tomorrow?" (164). But lastly they accept the offer and reach Gambhir Singh's *haweli* to mourn for his death. Outwardly, the other zamindars feign sorrow or disappointment on Gambhir Singh's death but inwardly they do have not any consideration for his death. The following dialogue between Madho Singh and Gambhir Singh's son is quite suggestive.

> *MADHO SINGH:* Your inheritance papers are all in order, I hope, Gajanan?
>
> *GAJANAN:* Oh yes, that was all done while he was still alive... (166).

The *coup de grace* is attained here with Sanichari's sole appearance on the stage. She remains now alone in life. The loneliness is countered on the both physical and mental level. Bikhni brings some pleasurable moments in her life but now she is no more with her. Though everything ends for her, she can't keep away from working because she has to survive. Survival despite obstacles remains indeed forever. Hence "Survival despite despair is the message of the play" (68).

Works Cited

Deshpande, G.P. "Introduction" in Mee, Enn.B. (ed). *Drama Contemporary India*. The Johns Hopkins University Press: London. pp111-168.

Ganguli, Usha. (2001).*Rudali* in Mee, Enn. B.(ed). *Drama Contemporary India*. The Johns Hopkins University Press: London. pp111-168.

Katyal, Anjum.(1997)."The Metamarphosis of Rudali" in trans. *Rudali*. Seagull Books: Calcutta. pp1-69.

Subramanyam, Laxshmi. (2002). *Muffled Voices: Women in Indian Theatre*. Har Anand Publications Pvt. Ltd: New Delhi. p. 272.

www.allacademic.com

www.mumbaitheatreguide.com

www.googlebooks.com

Index